Schweizer Anglistische Arbeiten
Swiss Studies in English

Begründet von Bernhard Fehr
Herausgegeben von Andreas Fischer (Zürich), Henri Petter (Zürich),
Werner Senn (Bern)

Band 118

Karin Schmidli

Models and Modifications Early African-American Women Writers

From the Slave Narrative to the Novel

francke verlag

Die Deutsche Bibliothek – Cataloguing in Publication Data

Schmidli, Karin:
Models and modifications : early African-American women writers ; from the slave narrative to the novel / Karin Schmidli. – Tübingen ; Basel : Francke, 1995
(Swiss studies in English ; Bd. 118)
Zugl.: Zürich, Univ., Diss., 1994
ISBN 3-7720-2430-0
NE: Schweizer anglistische Arbeiten

This thesis was accepted as a doctoral dissertation by the Faculty of Arts of the University of Zürich in the Summer Semester of 1994 on the recommendation of Professor Dr. Henri Petter.

Dischingerweg 5 · D-72070 Tübingen

Printed by Müller + Bass, Tübingen
Bound by Braun + Lamparter, Reutlingen
Printed in Germany

ISBN 3-7720-2430-0

To my parents

who awakened in me the love of literature

and

to Armin

whose great interest in my work has been a constant source of

encouragement

Acknowledgements

I wish to express my appreciation and gratitude to Professor Henri Petter for his support, advice, and encouragement and, most importantly, for his great interest in and his promotion of African-American Women's Literature.

For her generous invitation to attend her courses on contemporary African-American Women Authors, held at the University of East Anglia in Norwich, I thank Helen McNeil. I also owe thanks to the extremely helpful staff of the "Nordamerika-Bibliothek" (NAB), in particular to Rosmarie Zimmermann for her inestimable assistance. Thanks are certainly due to Peter Bitterli, who gave invaluable support whenever my computer tried to play tricks on me, and to Patrick Henderson, who read and critiqued my first chapters. I am greatly indebted to Norman Coleopy for his careful reading and his thoughtful and stimulating corrections of my manuscript. Finally, I would like to thank all my friends for sharing with me my love of African-American Literature.

CONTENTS

Preface

It had been my accidental reading of fiction and literary criticism that had evoked in me vague glimpses of life's possibilities. Of course, I had never seen or met the men who wrote the books I read, and the kind of world in which they lived was as alien to me as the moon. But what enabled me to overcome my chronic distrust was that these books ... seemed defensively critical of the straitened American environment. These writers seemed to feel that America could be shaped nearer to the hearts of those who lived in it. And it was out of these novels, stories and articles, out of the emotional impact of imaginative constructions of heroic or tragic deeds, that I felt touching my face a tinge of warmth from an unseen light; always trying to keep my face so set and turned that I would not lose the hope of its faint promise, using it as my justification for action.

Richard Wright, *Black Boy* (1945)

As a teenager in Switzerland, while still at high school, I was browsing through my parents' bookshelves one day, looking for something special to read. *Black Boy* caught my attention and for several days I was entirely enrapt by Richard Wright's narrative. That was my unwitting introduction to African-American literature.

As it turned out, from the first semester of my studies of English at the university, I had many opportunities to attend courses on the Literature of Black Americans. While I was acquiring a general knowledge of English and American Literature, those courses gave me an insight into something special, making for a new experience, an awareness of quasi-taboo topics such as racism and sexism.

Courses offered in Zürich by Dr. Gröflin, Dr. Stetson, and Prof. Gysin covered the 20th century from the Harlem Renaissance to the 1980s, including special areas such as women's writing, and Blues and Jazz. During a 10 months' stay in Vancouver, I was introduced to Alice Walker's powerful *The Color Purple*. Later, after writing a paper on Ralph Ellison's *Invisible Man*, I chose to analyze novels by Paule Marshall, Toni Morrison, and Alice Walker in my final paper ("Lizentiat"), *The Female Quest in Afro-American Women's Literature: A Study of Three Representative Novels*. By the time I had completed this study of the heroines' search for identity and self-assertion in various black communities of the United States, I knew that Wright, Ellison, and Baldwin were not alone the literary ancestors of today's black women writers (also including e.g. Maya Angelou, Gloria Naylor, Gayl Jones). Among others who had influenced them was Zora Neale Hurston, a well-known literary figure during the Harlem Renaissance, who died in obscurity and poverty.[1]

In the course of a Ph.D. project under the supervision of Professor Petter, I spent five months at the University of East Anglia (UEA) in Norwich. There, I had the privilege of attending Helen McNeil's courses on contemporary African-American Women Authors. I increasingly felt that I both wanted to and must first study the very beginnings of African-American Women's Literature, the source of Modern Black Literature. This happily coincided with the publication of the "Schomburg Library of Nineteenth-Century Black Women Writers". Whilst studying its 40 volumes,[2] I have become more and

---

1 In her essays, "Zora Neale Hurston: A Cautionary Tale and A Partisan View" (83-92) and "Looking For Zora" (93-116), in *In Search of Our Mothers' Gardens*, Alice Walker stresses her great indebtedness to Zora Neale Hurston's work: "I became aware of my need of Zora Neale Hurston's work some time before I knew her work existed" (83). She insists on the importance of collecting the work of the black woman writer that has been discarded and forgotten:

> *We are a People. A People do not throw their geniuses away.* And if they are thrown away, it is our duty *as artists and as witnesses for the future* to collect them again for the sake of our children, and, if necessary, bone by bone. (Italics in original, 92)

Alice Walker's two essays answer part of my question concerning the literary models of contemporary black women writers. Zora Neale Hurston is definitely one of them, and a decisive contributor to Afro-American culture. An anthropologist and a writer, in *Mules and Men* she collected and thus helped preserve hundreds of folk and trickster tales, which are part of the oral tradition brought over from Africa by the slaves. In her most famous novel, *Her Eyes Are Watching God*, Hurston depicts a woman's quest for a fulfilled life. It is a celebration of black folk culture, of love between equals (Janie and Tea Cake), and of a woman's self-discovery.

2 My research was greatly facilitated by the "Nordamerika-Bibliothek" (NAB) in Zürich; this is an excellent research library, which was founded in 1970 and is about

more interested in the abundance and variety of this hitherto neglected material, in response both to the appeal of the texts and the writers' personal commitment.

With ever watchful eyes and bearing scars, visible and invisible, I headed North, full of a hazy notion that life could be lived with dignity, that the personalities of others should not be violated, that men should be able to confront other men without fear or shame, and that if men were lucky in their living on earth they might win some redeeming meaning for their having struggled and suffered here beneath the stars.

Black Boy

---

to be amalgamated into the Zürich "Zentralbibliothek" (ZB). I am most grateful to the staff of the NAB for their invaluable assistance.

Introduction

One muffled strain in the Silent South, a jarring chord and a vague and uncomprehended cadenza has been and still is the Negro. And of that muffled chord, the one mute and voiceless note has been the sadly expectant Black Woman, ... The "other side" has not been represented by one who "lives there." And not many can more sensibly realize and more accurately tell the weight and the fret of the "long dull pain" than the open-eyed but hitherto voiceless Black Woman of America. ... as our Caucasian barristers are not to blame if they cannot *quite* put themselves in the dark man's place, neither should the dark man be wholly expected fully and adequately to reproduce the exact Voice of the Black Woman.

Anna Julia Cooper, "Our Raison d'Etre",
A Voice From the South (1892)

The above quotation is taken from the "Foreword" to the Schomburg Library of Nineteenth-Century Black Women Writers. Its general editor, Henry Louis Gates Jr., intends the re-publication of early black women's writings to give a new voice to the 'other side'; the present study, too, is meant to contribute to its rediscovery.

In general, people's knowledge of 19th-century American women writers does not go beyond Emily Dickinson, Harriet Beecher Stowe or local colour writers such as Sarah Orne Jewett and Kate Chopin, and people's knowledge of the black writers of the same period is limited to Frederick Douglass, Booker T. Washington, and W.E.B. Du Bois. There have, however, been many other writers who also deserve attention and re-consideration. Howard Dodson, in "A Note from the Schomburg Center", states the "Library's" claim to establish a more complete presence of black women authors in the literary canon:

> Most of the nineteenth-century titles reprinted during the 1960s [...] were by and about black men. A few black women were included in the longer series, but works by lesser known black women were generally overlooked. The Schomburg Library of Nineteenth-Century Black Women Writers is both a corrective to these previous omissions and an important contribution to Afro-American literary history in its own right. (xxv)

Prior to Gates' pioneering project, black women authors were neglected on two counts: as blacks and as women. For this reason I am going to discuss exclusively black women authors.

The Schomburg Library helped to provide the necessary source material for this project, offering insight into a little known but vast section of Black American Literature. I was amazed at the variety of the literary texts now available again: poems, Antebellum and Postbellum narratives, journals, biographies, autobiographies, short stories, plays, essays, novels, bibliographies, and anthologies.

After familiarizing myself with the early African-American woman's writing tradition, I have pursued two related aims in this study: firstly, to contribute towards closing a gap in the literary canon by helping to revive the works of forgotten women authors, and secondly, to suggest a scholarly approach to those authors that may also appeal to the layperson. My discussion will focus on several representative texts, defined as either "Antebellum Narratives" or novels written during "The Woman's Era" - a term created by Frances Ellen Watkins Harper to characterize the great productivity by African-American women writers in the 1890s. The following six authors provide the base for this study:

Antebellum Era

1. Mary Prince, *The History of Mary Prince, A West Indian Slave* (1831);
2. Harriet Wilson, *Our Nig; Or, Sketches from the Life of a Free Black* (1859);
3. Harriet Jacobs [Linda Brent], *Incidents in the Life of a Slave Girl* (1861);

Woman's Era

4. Emma Dunham Kelley, *Megda* (1891);
5. Frances E. W. Harper, *Iola Leroy, Or, Shadows Uplifted* (1892);
6. Pauline Hopkins, *Contending Forces: A Romance Illustrative of Negro Life North and South* (1899).

The Schomburg Library with its forty volumes is but a selection of the works written and published by African-American women during the 19th century. Although Henry Louis Gates included some better-known writers such as Phillis Wheatley, Alice Dunbar-Nelson, and Angelina Weld Grimké, he was especially interested in reprinting the works of the lesser-known writers, the ones who have so far simply been overlooked.

From this core collection of authors and texts, I have in turn singled out six works that I consider representative of the 19th-century Black Women's literary tradition, works that should enable me to trace a development from the first Slave Narrative to the novels of the 1890s.

As my aim in this study is to analyse Early African-American Women's Literature, I am, of course, especially intrigued by the very first texts by black women, that have at their centre the portrayal of the black woman's particular experience in 19th-century America. Thus, I chose *The History of Mary Prince*, the first Slave Narrative published by a woman in 1831, and *Our Nig*, the first novel by a black woman in America. Mary Prince, whose text was published in London, not the Unites States, deserves special attention because her experience differed from the others in that she was a slave in one of the British colonies, the Antilles. Although Mary Prince was actually a British subject, her narrative can, nevertheless, be considered representative of the Slave Narrative in general. *Incidents* was selected because I consider it, taken together with Frederick Douglass' *Narrative*, one of the major Slave Narratives. It is an important testimony of a woman slave's specific trials. In addition, it plays with elements from sentimental fiction. *Incidents* can therefore be considered a transitional work, inasmuch as it anticipates the novels of the Woman's Era published in the 1890s. *Iola Leroy*, similarly to *Incidents*, builds a bridge between the two Eras by opening during the Civil War and by presenting the 'Peculiar Institution' to the reader. I selected *Contending Forces* because of its parallels with *Iola Leroy*. In both novels the heroines are women who belong to an intellectual elite; they are self-sufficient and rather outspoken about racism, segregation, and the inequality between the sexes and races. They want to fight for the improvement of their race, in a joint effort with their husbands. The inclusion of Kelley's *Megda* is indeed problematic, as the novel neither reveals the characters' race nor voices any social protest.

Nevertheless, it is an interesting text that, taken together with Mrs. A. E. Johnson's *Clarence and Corinne; Or, God's Way,*[1] opens the Woman's Era. I chose it especially because it adds to the diversity of the material published by black women during the 1890s.

While studying representative texts, two contexts must be kept in mind: First of all, I want to integrate early Afro-American woman's fiction into the literary canon by comparing it with various other subgenres, above all 'Early Fiction', African Narratives, Captivity Narratives and Plantation Novels.[2] Here, the following questions have to be raised. What are the intrinsic features of the Afro-American literary tradition? Can such a 'young' tradition, which developed under quite particular conditions, be compared with other literary traditions? If it can, what are they, and in what way were the early women writers influenced by them? By answering these key questions it will be possible to detect the idiosyncratic features of early African-American woman's fiction.

Secondly, by studying the several heroines' development within their fictional worlds, we can prepare for an appreciation of the Black Heroine's literary birth and her development from the early narratives to the novels of the 1890s. Slave Narratives have been neglected long enough, even as historical and sociological documents of the Antebellum Era. It is time that not only historians but also scholars of literature give it more attention. Here again, some questions have to be considered. Why has the Slave Narrative been neglected, both as a historical and as a literary document? Does the slave heroine develop within the Slave Narrative? If she does, in what way do the heroines of the two Eras differ from each other? And in what way do they differ from white heroines and black heroes?

In Part One of this study, after a general introduction, I shall discuss the three Antebellum Narratives under the above aspects. A

---

1 Johnson's *Clarence and Corinne; Or, God's Way* (1890) and *The Hazeley Family* (1894) are both similar to *Megda* in that the question of race is absent. I preferred *Megda* to *Clarence and Corinne* because the latter does not have a heroine at its centre, but has a brother/sister relationship. Moreover, *Megda* seemed more promising for an analysis because of the novel's preoccupation with colour.

2 'Early Fiction' is a short term to describe the prototypical novel developing in the early 18th century, the age of Defoe, Swift, and Richardson.

formal analysis of the texts will be followed by a detailed treatment of the heroine's development along her path from slavery to freedom, or from childhood to adolescence, and a depiction of the 'Peculiar Institution', with a special focus on female friendships, 'family', 'marriage', motherhood, and the relationship between mothers and daughters.

Part Two, which is devoted to three novels of 'the Woman's Era', will offer a short general analysis of each of the texts and their plots. Some particular aspects will then be discussed, such as: the narrators' representations of their heroines and their experiences in the fictional worlds established by the authors; the characters' cultural bonds and their feelings towards the black community; female relationships, marriage and motherhood; black and white symbolism; and the all-important topic of 'passing' for white.

In Part Three, I shall summarize the critical reception given to the six authors in the 19th and 20th centuries.

Part Four, in conclusion, will delineate the connection between the Antebellum Era and the later novels of the Woman's Era. A development - from Mary Prince to Pauline Hopkins - will be outlined by concentrating on features common to the six authors, such as 'the decision to write', 'the choice of form', 'the heroine's source of strength', and 'the representation of reality'.

Before the abolition of slavery, black women like Mary Prince, Harriet E. Wilson and Harriet Jacobs were quite often approached by white abolitionists and encouraged to publish their life stories. For such narratives would propagate abolitionist thought and would intensify, among an English and North American audience, disapproval of slavery. Looking at these earlier Slave Narratives from a historical point of view, it is clear that the 'political' (abolitionist) message took precedence over the wish to create literature for the sake of literature only. But what about the novels written during the Woman's Era? Were they perhaps written in order to prove, to a mainly white audience, that black women were also capable of producing novels? What other motives could have led to the black women writers' immense productivity in the 1890s?

Frederich Douglass, in a letter to M. A. Majors, mentions a crucial issue raised again and again in this study, the omission of these 19th-century black women writers from the literary canon:

> In the very year that Cooper published *A Voice from the South,* Frederick Douglass, when asked by historian M. A. Majors to name some black women for inclusion in Majors' biographical work on black women, responded: "I have thus far seen no book of importance written by a negro woman and I know of no one among us who can appropriately be called famous." (Quoted in Mary Helen Washington's introduction to *A Voice from the South* xxxix-xl)

Douglass' above remark clearly shows that African-American women writers have suffered unjustified neglect not only at the hands of prejudiced white critics but also at the hands of their black male colleagues.

Part One

Antebellum Era: The Black Heroine's Awakening

Chapter 1

The History of Mary Prince: First Slave Narrative Published by a Woman

(a) Preliminary Remarks

On being brought from AFRICA to AMERICA.

'Twas mercy brought me from my *Pagan* land,
Taught my benighted soul to understand
That there's a God, that there's a *Saviour* too:
Once I redemption neither sought nor knew.
Some view our sable race with scornful eye,
"Their colour is a diabolic die,"
Remember, *Christians, Negros,* black as *Cain,*
May be refin'd, and join th' angelic train.

Phillis Wheatley, *Poems on Various Subjects* (London, 1773)

Fifty-eight years after the publication of Phillis Wheatley's *Poems on Various Subjects, Religious and Moral,* another black woman, Mary Prince ("c. 1788-after 1833"),[1] was 'inscribed' in literary history with "the first female slave narrative" written in America (William L. Andrews, in his introduction to *Six Women's Slave Narratives,* xxix). Wheatley, as an enslaved poet of the Age of Enlightenment, set out to prove to the world that, contrary to people's conviction of black inferiority and illiteracy, blacks *could create* (their own) literature. The year 1773 may therefore be considered to mark "the birth of the African-American literary tradition" in general, and the birth of African-American women's literature in particular (Gates, in his Foreword to the Schomburg Library, vii). Whereas Phillis Wheatley's urge for freedom is only implicitly manifest in her poems, Mary Prince could, in her dictated autobiography, give vent to her suppressed

1 Margaret Busby, *Daughters of Africa* 27.

feelings and express the horrors of enslavement, which Wheatley, being the 'protégée' of a rich, white Bostonian family, had never experienced to any comparable extent. Moreover, before the American Declaration of Independence it would have been simply impossible to publish anything derogatory about the British Colonies.

(b) The Slave Narrative: Formal Devices and Characteristic Features

The 'fabrication' and the publication of this Slave Narrative, which took place in the London of 1831, warrants closer analysis. The following discussion of the formal aspects of *Mary Prince* will bring out the characteristic features of the Slave Narrative per se, and will then go on to argue whether there is an affinity with other literary genres, above all with 'Early Fiction' and African Narratives. The aim of this approach is to assign a place in 19th-century literary history to this first text of early Afro-American woman's fiction .

When *Mary Prince* is compared with other Slave Narratives, it becomes strikingly clear that they obey a structural convention: the actual narrative of *Mary Prince* is preceded by a front page with a title and subtitles, together with an epigraph, and a preface, and is followed by a supplement with testimonials and an appendix containing the additional narrative of "A Captured African". With but slight variations, the same structure can be found in every Slave Narrative, from Olaudah Equiano (1789) to Frederick Douglass (1845) and Harriet Jacobs (1861). An analysis of the narrative's individual parts will bring out their intrinsic features and message.

The title and the subtitles, *The History of Mary Prince, A West Indian Slave. Related by Herself,* introduce the reader to a narrative which was dictated by a female slave who grew up in the British West Indies (specifically, Bermuda, Turk's Island, and Antigua). The subtitle 'Related by Herself' does not primarily state the veracity of the slave's tale, but it evokes for the first time the slave's 'existence' in the narrative. As the slave's humanity was under close scrutiny, and as the realities of slavery were concealed by the South, it was crucial for the narrative's author to repeatedly claim her existence. The message of the title is thus: 'I exist and therefore I am a human being'.

The epigraph on the front page, which is by the English poet, William Cowper, appeals to the white people to cease to stand in judgement of the black people, that is, not to make them suffer in slavery any longer. Cowper's direct verse with its simple human themes seems to have been a favourite among the editors of Slave Narratives, who showed preference for his poetic epigraphs (James Olney, "I Was Born", 152). Most epigraphs for Slave Narratives mention the cruelties and injustice of the 'Peculiar Institution' and by suggesting the equality of all people, consequently advocate the abolition of slavery. William Wells Brown even quotes part of the Declaration of American Independence on the title page of his novel, *Clotel* (1853), in order to remind people of the gap between what it says and what the slaves experience.

The "Preface", written by the British white abolitionist and editor Thomas Pringle, elaborates the importance of this narrative told by a slave, "... that good people in England might hear from a slave what a slave had felt and suffered ...." (Preface). The readers who should be stirred by this personal account from the mouth of a woman slave are English. Pringle's opening sentence is indeed quite uncommon, in that it assigns an active role to a slave, and above all to a woman, who wanted to have her life story published: "The idea of writing Mary Prince's history was first suggested by herself" (Preface).

The story told by Prince was written down by a female amanuensis. Why Pringle did not write down the narrative himself is open to speculation, but an amanuensis of the 'fairer' sex was probably better suited to the task of listening to and writing down the ghastly account of Mary Prince's life in bondage. In the preface, the reader is assured by the editor that nothing of importance has been omitted, and that Mary Prince has been "carefully [examined] on every fact and circumstance detailed". This assertion as to the veracity of the tale is characteristic of the slave narrative, and normally appears in letters appended to the narrative and in prefaces written by public figures of the time. Similarly to Mary Prince, Phillis Wheatley had to undergo an examination by "the most respectable Characters in Boston" in order to prove that she was indeed the author of a manuscript of poems (*Poems on Various Subjects*, in *The Collected Works of Phillis Wheatley*, 7). This exemplifies the odds against which blacks had to struggle in order to have their work published and taken seriously by the readers and critics of the time.

Another point stressed in Pringle's preface is that the amanuensis and the editor tried to preserve "Mary's exact expressions and peculiar phraseology". However the final text of Mary Prince's *oral account* of her life, was not just written down by a listener but "afterwards *pruned* into its present shape" by the editor (my emphasis, Preface). Therefore a certain censorship can be felt throughout the narrative, a sense that the narrator must have been questioned frequently and that certain particular situations must have been commented upon. This is illustrated by the following citation, in which Mary Prince recalls the scene of her sale on the auction block:

> Did one of the many by-standers, who were looking at us so carelessly, think of the pain that wrung the hearts of the negro woman and her young ones? No, No! They were not all bad, I dare say, but slavery hardens white people's hearts towards the blacks .... (4)

Her sudden exclamation "No, No!" may be a rhetorical device, or it may be a reaction to the amanuensis' probable remark that not all whites can be as bad as all that. Whatever the case, both the amanuensis and the editor knew that the book was addressed primarily to a white audience who were not to be shocked and put off by the caustic remarks made by a black woman about the whites. This 'double influence' on the oral text - by a white amanuensis *and* a white editor - must always be taken into account.

As the editors, amanuenses and readers of Slave Narratives must have been well acquainted with the representatives of 'Early Fiction' such as Defoe, Swift, and Richardson, it is not surprising that Slave Narratives show certain structural parallels to these early novels.[1] If we

---

1 Fictitious editors' prefaces underline the truthfulness of the tale as, for example, in Defoe's *Robinson Crusoe*: "The editor believes the thing to be a just history of facts; neither is there any appearance of fiction in it ...." (25). Then in Swift's *Gulliver's Travels* we see "A Letter from Capt. Gulliver to his Cousin Sympson" and the note "The

compare their fictitious editor's prefaces and their evocation of the respective authorship ("Written by Herself") on the front page with the corresponding part in the slave narrative, it can be concluded that both want to stress the veracity of the tale. There is, however, an important difference: in the case of our examples of 'Early Fiction', the above points are intended to give a realistic appearance to the related tale, while in the case of Slave Narratives they underline the fact that the story has really been experienced by a slave and is not simply made up by politically motivated abolitionists.

The preface serves a double purpose: firstly it introduces the subject of slavery as experienced by a woman, the narrator, and secondly, it further confirms the slave's existence.

The actual slave narrative, *The History of Mary Prince,* is a short 'I'-narrator's account (approximately 14,000 words) of a courageous woman's life and struggles while in bondage, up to the moment when she obtained her freedom in England in 1828 (1-23). The typographical division of the text is done, not by chapters but by paragraphs only. The story as narrated spans a time of over 40 years, beginning with Mary Prince's birth at Brackish-Pond in Bermuda towards the close of the 18th century. Many footnotes are added by the editor. In some of them unfamiliar expressions such as "Buckra men" (13) are explained, in another her name is commented upon (17).[1] Other notes provide

---

Publisher to the Reader", and in Richardson's *Pamela* in the "Preface by the Editor", we have: "the following letters ... have their foundation both in *Truth* and *Nature*" (31); these are a means of corroborating the fact that the story the reader is holding in his hands has actually taken place. Moreover, the preface to Defoe's *Moll Flanders* acknowledges certain alterations to the original text: "... the style of the famous lady we here speak of is a little altered; particularly she is made to tell her own tale in modester words than she told it at first ...." (28). Here there is a similarity between the preface to *The History of Mary Prince* and the preface to *Moll Flanders,* in both of which the genuineness of the account is verified and the style and language are pruned to their present state. The front pages of both types of texts also underline the respective authorship in the same way "Written from her own Memorandums" (*Moll Flanders*), "Written by Himself" (*Robinson Crusoe*), "Written by Himself" (*Narrative of the Life of Frederick Douglass*), and "Related by Herself" (*Mary Prince*).

1 'Mary, Princess of Wales' was the ironic name given her by her owners; and Pringle re-names Mary by giving her her paternal name of Prince. This 'name giving' is

further details concerning the whereabouts of her family (12/13), or information to support the veracity of her tale (17). Last but not least some of the footnotes stress the dehumanizing effects of slavery (5).

As regards the text before us, it can be assumed that, before its final transition from an oral to a written state, Mary Prince must have repeatedly related her life story to other friends and relatives while she was in bondage, and later to her abolitionist friends in England. The fact that families were separated and sold into different states must have influenced and even furthered the oral tradition of story-telling brought from Africa, and as slaves were not allowed to read or write, this was the only way in which shared experience could continue to be transmitted from one generation to the next. Thus, by telling his or her life-story, the narrator could establish a relationship between himself or herself and the listener; in addition, there was always the possibility that lost family members could be tracked down, which then again helped to fill the lacunae in the narrative of the storyteller. Similarly to the medieval ballad, Prince's story has developed and also has probably been 'embellished' by her over the years until its fixation in 1831. Walter J. Ong, in *Orality and Literacy*, stresses the functionality of narrative in primary oral cultures:

> In a writing or print culture, the text physically bonds whatever it contains and makes it possible to retrieve any kind of organization of thought as a whole. In primary oral cultures, where there is no text, the narrative serves to bond thought more massively and permanently than other genres. (141)

A "Supplement" of 17 pages is appended to the narrative, in which the editor explains the relationship between Mary Prince and her last owner, Mr. Wood (24-40). He also adds several letters in order to show the reader that many influential people have spoken and acted in support of Mary's freedom. A paper which Mr. Wood had given to

---

a recurrent element in Slave Narratives and symbolizes, on the one hand, the fugitive's passage from bondage to freedom and asserts, on the other hand, that she or he is part of mankind. Both William Wells Brown and Frederick Douglass changed their names several times, and on reaching freedom were re-named by their friends. However, it was essential for both of them to keep their Christian names in order to "preserve a sense of [their] identity" (*Narrative of the Life of Frederick Douglass* 110).

Mary before she left his house and also a letter which he had written to the Governor of Antigua describe the various reasons why he 'cannot' and does not want to grant her manumission. Both testimonies attempt to prove Mary's deceitfulness and disreputable character. A letter by Mr. Joseph Phillips,[1] who lived in Antigua at one time and had known Mary there, contradicts what Mr. Wood says about her. All of this is backed up by the editor's praise of Mary's good character: her "*decency* and *propriety* of conduct", as well as "her *delicacy*, ... [which] has been a trait of special remark by the females of my family" (35). He also exposes the contradictions in Mr. Wood's account.

In the belief that some readers might find parts of Mary's narrative exaggerated, especially her account of the manufacture of salt on Turk's Island, Pringle adds a number of facts taken from the "Anti-Slavery Reporter", where the interested reader could find more evidence of similar cases. He also quotes a passage by Dr. Walsh, a friend of his, who in his "'Notices of Brazil' ... vividly illustrated the true spirit of Negro Slavery ...." (Supplement 38-39).

In his concluding statement, the editor points out that Colonial Slavery actually extends its devastating influence to Great Britain because its Legislature accepts, as we can see in the case of Mary Prince, that slaves "can exist within the shores of Great Britain" (40).[2]

The supplement to the narrative confirms the truth of Mary's story, and spells out the abolitionist position that the system of slavery is evil, for both blacks and whites alike. It is also the final proof of Mary's identity.

---

1 Joseph Phillips, the agent of the "Ladies' Society of Birmingham for the Relief of British Negro Slaves", was also subject to calumnies at one time. These brought him nearly five months of imprisonment, and resulted in the loss of his business. Poverty followed, and all this only because he "... disinterestedly exerted himself in the distribution of the money from England among the poor deserted slaves ...." (Supplement 33).

2 Although the British slave trade had been abolished in 1807, some British colonies (the Antilles) still had their own laws concerning the 'peculiar institution' and then started abolishing slavery only in 1833. While the first Northern States had decided to free their slaves shortly after the War of Independence, and Congress had even prohibited slavery in 1807/08, its abolition in the South could only be enforced after the defeat of the Confederacy in 1865 (Abraham Chapman, in his introduction to *Steal Away* xviii-xix).

The slave narrative closes with the appended *Narrative of Louis Asa-Asa, A Captured African* (41-44), to which attention has already been drawn in T. Pringle's preface. "The Negro Boy's Narrative" (1831) is an effective addition to *The History of Mary Prince,* because it describes the way whole tribes of Africans were hunted down and shipped to the Americas, even after 1815 when at the Congress in Vienna it had been decided that transatlantic slavery should be abolished. "While Mary's narrative shews the disgusting character of colonial slavery, this little tale explains with equal force the horrors in which it originates" (41). For the English reader, moreover, Louis Asa-Asa's narrative must have been a reminder of another famous narrative: *The Interesting Narrative of The Life of Olaudah Equiano, or Gustavus Vassa, The African. Written by Himself* (1789).

This final part of the narrative therefore establishes a link between Mary Prince's text, the first slave narrative by a woman, and Equiano's *Interesting Narrative,* which Henry Louis Gates considers to be "the prototype" of the nineteenth-century slave narrative (Introduction to *The Classic Slave Narratives* xiv). Thus the allusion to the source of Slave Narratives forms a bridge between two continents and links Black American Literature with African Literature.

In summary, we can see that the different parts which frame the actual narrative serve two purposes: first, to ascertain the I-narrator's, that is, the slave's existence and second, to corroborate the slave's account. This characteristic feature can be found in all Slave Narratives, regardless of whether the author is male or female. Thus the slave narrative is both a historical and a literary document with a political and Christian aim, namely to abolish slavery.

The structural parallels with Early Fiction and African Narratives such as Equiano's exemplify how the black authors have adapted certain literary conventions, and demonstrate their ability to shape these conventions to suit their personal experience. The parallels also indicate that black authors were influenced by the editors, abolitionists, and amanuenses, who were representative of the 19th-century reader and his or her literary expectations.

(c) Slave Narratives Versus Plantation Novels: The Other View of the Patriarchal Institution

Justification of the need of the slave's reiterated claim, 'I exist', in the slave narrative will be offered by discussing a number of philosophical, religious, and literary arguments which were current on the question of human bondage.

In their introduction to *The Slave's Narrative,* Charles T. Davis and Henry Louis Gates quote part of Hume's major essay, "Of National Characters" (1748), in which Hume argues, in a footnote added to the original text in 1753, that blacks are naturally inferior to whites:

> "In Jamaica, indeed they talk of one negro as a man of parts and learning [Francis William, the Cambridge-educated poet who wrote verse in Latin]; but 'tis likely he is admired for very slender accomplishments, like a parrot who speaks a few words plainly". (xxv)

Davis and Gates write further that Hume's opinion on this subject was adopted by other philosophers such as Kant and Hegel, and was also shared by Thomas Jefferson:

> Of Wheatley ... Jefferson wrote: "Misery is often the parent of the most affecting touches in poetry. Among blacks is misery enough, God knows, *but not poetry*. ... The compositions published under her name are below the dignity of criticism". (My emphasis, xxvii-xxviii)

The authors of Slave Narratives had to face similar reactions to their literary productions. Their veracity was questioned, and the stories were considered to be inventions issued by white and black abolitionists from the North who wanted to condemn the South for upholding slavery. Nevertheless, Slave Narratives were extremely popular, which must also account for the vast number of more than

6000 extant narratives! (James Olney 148).[1] Davis and Gates state that "[a] more revealing indication of the extensive readership is, perhaps, the scores of pro-slavery confederate romances published to rebut the slave narrative's collective realism, as well as critical admonitions to Southern writers and readers to support such fictions" (*The Slave's Narrative* xvii).[2]

These pro-slavery romances, now referred to as Antebellum Plantation Novels, were in part a response to the Slave Narratives in that they praised the Slave System by painting a most peaceful picture of slave life in the South. They depict the happiest, most trustworthy and most innocent black characters, among the best masters and mistresses imaginable! The most notorious representatives of the plantation school were William Gilmore Simms, William John Grayson, and John Pendleton Kennedy, in their advocacy of a patriarchal Old South and their exultations in its in heaven ordained peculiar institution. In her account of "Plantation Fiction", Lucinda H. MacKethan writes that Kennedy's *Swallow Barn* (1832) is generally considered "the fountainhead of plantation literature" (*The History of Southern Literature* 210).

---

1 One of the reasons for the immense popularity of the Slave Narrative may well be the reader's tendency to identify with the heroine or the hero. Such a 'heroine-reader-interaction' can also apply to the novel. This phenomenon is described by Henri Petter in his study, *The Early American Novel,* in which he applied to the term "novel of victimization" a novel which

> relies for its success on the contrast between the reader's cozy comfort and the heroine's sorrows and insecurity. The reader of the tale ... is at home, as it were, enjoying the cheering warmth of the fire, while outside, in the sleet and cold blasts of winter, the heroine is looking for some hovel as a temporary shelter. Whether the reader truly sympathises with the heroine's plight or not depends ... to a considerable extent upon the reader's familiarity with situations similar to hers - perhaps through his own experience, but more probably because of their current use in fiction. (29)

2 For a chronological list of Slave Narratives, see Davis and Gates' "Selected Bibliography of Black Narratives, 1760-1865" (319-327); and for a list of "Autobiographies, Slave Narratives and Letters", see Ruoff and Ward's *Redefining American Literary History,* 297-312.

In Grayson's 66-page didactic poem "The Hireling and [the] Slave" (1851), the proslavery argument is unequivocally introduced in a 12-page preface in which the writer elaborates his views of slavery by comparing England's class of labourers (the hireling) to America's slaves. He chastises English and American abolitionists by arguing that the slaves receive even better treatment than England's paupers, for whom nobody cares and provides, and who are hired only on a daily basis. Slaves are only lightly punished by their master's hand, whereas British offenders against the law are to expect the "penal colony", the "convict ship" or even the death penalty (48/49). And slaves have the advantage of a life-long engagement with and attachment to their masters. It is further stressed that it was Providence that brought the uncivilized African to the Americas, which greatly improved his condition and which can be considered "the only means for civilizing" the entire African Continent (xii). Grayson's preface is followed by a short argument, which serves to summarize the preface and launch the first part of the poem. The second argument is even bolder than the first, in that it maintains that "[t]he Hireling in Europe [is] willing to exchange for the security of the Slave, his own precarious subsistence ...." (50).[1]

Grayson's arguments on the providential nature of slavery, and its justification, had probably been influenced by Thornton Stringfellow's essay "A Brief Examination of Scripture Testimony on the Institution of Slavery" published in the *Religious Herald* in 1841 (in Drew Gilpin Faust 138-167).

> [It] set[s] forth the biblical arguments for human bondage more fully and more systematically than had any previous proslavery treatment. Springfellow sought to counter the "bitter fruits" and "false doctrines" of abolitionism by setting forth the details of God's response to slavery in both the

---

1 To a twentieth-century reader this poem sounds strangely comical, and if it were detached from place and time, one could even consider it ironical.
The comparison between slave and hireling was a frequent argument in the proslavery discussions of the 19th century. While the advocates of slavery justly criticized the merciless treatment of the lowest class in Britain, the labourer, they were wrong in that they wanted to replace a system which everybody considered harmful and devastating for something which was even more so, namely slavery.

> Old and New Testaments. The Virginian also devoted considerable attention to refuting the abolitionist contention that the "servitude" discussed in the Bible was contractual in nature and thus markedly different from involuntary slavery in the South. (Drew Gilpin Faust 137).

William Gilmore Simms, "[t]he South's leading antebellum novelist" (Lucinda H. MacKetan 210), was a most fervent defender of the patriarchal Old South in which the bondsman was considered a 'natural' and 'providential' necessity - on the one hand, for the South's development, and on the other hand, for the 'uplift' i.e. 'civilization' of the black race. In *The Yemassee* (1835), and also in the "Revolutionary War romance, *Woodcraft* (1852, originally titled *The Sword and the Distaff*)", Simms painted an ideal picture of the South's possible social structure by depicting "happy, familial master-slave relationship[s]" (210). Harrison, the protagonist of *Yemassee*, and his servant Hector represent an early vision of Simms' proslavery views, a sketch of the devastating effect it would have on blacks if ever slavery were to be abolished:

> "Yes, Hector, - you are now free. I give you your freedom, old fellow. Here is money, too, and in Charleston you shall have a house to live in for yourself."
> "No, maussa; I can't go; I can't be free," replied the negro, shaking his head ... Wha' Hector done, you guine turn um off dis time o' day?"
> "Done! You have saved my life, old fellow - you have fought for me like a friend, and I am now your friend, and not any longer your master."
> "Ki, maussa! ... Enty you gib um physic when he is sick, and come see and talk wid um, and do ebbery ting he want you for do! ...
> "Yes, Hector, I have done for you all this - but I have done it because you were my slave, and because I was bound to do it."
> "I d - n to h - ll, maussa, ef I guine be free!" roared the adhesive black, in a tone of unrestrainable determination. "I can't loss you company ... 'Tis onpossible, maussa, and dere's no use for talk 'bout it. De ting aint right: and enty I know wha' kind of ting freedom is wid black man? Ha! you make Hector free, he turn wuss more nor poor buckrah-he tief out of de shop - he git drunk and lie in de ditch -

> den, if sick come, he roll, he toss in de wet grass of de stable ... he no hab parson - who know ... No, maussa-you and Dugdale berry good company for Hector. I tank God he so good - I no want any better." (ch. 51, 399-400)

In view of the tendencies to prove the inferiority of the black people and to degrade their accomplishments by branding them as mere imitations, the authors of Slave Narratives and their abolitionist 'sponsors' constantly had to refute these common ideas by asserting, on page after page, the slave's identity. Moreover, the Plantation Novels, which in part were a direct response to the Slave Narratives, further illustrate the slave's difficulty in making white people believe that what she or he says about slavery's horrors is true. These novels show the beauty of the Old South, and depict the slaves' happiness and comfort within the Patriarchal Institution. And finally, the various biblical arguments used and abused by some Southern representatives of the Church in order to justify chattel slavery made it hard for slaves to defend their position and to refute the prevailing assumptions.[1]

(d) From Slavery to Freedom

The I-narrator of each slave narrative follows a more or less similar pattern. This pattern has a tripartite structure: an account of her or his life in slavery, beginning with the slave's birth, parentage, daily routine and tribulations; a description of the gaining of literacy and religion; and finally, the slave's successful and 'heroic' escape from bondage. In general, each phase is closely connected with the heroines' or heroes' path to freedom.

When analysing the I-narrator's (heroine's) account of her experiences in slavery and her successful 'escape', we can establish a parallel with 'Early Fiction', Captivity Narratives and other Slave

---

1 For further information about the characterization of black figures in American literature see Jean Fagan Yellin's study, *The Intricate Knot: Black Figures in American Literature, 1776-1863.*

Narratives. In the following discussion, the heroine's path to freedom will be brought in relation with the structural and stylistic devices of the narrative.

The opening paragraph begins with: "I was born at Brackish-Pond in Bermuda, on a farm belonging to Mr. Charles Myners" and introduces the first phase of the narrative, an account of Mary's days in slavery (1).[1] The narrative is written in the first person (with a few exceptions) and abounds in reflective passages (pauses) in which the narrator, Mary Prince, comments on the events: "This was the happiest period in my life ...." (1). The narrative also contained moral lessons - on slavery's destructive effects on the human being, black and white alike - which were given to her amanuensis as the representative of a larger audience: "But who cared for that? ... Oh those white people have small hearts who can only feel for themselves" (4). Sometimes the reader is addressed directly in order to underline what the 'eyewitness' felt and suffered during slavery:

> I wish I could find words to tell *you* all I then felt and suffered. The great *God* above *alone* knows the thoughts of *the poor slave's heart*, and the bitter pains which follow such separations as these. All that we love taken away from us .... (My emphasis, 3)

The evocation of God at this point in the narrative is a didactic means of bringing the heroine closer to her readers by mentioning Christianity, and by affirming Mary's part in it as well. Only God, the Almighty, knows *how* and above all *that* slaves can feel. This implies that even when the narrator cannot fully express her thoughts, and the reader cannot understand or does not want to understand her plight, there is someone to turn to, someone who *knows it all*.

On a second level, the above quotation also refers to Prince's religious instruction, which the narrator discusses in more detail towards the end of her narrative (16-17/22). The gaining of literacy and of religious education play a major role in Slave Narratives. While the former enabled the slaves to write their own freedom papers in order to escape to the North, the latter indirectly furthered the path to freedom by inspiring the slaves with a sense of Godly justice and with

---

1 "I was born ...." is the formula by which Slave Narratives generally begin (James Olney 153).

the prospect of eternal bliss in paradise. Faith in the Almighty, inspired them with courage and endurance, and made them believe in His shaping of their destiny. In addition, it enabled the more 'privileged' slaves to attend church, either on Sundays or in the evenings, and thus to have a couple of hours off work. At these gatherings they sometimes even came into contact with abolitionist thought. Therefore planters quite often forbade their slaves to partake of religious instruction and preferred to keep them in ignorance as to the real content of the Bible. Planters often told their slaves that the Bible said that God had created the black man to serve the white man as his slave. As pointed out in Chapter 1 (c) their view was of course constantly nurtured by religious leaders who preached about the providential character of slavery and thus sought to justify it.

At one Methodist meeting which had a great impact on the narrator, Prince experienced "the first prayers [she] ever understood" (16). This event marks a decisive turning point in Prince's life; in Slave Narratives it is representative of the slave's search for and finding of God. As a result of her experience, she got in touch with the Moravian church, where three ladies taught her to read the Bible and gave her some religious instruction (17). This is the narrative's second phase, illustrating the heroine's gaining of literacy and faith.

The close link between physical and spiritual freedom (the narrative's third phase) manifests itself in Prince's account of the Rev. Mortimer's instructions while she was in England: "Mr. Mortimer tells me that he cannot open the eyes of my heart, but that I must pray to God to change my heart, and make me to know the truth, and the truth will make me free" (22).[1]

---

1 Readers of Slave Narratives were also acquainted with Captivity Narratives, i.e. accounts by Puritans, "usually autobiographical, of [their] forced participation in Indian life" (Vaughan and Clark 2). The similarity of the structure and subject matter of these two genres is striking, especially when considering the slave's and the captive's Faith in God. While Slave Narratives follow in general the triple structure of (a) an account of the narrator's enslavement, (b), his/her gaining of literacy and his/her religious conversion, and (c), his/her successful escape to freedom, Captivity Narratives have a parallel pattern: on a first level the narrator's captivity is elaborated, then, his/her finding of God, followed by attainment of God's redemption, and finally the captive's deliverance from the 'heathen'. The tradition of Captivity Narratives began with "Mary Rowlandson's story of capture during the later stages of

The heroine's self-assertion can be felt through her narrative pauses, which she repeatedly uses to address her English audience. By telling her readers that they do not really know the facts about slavery and that it is, therefore, her duty to relate those facts to them, she puts herself into the position of being a spokesperson for all enslaved blacks:

> *I* have felt what a slave feels, and *I* know what a slave knows; and *I* would have all the good people in England to know it too, that they may break *our* chains, and set *us* free. (My emphasis, 11)

The change from 'I' to 'we' underlines the transcendence from her personal 'history' to the 'History' of all African-Americans, and thus links her personal suffering to the suffering of every human being held in bondage. Prince also affirms her humanity by saying, "Oh the Buckra people who keep slaves think that black people are like cattle, without natural affection. But my heart tells me it is far otherwise" (9).

The final paragraph of her narrative "is given as nearly as was possible in [the narrator's] precise words" (see footnote, p. 22). It forms a conclusion to her story and presents a highly didactic argument in favour of the slaves' humanity and freedom. Prince condemns the slave owner, who shows neither modesty nor decency, and wonders about those English people who go to the West Indies and are able to "act in such a beastly manner" (23). She states that slaves do want their freedom, even if "good people" are told the contrary by slave owners. The narrator is not afraid to openly denounce as "ignorant" or a "lying person" any man who maintains that slaves are happy in slavery (23). She tells her English audience that she knows better because she has been a slave herself. Thus, she puts herself above the white man's authority.

The evocation of 'God' and 'the great King of England' at the very end of her 'history' is well designed. In this way, she shows the great faith she has in England and that its citizens will call upon their great

---

King Philip's War", which was published in 1682 (3). At the center of her account is her finding of God and His redemption (29-75). John Gyles' text, published in 1736, places more stress on his experiences while in captivity, giving a detailed ethnographical account of his life among the Indians (91-131).

King (ordained by God), who is in a position to intervene on behalf of the slaves.

Many readers must have asked themselves, how anyone could, over a long period of time, survive the sort of treatment related by the narrator, without suffering a physical and/or mental breakdown? Prince actually experienced both at one point, but it seems that her 'chief faults', as mentioned by the editor in the supplement to the narrative, saved her life: "Her chief faults, so far as we have discovered them, are, a somewhat violent and hasty temper, and a considerable share of natural pride and self-importance ...." (35). Without this natural pride she would not have been able to fight against the 'trespassings' of her indecent master, Mr. D__, and without a feeling of 'self-importance' she would not have survived the extreme mental anguish of being reduced to an object and offered for sale. As to her "violent and hasty temper" it must be said that there is nothing in her narrative testifying to such a characteristic, although circumstances would have fully accounted for it. Here again, it must be the censorship practised by both the amanuensis and the editor which accounts for this textual suppression of Prince's real character in her narrative.

It was also her natural pride and her self-importance which gave her the courage to finally leave the abusive Woods and, by that almost heroic act as a lonely and destitute woman in a foreign country, to gain her freedom. William L. Andrews, in his introduction to *Mary Prince,* maintains that "[i]n her verbal and physical resistance to her sadistic master and mistress, the black woman's determination not just to endure but to triumph over injustice is underlined" (xxx).

It can be concluded that in telling the story of her life in bondage, the female narrator has a two-fold intention: firstly, Prince wants to gain her permanent freedom and return to her husband in Antigua, and secondly, she is interested in bringing the horrors of slavery to the attention of the public, i.e., the English citizens, in the hope that they might then support the abolition of slavery in the British West Indies. Thus in her closing sentences she says:

> This is slavery. I tell it, to let English people know the truth; and I hope they will never leave off to pray God, and call loud to the great King of England,

> till all the poor blacks be given free, and slavery done up for evermore. (23)

Prince's account of her life up to the time of her acquiring freedom follows a tradition: the plot of her 'history' follows a pattern one can find in many other Slave Narratives, and also in Captivity Narratives. It contains detailed descriptions of the evil system of slavery: its slave auctions, whippings, killings of slaves and the heartbreaking separation of 'families'. Although at the beginning of her narrative Mary Prince mentions the way she learns to "say [her] letters [and] to spell many small words" (2), and later relates how the Moravian ladies taught her to read (17), the acquisition of literacy does not, in contrast to other Slave Narratives, play a crucial role in the heroine's path towards freedom. In *The Narrative of the Life of Frederick Douglass*, on the other hand, as in other "prominent male-authored accounts ... literacy, the physical mastery over the slaveholder or overseer, and the solitary journey North" were important steps to freedom (Valerie Smith, in her introduction to *Incidents in the Life of a Slave Girl* xxvii).

Prince's escape is not a 'real' escape, in the sense of the spectacular depictions in novels and other Slave Narratives (see "Eliza's Escape", in chapter 8 of *Uncle Tom's Cabin*; Linda Brent's escape in chapters 29/30 of *Incidents in the Life of a Slave Girl*; or Sojourner Truth's escape in the *Narrative of Sojourner Truth* 41-43). Instead, it is more an account of one woman's long struggle to survive in her cruel environment and to stay alive in the hope of being able to buy her legal freedom from her sadistic masters.

Being a woman, Mary Prince could not gain mastery over her slaveholders by physical violence as some male narrators of Slave Narratives did. Instead, she had to seek other ways to overcome her slaveholders, such as running away, or talking back when the treatment of her person (floggings) became unbearable (9; 13).

> I then told him I would not live longer with him, for he was a very indecent man - very spiteful, and too indecent; with no shame for his servants, no shame for his own flesh. (13)

Throughout Prince's narrative, a thread can be followed by which she repeatedly affirms the blacks' collective history. She pleads for freedom, urging the English people to act in order to free their black brothers and sisters. Freedom is mentioned again and again, until a climax is reached in the final passage in which Mary Prince clearly and logically argues for equal rights for blacks and whites: "[English servants] have their liberty. That's just what we want. We don't mind hard work, if we had proper treatment, and proper wages *like* English servants ...." (my emphasis, 23).

(e) Nurturing Female Figures in the Face of the 'Peculiar Institution'

The heroines of women authored narratives - contrary to the heroes of male authored narratives - display their reliance on other people in order to survive the horrors of slavery and to gain their freedom. The success of their endeavours is quite often brought about by a communal effort, whereas in male narratives we more often see the solitary and heroic quest for freedom. In women's narratives, moreover, the relationship between mothers and daughters is often stressed as a wholesome one.

In *Mary Prince* there are several persons to whom the heroine had a strong emotional attachment. At the beginning of her story, these persons are Mary's first mistress, Mrs. Williams, and her daughter, Miss Betsey, for whom she was bought, and Miss Fanny Pruden, to whose mother she was hired out at the age of 12, as well as the heroine's own mother.[1] Mary was greatly devoted to Mrs. Williams, who was herself a victim of her own husband's brutality:

> I was truly attached to her, and, next to my own mother, loved her better than any creature in the world. My obedience to her commands was cheerfully given: it sprung solely from the affection I felt for her, and not from fear of the power which the white people's law had given her over me. (1/2)

---

1 Interestingly enough, her mother's name is never mentioned.

As Betsey's playmate, she was almost considered her equal. Hence the first years of her childhood (related on the first page of her narrative) were passed in sheer 'happiness', as she was still quite ignorant of her real condition as a slave. Mary caught a first glimpse of her situation as a slave when, because of her Mistress' pecuniary difficulties, she was hired out to the Prunes. There she received some instruction in spelling from Miss Fanny: "Dear Miss Fanny! She was a sweet, kind young lady, and so fond of me that she wished me to learn all that she knew herself ... But this happy state was not to last long. Those days were too pleasant to last. My heart always softens when I think of them"(2). The brutal separation from her mother, who in one day lost all of her three daughters on the auction block, is depicted in detail. Here a parallel can again be drawn concerning the treatment of the loss of parents, mothers or protectors in 'Early Fiction', English novels of the 19th century, Woman's Fiction and Slave Narratives.[1]

Afterwards, her mother is only mentioned twice in the narrative. The first time is when Mary Prince escaped from her master after a severe punishment, and hid at her mother's. On being brought back by her father to Capt. I--- she "took courage" and told her master that

---

1 Some examples: Pamela is at Mr. B's mercy after her benefactress' death; Moll Flanders is left as an 'orphan' "in bad hands" after her mother's transportation to the plantations (34); Charlotte Brontë's protagonist, Jane Eyre, in the novel of the same name, is an orphan who spends her first ten years in the household of her uncle, Mr. Reed, where after his death Jane is constantly abused by his family, who treat her like a servant; In Emily Brontë's novel, *Wuthering Heights*, Heathcliff is an orphan whom Mr. Earnshaw found abandoned in the streets of Liverpool. After his protector's death Heathcliff was even more at the mercy of Earnshaw's son, who had always been jealous of his father's protégé and as a result had never accepted him as an equal; Dickens' heroines and heroes were also quite often reduced to the state of orphans at the beginning of their fictitious careers, and the most successful American sentimental novels at mid-century, such as Susan Warner's *The Wide, Wide World,* Maria S. Cummins' *The Lamplighter,* and E.D.E.N. Southworth's *The Hidden Hand,* all feature heroines who have either been abandoned by one of their parents, have been left alone in the world after their parents' deaths, or were separated from their mothers by force. Although Slave Narratives - in which the protagonists are made orphans by the slave system - are unique as regards their subject matter, a literary parentage can still be conjectured from the examples given above, thus fitting the Slave Narratives into the literary canon.

> [she] could stand the floggings no longer; that [she] was weary of her life, and therefore [...] had run away to [her] mother, *but mothers could only weep and mourn over their children; they could not save them* from cruel masters - from the whip, the rope, and the cowskin. (My emphasis, 9)

It is really most astonishing that the child Mary dares stand up for herself, and how she analyzes the slave mother's helpless situation, unable to protect her children from any injustice whatsoever.

The second instance occurs when she relates the sad circumstances under which she meets her mother again later. She saw her in "a sloop" loaded with slaves who were to work in the salt manufacture on Turk's Island. She had lost her mind owing to a violent storm at sea; with her was a four-year-old girl Mary Prince had never seen before (12).

The relationship between Mary Prince and her mother is actually representative of all blacks who lived in slavery. Mothers were considered by the slaveholders to be little more than 'breeding machines' and had no legal right to their children. While they sometimes had the chance of being bought together with their children, 'fathers' and 'husbands' were even worse off. They were usually sold separately, or had to live far away from their wives and children. 'Family life' or anything remotely resembling it was thus systematically and permanently destroyed. It was a common practice among slaveholders to keep slaves related by blood as isolated from one another as possible so that no emotional ties could develop. Thus, over the years, the various members of a family often became scattered throughout the Americas. Behind this policy was the idea that people who had no community to which they felt they belonged to were also less likely to revolt against the abominable conditions they were made to suffer.

Naturally enough, the above differences between a woman's and a man's experience in slavery also find expression in the form and content of their respective autobiographical narratives: the male-authored slave narrative focusses mainly on the narrator's *solitary* struggle for freedom, whereas the female-authored slave narrative embraces the important mother-daughter relationship, together with other relationships which were decisive along the heroine's path to liberty.

In Prince's narrative, one such relationship embodying a positive female figure is "[p]oor Hetty, my fellow slave, [who] was very kind to me, and [whom] I used to call my Aunt" (7). Hetty's miserable life, and her even more awful death, were stamped indelibly on Prince's mind. Hers was the example of the slave who worked day and night, but was nevertheless severely flogged and could never satisfy her master. Calling Hetty her 'Aunt' exemplifies the narrator's wish to restore the previously severed familial ties.

As is often the case in female-authored Slave Narratives, relationships with members of the other sex find little mention. Prince gives only a short account of her husband and of their marriage in 1826. In this context it has to be remembered that black women were considered to be 'licentious' and 'unstable' in their relationships to their 'husbands'.[1] Indeed, marriage was quite often not permitted them by their owners, and various churches, such as the English Church, did not sanction slave marriage. Hence, the female narrator (heroine) tries to preserve her dignity and humanity, which she was constantly being denied, by omitting certain facts which could have been considered harmful to her reputation, facts which, nevertheless, had been forced upon her by the whites' slave system.

Finally, it can be stated that the description of the heroine's close relationship to her mother, as well as to other people who supported her during her tribulations, presents her, not as a 'solitary hero' on 'his' spectacular quest for freedom, but as a heroine who manages to survive slavery's horrors with the help of nurturing women.

In the telling of the slave narrative, the narrator/heroine is constrained by the relatively fixed pattern, and is consequently limited in the representation of her personal development. Nevertheless, Mary Prince's narrative depicts a heroine who 'walks' her personal 'path' to freedom. Although the elements of literacy, religion and escape are there, they are not necessarily connected with the heroine's progress towards freedom. The narrator's liberty to arrange her story differently from the usual structure of the slave narrative, may be due either to the fact that it is dictated, or the fact that Frederick Douglass' 'master' narrative has not been published yet!

---

1 See Mr. Wood's letter to the Governor of Antigua, Sir Patrick Ross (27/28).

Chapter 2

Wilson's *Our Nig*: First Novel by a Black Woman in America

(a) The Re-Discovery of a Novel

I sat up most of the night reading and pondering the enormous significance of Harriet Wilson's novel *Our Nig*. It is as if we'd just discovered Phyllis [sic] Wheatley - or Langston Hughes .... She represents a similar vastness of heretofore unexamined experience, a whole new layer of time and existence in American life and literature.

Alice Walker (1983)

The year 1859 constitutes as much a landmark in literary history as did the years 1773 and 1831, which saw the publication of Wheatley's poems and Prince's slave narrative, respectively. This year there appeared two literary productions by Afro-American women, Frances Ellen Watkins Harper's first short story, "The Two Offers",[1] and the first novel by an Afro-American published in the United States, Harriet E. Wilson's *Our Nig; or, Sketches from the Life of a Free Black, in a Two-Story White House, North. Showing That Slavery's Shadows Fall Even There. By "Our Nig"*.[2]

The re-discovery of Harriet Wilson (1827? - ?) and her novel, *Our Nig*, and Henry Louis Gates' verification of the repeatedly questioned

---

1 In "The Two Offers", the I-narrator adopts a 'proto-feminist' and autobiographical approach and uses the example of two cousins to convey the idea that for a woman, there are various ways to a fulfilled life, other than marriage: "She had a higher and better object in all her writings than the mere acquisition of gold, or acquirement of fame. She would willingly espouse an unpopular cause ... In her the down-trodden slave found an earnest advocate ...." (*The Anglo-African Magazine* 313). The idea of an independent woman who fights for the rights and the elevation of her 'race' is further developed in her novel *Iola Leroy*, published in 1892 (see Chapter 4 of this thesis).

2 It should be noted that Brown's *Clotel* - the first novel written by an Afro-American - was published *in London* in 1853.

authenticity of her authorship, one hundred and twenty-four years after the novel's first publication, represent an important contribution to literary studies, because the novel constitutes an important link between the Slave Narrative of the period before the Civil War and the Woman's Era Novels of the 1890s.[1] Both writers and social historians also find valuable new aspects and insights in this text. In *Our Nig*, a fictional third person autobiography, Wilson combines the structure of the Slave Narrative with certain forms of the Sentimental Novel to create a unique work of art, portraying the growing-up of a 'free' black girl in the North.

Who was this bold woman, this "Mrs. H. E. Wilson", who entered the copyright of her novel "according to Act of Congress, in the year 1859, ... [i]n the Clerk's office of the District Court of the District of Massachussetts" (2)? The following conjectural biographical data of H. E. Wilson's life are taken from David A. Curtis' "Chronology of Harriet E. Adams Wilson", which is appended to Gates' 1983 edition of the novel (*Our Nig xiii-xxvii*). Harriet Adams was probably born in Milford, New Hampshire in 1827 or 1828. "Her race is listed as 'B[lack]'" (*xiii*). In 1850, at age 22, a Harriet Adams was living with the white family of Samuel Boyles in Milford, New Hampshire. In 1851 she lived in W__, Massachussetts. The same year, a Thomas Wilson, probably from Virginia, married a Harriet Adams in Milford, New Hampshire; a year later, in 1852, her son, George Mason Wilson, was born at the Hillsborough County Farm (which is for the poor of the county) in Goffstown, New Hampshire. "His race is listed as "Black"" (xix). From 1855 to 1863 Harriet Wilson, listed as a widow, probably lived in Boston, Massachussetts. Her novel was published on 5th September, 1859. George Mason Wilson, however, for whose support his mother launched this experiment i.e. the publication of a novel (see Chapter 2 (b) in this thesis), died in Milford at the age of seven years eight months, on 13th or 15th February, 1860. There is no further evidence of Wilson's life after her son's death.

In Henry Louis Gates' introduction to *Our Nig*, he gives three speculative reasons for the novel's oblivion: firstly, the anonymous

---

1 For more information about Harriet Wilson, see the account of David Ames Curtis and Henry Louis Gates, "Establishing the Identity of the Author of Our Nig", in *Wild Women in the Whirlwind;* and Barbara A. White, "'Our Nig' and the She-Devil: New Information about Harriet Wilson and the 'Bellmont' family", in *American Literature.*

author states (and that already in her title) that racism exists in the North as well as in the South. As the potential readers of the book were white abolitionists living in the North, they were probably alarmed by a book which challenged the common stereotypes of a 'racist' South and a 'free' and 'humanitarian' North. Secondly, it is likely that the narrator's neutral representation of the marriage and relationship between the heroine's white mother and her black father did not have a particularly promotive effect in either the North or South. And thirdly, there was the author's ironical use - in her title and for her anonymous identity - of the denigrating name Nig which the family used for the protagonist (xxvi-xxix). Moreover, some abolitionists probably disliked the narrator's critical remarks about them in the last chapter of her novel:

> Strange were some of [Nig's] adventures. Watched by kidnappers, maltreated by professed abolitionists, who didn't want slaves at the South, nor niggers in their own houses, North. Faugh! to lodge one; to eat with one; to admit one through the front door; to sit next one; awful! (ch. 12, 129)

The depiction of Samuel, the protagonist's husband, as a fake fugitive slave is another point which might have raised strong criticism among abolitionists; it could have been used to underline one of the main pro-slavery arguments, that slavery's horrors were all made up by liars and politically motivated abolitionists.

It should also be noted that the protagonist's free interpretation of the Bible, which results in her amusement at the death of Mary, one of her tormentors, and also her secret thoughts of poisoning "her mistress to rid herself and the house of so detestable a plague" almost certainly would deter further publication (108).

(b) The Novel: Formal Devices

The 19th-century readers from the North must have been at least puzzled by the novel's provocative title. They were used to more or less neutral titles such as *The History of Mary Prince. A West Indian Slave; Narrative of the Life of Frederick Douglass, an American Slave; Narrative of Sojourner Truth, A Bondswoman of Olden Time; Uncle Tom's Cabin;* and *Incidents in the Life of a Slave Girl.* With *Our Nig,* however, the immediate intimacy of the first word, "Our" - establishing a link between the protagonist and the reader - must have antagonized many, all the more so because of its connection with the abusive term 'Nig'. Thus from the very start, the readers cannot hope to escape a certain implication in the story, as the title says that the protagonist, Nig, is also the readers' Nig, whether they like it or not. With these rather ironical first two words, the author strikes a personal note; this leads smoothly into the long subtitles, as Wilson changes from a personal to a more general level. While the titles of the other narratives mentioned above do not reveal much about the text to be read, the subtitles of *Our Nig* point directly at the main topic of the novel: the existence of racism in the North.

Another striking thing is that Harriet Wilson signs her title page with "By 'Our Nig'" and in so doing reveals that the protagonist and the author-narrator are one and the same.

The epigraph by Josiah Gilbert Holland on the title-page foreshadows the heroine's deep affliction (see Gates' "Notes to the Text" in *Our Nig iii*): "'I know / ... that sorrow sits and drinks / At sweetest hearts, till all their life is dry; / ....'" (1). This is a first epigraph, to be followed by others heading the twelve chapters of the novel; they all serve as introductions to the respective chapters and bear witness to the author's wide reading and her knowledge of literature.

Wilson's "Preface", signed only with her initials "H.E.W.", begins in the third person "... the writer confesses her inability to minister to the refined and cultivated ...." but changes, two sentences later, into the first person:

> Deserted by kindred, disabled by failing health, I am forced to some experiment which shall aid me in maintaining myself and child without extinguishing this feeble life. (3)

The preface repeats the claim - already made in the title - that the novel is indeed an autobiographical novel. Some points mentioned in Wilson's preface are conventionally used in the prefaces of Slave Narratives. Firstly, she states that the readers should not criticise too severely the writer's attempt at erudition, and continues the apologia by mentioning that she is aware of "errors" and "defects" in her narrative.[1] Secondly, she declares that there will be omissions owing to the fact that the whole truth would "provoke shame in our good anti-slavery friends at home"; and thirdly, she appeals to "her colored brethren" to support her project.

Apart from this, Wilson's preface is exceptional in that it addresses not the "refined" and "cultivated" - i.e. the white Northern middle class usually addressed by authors of Slave Narratives, as it were - but a poor, black audience. Furthermore, her motive in writing and publishing her life story is not primarily an abolitionist matter. It is an "experiment" to help support herself and her sickly child. By thus attempting, for financial reasons, to set down her life story in writing, Wilson confirms that writing is work.[2] Whereas Phillis Wheatley had

---

1 In her preface and final chapter, Harriet Wilson, in common with many authors of Slave Narratives, and with other 18th and 19th-century novelists, has recourse to the apologia classica, as in Olaudah Equiano's

> Dedication to the Lords Spiritual and Temporal, and the Commons of the Parliament of Great Britain ... I am sensible I ought to entreat your pardon for addressing to you a work so wholly devoid of literary merit; but, as the production of an unlettered African, who is actuated by the hope of becoming an instrument towards the relief of his suffering countrymen, I trust that *such a man*, pleading in *such a cause*, will be acquitted of boldness and presumption. (Gates, *The Classic Slave Narratives* 3)

2 Nancy Prince - another free black woman (born in Massachussetts) - who published her *Life and Travels* in Boston in 1850, similarly uses writing as a means to economic independence: "... by the sale, I hope to obtain the means to supply my

literary encouragement and financial support from the Wheatleys while she was their slave and protégée, Harriet Wilson, almost a century later, had the courage to undertake this experiment with no sponsor at hand. This also differs from the authors of Slave Narratives, who were almost always sponsored by white abolitionists. Wilson also insists that it is not her intention to "palliate slavery at the South" by dwelling on its existence in the North. Henry Louis Gates considers Wilson's preface to be "an extraordinary document in the Afro-American literary tradition; it is, if not unique, certainly one of the rare instances in which a black author has openly anticipated a hostile reaction to her text from 'our good anti-slavery friends at home'" (Introduction to *Our Nig* xxxiv-xxxv).

The eight-page "Appendix" (133-140) and the preface (i.e. the nonfictional discourse) form a whole, inasmuch as they give information about the author's life which goes beyond that in the fictional discourse (i.e. the actual narrative). The initials "H. E. W." at the end of the preface and the three letters added in the appendix serve to confirm the truth of *Our Nig*'s plot.

The appendix is subdivided into three parts which read like letters. First, there is a letter by Allida (aunt J---), which begins with the words "Truth is stranger than fiction". It contains a quotation of part of a letter written by Alfrado (Frado for short, the novel's protagonist) to her friend Mrs. Walker, followed by a poem by Frado, and then a passage by Allida, who also added a poem which was probably written by herself. Second, there is a letter by Margaretta Thorn. Third, there is a letter dated 20th July, 1859 in Milford and signed with the initials C.D.S. All three letters confirm the author's good reputation and the truth of Frado's narrative. They also appeal to "all the friends" (137), the "friends of our dark-skinned brethren", or to "all Christians" (140) who should support the writer by buying her narrative.

In her letter, Allida states that she has known Frado for the last eight years. Here, Allida recounts in more detail what is only briefly hinted at in the last chapter of Frado's narrative - Frado's experiences at Mrs. Walker's as a "'straw sewer'" (133), and her acquaintance with Samuel, their marriage, his desertion, and the birth of a son.

---

necessities. ... I take this method to help myself, as health and strength are gone" (Nancy Prince, in her preface in *Collected Black Women's Narratives*).

Henry Louis Gates maintains that Allida actually tries to direct the reader's attention away from the narrative's main theme, the appearance of 'slavery' in a Northern household, by suggesting that the main topic is love betrayed (Introduction xxvii). It is more likely that Allida wanted to give an account of the author's blameless character - as is usually done in Slave Narratives - from the time she first knew her eight years earlier. This enables readers to see beyond the narrative and to gain an impression of Harriet Wilson's biographical background, so that they can compare it with what they are reading in the narrative. The narrator of the novel has been quite outspoken about her 'bondage' as an indentured servant in the North, so that Allida need not refer to this part of Frado's life. The other two letters do to some extent touch upon the subject of her terrible experiences during her childhood and adolescence, which were so destructive to her health.

The novel is written almost exclusively in the third person. In a few instances the narrator 'slips' (on purpose?) into the first person, e.g. in the first three titles, "Mag Smith, *My* Mother", "*My* Father's Death", and "A New Home For *Me*", and in the first sentence of the novel's last chapter, "A few years ago, within the compass of *my* narrative, there appeared often in some of *our* New England villages ...."(my emphasis). This confirms that third person narrator and first person narrator are identical, and merge with the narrative's heroine, Frado. This conscious or subconscious change of narrator might result from Wilson's difficulties in choosing the form and structure to suit her 'new' subject matter. The epigraphs at the beginning of each chapter testify as to the author s wide reading, and no doubt Wilson was influenced by the Slave Narrative and by Woman's Fiction.[1] The first three chapters and the last one, "The Winding Up of The Matter", serve respectively as an introduction and a conclusion to the novel. This is underlined by the above mentioned change of narrator in these

---

1 In her study, *Woman's Fiction,* Nina Baym criticizes the labels, "sentimental fiction", "fiction of sentimentality", "domestic fiction", and "domestic sentimentalism" often used by scholars when discussing this specific genre. She maintains that "[t]his terminology is misleading ... because it puts the emphasis on a presumed ambience in the fiction rather than on the implications of the basic plot" (24). Hence in order to avoid "distorting presuppositions", Nina Baym's term, "Woman's Fiction", is used in this thesis when referring to these novels.

chapters. Although Slave Narratives generally begin with the formula "I was born ....", to introduce the protagonist, *Our Nig* does not; instead of that it devotes its first chapter to the protagonist's white mother (see Chapter 2 (d) in this thesis). In that way, the protagonist's parentage is established - which is also an important feature in Slave Narratives, with the difference that the father is usually a white planter and the mother his slave. The opening lines of the novel, "Lonely Mag Smith! See her as she walks with downcast eyes and heavy heart" present an omniscient narrator who periodically interrupts her narrative in order to insert some moral lesson by addressing or including the reader (ch. 1, 5):

> Blessed release! may *we* all respond. How many pure, innocent children not only inherit a wicked heart of their own, claiming life-long scrutiny and restraint, but are heirs also of parental disgrace and calumny ... Alas, how fearful are *we* to be first in extending a helping hand to those who stagger in the mires of infamy .... (My emphasis, ch. 1, 6-7)

Faithful to the generic structure of the Slave Narrative, *Our Nig* follows a tripartite pattern, which includes:

(a) An account of the protagonist's family (Frado's) and her relation to the Bellmonts (chs. 1-2), with a detailed description of her daily work routine in the service of the Bellmonts (ch. 3).

(b) Frado's gaining of literacy: school (ch. 3) and religious instruction, discussions and religious meetings with Aunt Abbey (chs. 7-10).

(c) Alfrado's growing desire to escape, and increasing resistance to Mrs Bellmont's brutality (ch. 10); Frado's final 'freedom' at the age of 18, but loss of health (chs. 11-12).

Both the Slave Narrative and Woman's Fiction have a didactic purpose. The former is enriched by inserted reflections on the horrors of slavery, and the latter as a whole conveys a moral lesson to its women readers, who identify with the heroine in her trials and triumphs. The heroines of both genres encounter impediments which they have to overcome, but whereas the slaves are depicted as 'victims' of a corrupt, inhumane and unchristian institution, the heroines in Woman's Novels are made responsible for overcoming their difficulties. Thus, Nina Baym states that these books "separate cause from effect and insist that in nineteenth-century America, women have the opportunity and responsibility to change their situation by changing their personalities" (*Woman's Fiction* 19). This observation might explain further Wilson's dilemma in searching for a suitable form for her 'bildungsroman' of a black girl.

(c) From Childhood to Adolescence: A Heroine's Growth

In this chapter, I will analyse how the protagonist is shown to develop from childhood to adolescence, and the way she experiences herself in her fictional world. Moreover, there will be a discussion of the limitations on the black heroine's representation in 19th-century American literature, and an elucidation of how she differs from her white contemporaries as depicted in Woman's Fiction. In her 'Guide to Novels by and about Women in 19th-century America', Nina Baym gives a very apt outline of these white heroines:

> The thrust of all this fiction has to do ultimately, and obsessively ... with how the heroine perceives herself. At the outset she takes herself very lightly - has no ego, or a damaged one, and looks to the world to coddle and protect her. She makes demands on others as a function of not making demands on herself. She expects nothing from herself because she recognizes no inner capacities. To some extent, her demands are unreasonable. But the failure of the world to satisfy either reasonable or unreasonable expectations awakens the heroine to inner possibilities. By the novel's end she has developed a strong conviction of her own worth as a result of which she does ask much from herself. She can meet her own demands and, inevitably, the change in herself has changed the world's attitude toward her, so that much that was formerly denied her now comes to her unsought. (*Woman's Fiction* 19)

The first time the reader is introduced to the child/heroine, Frado, is in chapter 2, while she is still at her mother's. She is portrayed from Mag's (her mother's) and Seth's (her stepfather's) perspective:

> "Who'll take the black devils?" snarled Mag ... "There's Frado's six years old, and pretty, ... She'd be a prize somewhere," [Seth said]. (16-17)
>
> "Frado is such a wild, frolicky thing, and means to do jest as she's a mind to; she w on't go if she do n't want to" [Mag remarked] ... He took her hand and said: "We're going to move, by-'m-bye; will you go?" "*No*!" 'screamed she; and giving a sudden jerk which destroyed Seth's equilibrium, left him sprawling on the floor, while she escaped through the open door. "She's a hard one," said Seth, brushing his patched coat sleeve. "I'd risk her at Bellmont's." (My emphasis, 18-19)

At the same time, the narrator presents her point of view:

> Frado ... was a beautiful mulatto, with long, curly black hair, and handsome, roguish eyes, sparkling with an exuberance of spirit almost *beyond restraint*. (My emphasis, 17)
>
> Why the impetuous child entered the house we cannot tell .... (16-23)

The omniscient narrator's description and the two adults' description of six-year-old Frado are identical in that they stress her wild, unrestrained temper, her beauty, wit and energy. The readers are thus shown a wilful child/heroine, about to embark on her long road of trials. The first time the narrator gives the heroine a voice of her own, she utters an imperative "No!", and her 'running away' from the house after Mag and Seth's discussion shows her to be a girl of courage and determination, similar, for example, to the child/heroine, Cap, in *The Hidden Hand*.

The difficulty and hardship of her future path are already foreshadowed by her mother's intention to give her away; this idea is conveyed by the narrator's statement, "Mag Smith was relieved to know her child was not driven to desperation by their intentions to relieve themselves of her, and she was inclined to think *severe restraint* would be healthful" (20), and also by the conversation between the two adults: "'Would n't the Bellmonts take her?' asked Seth. 'Bellmonts?' shouted Mag. 'His wife is a right she-devil! ... She can't keep a girl in the house over a week; ... she's so ugly ....'" (my emphasis, 17-18).

At the end of chapter 2, Frado, now a six-year-old child, enters the Bellmonts' household (22); she is allowed to 'leave' for the first time as an adolescent of 18, at the end of her prolonged indenture, in chapter 11 (117). The 'healthful', 'severe restraint' Frado is subjected to at the hands of the Bellmonts turns out to be an ironic understatement of the treatment she suffers. It can be argued that this 'two-story white house' with its various inhabitants (all members of one family) is symbolic on two levels. Firstly, it represents a microcosm of the racism and cruelty which - similar to slavery in the South - also exists in the North, and secondly, it stands at the same time for the confinement experienced by the heroines of 19th-century Women's Novels. The overpowering effect of this long indenture on the protagonist's future outlook on life is even underlined by the novel's structure. Of *Our Nig*'s 12 chapters, a total of 10 deal with the heroine's life of confinement to the Bellmonts' house and family, where little contact to the world outside is possible.

During the first weeks at the Bellmonts', Frado still *hopes* that her mother might return. 'Hope' for change from outside her own realm of action is later the main steadying force while passively 'tolerating' Mrs. Bellmont's and Mary's cruelties towards her. For many years, she secretly cherishes a 'dream' that James, Jane or Jack might take her along with them to their new homes. That this dream cannot come true is abruptly brought home to her when James, her favourite, dies of consumption.[1] In this situation, Frado shares the lot of her white sister as depicted in Woman's Novels. They, too, can change their lives in a positive way only by using their "inner possibilities", and not just by hoping for others to bring about change. From the very beginning of Frado's indenture, she has been waiting for others to change her desperate situation. Similar to the slaves in the South, her fate was put at an early age into the hands of white people.

---

1 At St. Clare's sudden death, Uncle Tom's hope for freedom is also destroyed (Harriet Beecher Stowe, ch. 29, 342-349).

Frado fights back only once, otherwise the narrator describes her as being naturally merry: "Her jollity was not to be quenched by whipping or scolding" (38). In the house (71), at school (37-39), on the way back from school (33), and at work (54-55) she manages to trick her 'adversaries' intelligently, in the manner of the rabbit in the "trickster tales".[1] It is strange that "one spark of playfulness could remain amid such constant toil; but her natural temperament was in a high degree mirthful ...." (53). Many Slave Narratives have a tendency to define their protagonists solely through the brutality of their master class. This is understandable if we bear in mind that Slave Narratives were used by abolitionists as a political weapon in order to convince people of the horrors of slavery. Authors of Slave Narratives who had to adapt their story to a more or less rigid form were therefore limited in the portrayal of their protagonist's personality. The narrator in *Our Nig* is free of such obligations to sometimes overly eager abolitionists, and hence depicts the protagonist, not simply as a helpless victim, but as a girl or woman with a personality of her own. Frado suffers tremendously, but nevertheless manages to preserve certain character traits such as her urge for independence, her aversion to injustice, her wit and her mirth, which will later also find expression in her naive interpretation of the Bible.[2]

---

1 For further information on the trickster tales, see ch. 2 "The Meaning of Slave Tales", in *Black Culture and Black Consciousness* by Lawrence W. Levine; Part I, "Folk Tales" in *Mules and Men* by Zora Neale Hurston; and Part IV, "How Clever Can You Get? Tales of Trickery and its Consequences", in *Afro-American Folktales* edited by Roger D. Abrahams.

2 In his preface to *Black Culture and Black Consciousness* (1977), Levine demands of today's scholars what Harriet Wilson managed to do with her novel in 1859:

> This book may dismay some because it abandons the popular formula which has rendered black history an unending round of degradation and pathology. The familiar urge to see in heroes only virtue and in villains only malice has an analogue in the desire to see in the oppressed only unrelieved suffering and impotence. This ideal construct - the pure victim - is no more convincing or supported by what we know of human psychology and history than the ideals of pure hero or villain. Yet such are the realities of our current racial and political situation that it remains necessary to stress that which should be obvious: to argue, as this book does, that even in the midst of the brutalities and injustices of the antebellum or postbellum racial systems black men and women were able to find the means to sustain a far

A positive change in the protagonist's miserable life is brought about by her act of rebellion, shortly after she has "resolved to give over all thought of the future world", i.e. hope of redemption and consequent eternal life in heaven close to James (104). She finally manages to stand up to her mistress, for the first time defying her when threatened with a beating:

> "Stop!" shouted Frado, "strike me, and I'll never work a mite more for you;" and throwing down what she had gathered, stood like one who feels the stirring of free and independent thoughts. (105)

This act of rebellion actually has been encouraged by Mr. Bellmont, who has told her that he cannot protect her as his sons could, and that she should try to avoid any undeserved punishments (104). As a consequence of her open protest, Frado has to endure fewer whippings. In his *Narrative of the Life of Frederick Douglass,* Frederick Douglass describes a similar act of resistance which also marks "the turning-point in [his] career as a slave" (74).

Frado's sudden act of rebellion, narrated in chapter 10, constitutes the turning-point in her life. After years of hard labour and brutal treatment, even Frado's natural mirth seems somewhat subdued, while her health is completely destroyed: "The past year had been one of suffering resulting from a fall, which had left her lame" (ch. 11, 117). Frado, not a child any more, tries to be the doer in her own life. Her secret hope - that someone will bring relief to her sufferings by taking her away - has disappeared. She finally realizes that she herself possesses the power to protect herself from her mistress. The knowledge of her new weapon, namely self-assertion, also inspires her with self-confidence, courage, and patience. These are important qualities (also found in the heroines of Woman's Novels), which enable her to endure the remaining years of her servitude and to face life's struggle on her own. Frado's determination at the end of her indenture to try her own luck, i.e. "to flee from any and every one having [Mrs. Bellmont's] similitude of name or feature", shows, on the one hand, the intensity of her frustration and desperation while, on

---

greater degree of self-pride and group cohesion, individual autonomy, and self-worth than a number of recent scholars have maintained. (x-xi)

the other hand, demonstrating the strength of her wish to be free and independent of the family's influence (110).

Although the protagonist is afraid of the future, when she will have to provide for her own needs and wants, she is determined to leave the Bellmont household and thus to liberate herself. That her wit has not fully left her can be seen when she argues logically with Mrs. Bellmont's ally, Mrs. Smith, "that she had enough of such comforts ... and as it was so wicked to be ungrateful, she would go from temptation; Aunt Abby said 'we mustn't put ourselves in the way of temptation'" (116). The irony in Frado's logic is obvious, and underlines the fact that she not only uses 'religion' in a very personal way but also quite freely adapts the commandments to her personal needs.[1]

When the protagonist finally leaves the Bellmonts at the age of 18, she is - although determined to support herself - repeatedly taken sick. At a very critical moment in her illness, the family she is currently working for brings her back to the Bellmonts. Although she feels ashamed to ask for something that Mrs. Bellmont does not want to give, she nevertheless feels that "they owed her a shelter and attention, when disabled, and she resolved to feel patient, and remain till she could help herself" (120-121). Here the narrator is relating the only instance in which Frado actually expects something from her former employers in return for her long years of free labour.

The protagonist's sudden and unexpected act of self-assertion - when she finally rebels agains her mistress - signifies Frado's change from a girl who hopes for a rescuer from outside, to a woman who is ready to take on the responsibility for her own life. Here again Frado strongly resembles the heroine in Woman's Fiction, as outlined by Nina Baym. This act of rebellion is also an expression of her maturity and her urge for personal freedom. It gives her the power to overcome her spells of sickness and to search for employment again and again. She does achieve independence as a milliner, and enjoys her happy and inspiring stay at her instructress' place somewhere in Massachusetts, but these periods are only short: "Thus she passed months of quiet, growing in the confidence of her neighbours and new found friends" (ch. 11, 125).

---

1 Chapter 2 (d) of this thesis will deal in more detail with the protagonist's personal interpretation of the Bible.

Readers familiar with 19th-century Woman's Fiction must have been astonished, if not shocked, at the novel's ending (ch. 12). Instead of the expected 'happy ending' resulting in marriage, and instead of the picture of a fulfilled heroine surrounded by her caring friends (her surrogate family), husband and children, we are confronted with love betrayed, sickness, fever, and death. In the final chapter, "The Winding up of the Matter", the omniscient narrator briefly summarises the protagonist's meeting with and marriage to Samuel, a fake fugitive slave. The shortness of the account and the narrator's explanation, if not excuse, of her heroine's behaviour suggest that 19th-century readers expected a very different ending:

> ... and as people of colour were rare there, was it strange she should attract her dark brother ... that they should marry? A short acquaintance was indeed an objection, but she saw him often, and thought she knew him ... There was a silent sympathy which Frado felt attracted her, and she opened her heart to the presence of love - that arbitrary and inexorable tyrant. (126-127)

For Frado to leave her first secure dwelling and her hard-won independence in order to rely on a man she has not known for long is to break entirely with the tradition of white heroines in Woman's Novels. The narrator's definition of love as an "arbitrary and inexorable tyrant", as well as her description of Samuel "whose back showed no marks of the lash, erect as if it never crouched beneath a burden" foreshadow Samuel's betrayal of Frado (127). His "disclosure that he had never seen the South" suddenly reveals him to be a fake fugitive slave as well as a 'fake' husband: "He left her to her fate - embarked at sea ... Once more alone! Yet not alone" (127-128). The last chapter can also be seen as a new beginning, a new phase in the life of the heroine, who again stands at the beginning of new trials because she has been left by her husband. Her loneliness and desperation after her husband's desertion again bring her closer to the white heroine's representation in Woman's Fiction, and even link her fate to that of her mother at the very beginning of the novel.

The narration could well have ended with chapter 11, and chapter 12 with its six pages does not contribute greatly to the development of the plot. It may be considered as an account in itself, a supplement.

Author, narrator and protagonist merge into one voice urging readers to buy the book in order to support Frado and her sick child:

> Still an invalid, she asks your sympathy, gentle reader. Refuse not, because some part of her history is unknown, save by the Omniscient God. Enough has been unrolled to demand your sympathy and aid. (130)

With the second but last paragraph of chapter 12, the story which opened with the writer's 'advertisement' of her experiment (the writing of this novel) in her preface has come full circle. Fiction and reality merge as the narrated persona and the narrating persona approach the end of the novel, until they become one and the same voice in chapter 12. As the narrator and protagonist become identical, it is likely that the narrator-writer tried to protect herself from undue exposure to the public. This probably accounts for the brevity of and the lacunae in the final chapter, which could be considered more a beginning than an ending, and which does not follow the tradition of the Woman's Novels. However, its final paragraph, which supplies information concerning "the destiny of those connected with [Frado's] *early* history", again uses elements taken from Woman's Fiction (130). The reader is informed that Frado's antagonist, Mrs. Bellmont, has been punished terribly, by "an agony in death unspeakable", for her treatment of an innocent and defenceless child (130). Her awful death symbolises the heroine's victory over her tormentor, and thus the world of fiction is at least partly in order. Although the heroine will have to face new trials at the end of the novel, she is nevertheless represented as someone who is actively trying to improve her desperate situation and who, because of her endearing personality, encounters many friends who help her along her way.

> In one of her tours, Providence favored her with a friend, who pitying her cheerless lot, kindly provided her with a valuable recipe, from which she might herself manufacture a useful article for her maintenance. (129)

Harriet Wilson's experiment, the creation of the novel, *Our Nig*, is, on the one hand, a success in that a black woman's voice has been added to the literary canon on the other hand however, it failed in one of its purposes, prolonging her son's life: George Mason Wilson, aged seven, died of fever in 1860, shortly after the book's publication.

(d) Mothers and Surrogate Mothers

In the novel, the first person the reader meets is Mag Smith, the protagonist's white mother. Her representation is unlike that of the mothers generally depicted in Slave Narratives authored by women or in 19th-century Woman's Fiction. These women are portrayed as heroic mothers or grandmothers who hold the family together.[1] Both genres usually portray the mother as a magnanimous person, loving her children; in Slave Narratives, she falls 'victim' to Slavery's conventions in the South, whereas in Woman's Fiction, she either is wrenched from her child through severe illness (Mrs. Montgomery in *The Wide, Wide World*) or is forced to give her child away because she is at the mercy of a devilish relative (Mrs. Le Noir in *The Hidden Hand*).

Our protagonist's mother, Mag Smith, is different. Although having herself been orphaned at an early age, she nevertheless abandons her daughter Frado for no greater reason than poverty. Mag Smith, however, cannot simply be considered as antagonistic to Frado, even though her act is the cause of the protagonist's miseries. Here the author breaks doubly with the structure of the Woman's Novel: firstly, she does not depict the mother as a 'safe harbour' and secondly, she does not adhere in a simplistic way to the friend-foe dichotomy so common in 19th-century Woman's Fiction.[2] This is evident in the first chapter, where the narrator describes Mag Smith's miserable life. Mag Smith, we are told, "[e]arly deprived of parental guardianship", has

---

1 See Jackson, 1866, Delaney, 1891, Burton, 1909, in *Six Women's Slave Narratives* and *Incidents in the Life of a Slave Girl* 1861.

2 For further analysis of 19th-century novels by women, see Nina Baym, *Woman's Fiction. A Guide to Novels by and about Women in America, 1820-1870*; consider also H. L. Gates' succinct summary, in his introduction to *Our Nig* (xli-xliii), of the main characteristics which Baym attributes to Woman's Fiction.

become the victim of a society whose rigid moral and social standards lead to her ostracism after she is deserted by a lover who leaves her pregnant. Later, her poverty and her subsequent marriage to a black man further ostracize her from society (ch. 1, 5). The description of Mag Smith's life before Frado's birth is complex and controversial because it also introduces two important topics in American social life, poverty and amalgamation. Mag Smith is presented to the readers as a victim, with whom they should truly sympathize. Thus, her abandonment of Frado is anticipated in the first chapter by the description of her alienation from society. Mag Smith, instead of growing and developing in response to her difficulties in life - as expected of heroines in Woman's Fiction - falls deeper and deeper into the abyss of poverty and shame until there is no return. It is obvious that under these circumstances, Mag Smith cannot be a nurturing figure to her daughter, the novel's protagonist. Frado must, at the age of six, face the hardship of a life alone, deserted by her kindred, like so many of her white contemporaries in Woman's Fiction. It is only in the first two chapters that the readers learn anything about Frado's black father, Jim, "a kind-hearted African", her white mother, Mag, or her 'stepfather', Seth (9).

From the age of six to the age of 18, Frado had to endure a life similar to that of a slave in the deep South. During her time as an indentured servant in the house of the Bellmonts, and afterwards up to the birth of her child in her twenties, the heroine encounters a dozen people of both sexes who exercise a decisive influence on her life. H. L. Gates holds that, of all the women characters, there are only two (Mrs. Bellmont and her daughter Mary) who do not befriend her. And of all the male characters there is only one, namely her future husband, Samuel, who actively abuses her and betrays her love and confidence (xlv). All of the other characters - themselves victims of Mrs. Bellmont or Mary - though not able to shield Frado from being physically and mentally maltreated, are nevertheless in one way or another responsible for her survival. Dependent on Mrs B. and her daughter, one "wholly imbued with *southern* principles", the protagonist has virtually to go through hell (Preface).

Finally, it will be shown how the women in and connected to the Bellmonts' household influenced Frado's outlook on life. Special attention will be given to those who introduced Frado to "book information" (ch. 11, 124).

Literacy plays a major role in the slaves' lives, in the planning and successful execution of their escape; it is a symbol of the slave's rejection of white control and is an important step towards the slave's self-assertion. Similarly, 'book knowledge' is also accorded an important role in *Our Nig*.

Although the 'positive' male characters' contributions are not minor ones, they will be referred to only in connection with the women characters who have a nurturing influence on the protagonist. These women include Miss Marsh, her teacher, Aunt Abbey (Mr. Bellmont's sister), Jane (the Bellmonts' invalid daughter), Susan (James' wife), Mrs. Moore and, finally, "a plain, poor, simple woman" (nameless in the narrative, but referred to by Allida in the Appendix as Mrs. Walker).

Miss Marsh, the protagonist's teacher, may be considered a first substitute for the 'absent' mother. She 'will love' Frado because she believes her to be a "good girl". This teacher defends Frado actively against Mary's and the other children's cruelties on her first day at school:

> She then reminded them of their duties to the poor and friendless; their cowardice in attacking a young innocent child; referred them to one who looks not on outward appearances, but on the heart. 'She looks like a good girl; I think I shall love her, so lay aside all prejudice, and vie with each other in shewing kindness and good-will to one who seems different from you," were the closing remarks of the kind lady. Those kind words! The most agreeable sound which ever meets the ear of sorrowing, grieving childhood. (Ch. 3, 32)

By intervening and giving a lesson on true Christian behaviour to the children, she manages to turn the tables and, in consequence, makes school a pleasurable place for Frado:

> Example rendered her words efficacious. Day by day there was a manifest change of deportment towards "Nig." Her speeches often drew merriment from the

> children; no one could do more to enliven their favorite pastimes than Frado. (32-33)

Although Mrs. Bellmont is absolutely opposed to her going to school, because she "was in doubt about the utility of attempting to educate people of colour, who were incapable of elevation", her husband nevertheless decided that "she should go to school" (32). "[T]hree months of schooling, summer and winter, she enjoyed for three years" (37). Not only was she safe from Mary and her mother's cruelties during school hours, but these years of schooling enabled her to read books later in life. This ability afforded her some "soul refreshment" and also gave her new impulses (ch. 11, 116).

The second nurturing character is Aunt Abbey, John Bellmont's "maiden sister [who] shared with him the estate on which he resided, and occupied a portion of the house" (ch. 2, 22). She represents the Woman's Novel's recurring figure of the motherly character - often childless herself - who guides the orphaned child through all the difficulties of the harsh outside world. Aunt Abby is very good, educated, and truly religious in comparison to her sister-in-law, Mrs. Bellmont, who although "a professor of religion" (ch. 10, 104), is incapable of applying Christian ethics to her everyday life. Thus "[Frado] was never permitted to attend church with her mistress. 'Religion was not meant for niggers', *she* said" (68).[1] Mrs. Bellmont is the absolute opposite of good-hearted Aunt Abby, who not only tries to shield the girl from her tormentors (Mrs. Bellmont and Mary) but also strives to give her some moral and religious teaching: She "... looked within [and] saw a soul to save, an immortality of happiness to secure"

---

1 In numerous narratives, similar examples are given of so-called 'religious' masters and mistresses who were notorious for excelling in their brutality towards their slaves or servants. Thus, Nancy Prince in her narrative also questions her employers' 'religion':

> Hard labor and unkindness was too much for me; in three months, my health and strength were gone. I often looked at my employers, and thought to myself, is this your religion? I did not wonder that the girl who had lived there previous to myself, went home to die. They had family prayers, morning and evening. Oh! yes, they were sanctimonious! (*Collected Black Women's Narratives* 11-12)

(ch. 6, 69). In Aunt Abby's 'quarters', Frado can feel secure from the cruelties of the two 'villainesses', and in her room she can relax from the day's toil. It is there that Frado learns about God in discussions with Aunt Abby and by reading the Bible. Frado is also greatly affected by what she hears at the religious evening meetings, to which she is invited by Aunt Abby. Although religion, God, and eternal paradise are still something strongly associated with people she loves, such as James, Mrs. Bellmont's returned son, and Aunt Abby, she nevertheless experiences something new during those meetings. James - who is severely ill and will not recover from his consumption - is Aunt Abby's ally; together with his brother Jack, his sister Jane and their father they support Frado against his mother and his sister, Mary. Thus, Frado is caught between two forces, the 'good' and the 'bad'. While on the one hand she is told that prayer and heaven are for blacks and whites alike, Mrs. Bellmont says to her that "it would 'do no good for her to attempt prayer; prayer was for whites, not for blacks ....'" (94) and that "she could not go [to heaven] where James was; she need not try" (ch. 9, 100).

Frado's personal, innocent conception of religion is sometimes close to becoming comically ironic, and her teachers and moral guides, Aunt Abby and James, have difficulty in bringing their 'pupil' back to reason. This happens, for example, after Mary's departure on a longer trip, and again when Frado hears of her sudden death:

> "Well, she's gone, gone, Aunt Abby. I hope she'll never come back again."
> "No! no! Frado, that's wrong! you would be wishing her dead; that won't do."
> "Well, I'll bet she'll never come back again ...."
> "But you forget what our good minister told us last week, about doing good to those that hate us."
> "Did n't I do good, Aunt Abby, when I washed and ironed and packed her old duds to get rid of her ...."
> (ch. 8, 80-81)

> "She's dead, Aunt Abby!" ... It seemed a thanksgiving to Frado. Every hour or two she would pop in into Aunt Abby's room with some strange query: "She got into the *river* again, Aunt Abby, did n't she; the Jordan is a big one to tumble into, any how. S'posen she goes to hell, she'll be as black as I am. Would n't mistress be mad to see her a nigger!" and others of a similar stamp, not at all acceptable to

> the pious, sympathetic dame; but she could not evade them. (Ch. 10, 106-107)

Frado's naive image of God, heaven, and hell is strongly related to her personal life and experience with the people around her. She does not like God, because he created Mrs. Bellmont as well as her (ch. 4, 51); finally, she even gives up the prospect of eternal life in heaven, because there she might have to put up with Mrs. Bellmont. Although Frado could fancy Mary in hell, she cannot imagine the same of Mrs. Bellmont. Her mistress exerts such power in her environment - everyone has to submit, even her husband - that Frado can only picture her continuing her abuses in heaven.

> Frado pondered; her mistress was a professor of religion; was *she* going to heaven? then she did not wish to go. If she should be near James, even, she could not be happy with those fiery eyes watching her ascending path. She resolved to give over all thought of the future world, and strove daily to put her anxiety far from her. (104)

Although the comical aspect of Frado's religious views should not be dismissed, there is also a more serious side to her superstitious idea that her mistress will control over her even after death. Levine refers to various superstitious beliefs among Antebellum blacks, which depict the return of their bad masters after death.[1] It is not simply Frado's "rejection of Christian religion" which makes her give up the prospect of heavenly eternity, as H. L. Gates maintains (in his introduction xlix), but rather an interplay between the Christian religion and African superstition, which is strongly related to the blacks' collective history and experience.

---

1 There were

> ... the spirits of masters who returned after death to continue the torment of their black bondsmen. Lewis Clarke watched two of his fellow slaves dig their master's grave six or seven feet deep and then helped them place a large stone on his coffin 'so as to fasten him down as strong as possible'. 'Slaves', he commented, '... are all superstitious ... I was actually as much afraid of my old master when dead ... and thought he had actually come back again, to torment me more'. (*Black Culture and Black Consciousness* 79)

Jane and Susan, although minor characters in the novel, nevertheless play an important nurturing role in Frado's life while she is living with the Bellmonts. Jane, being an invalid and utterly dependent on her mother and sister, cannot openly intervene on Frado's behalf:

> Jane went to confer with her Aunt about the affair; and learned from her the retreat. She would gladly have concealed her in her own chamber, and ministered to her wants; but she was dependent on Mary and her mother for care, and any displeasure caused by attention to Nig, was seriously felt. (ch. 4, 46)

Harriet Wilson devotes almost a whole chapter, "Departures", - to Jane, in which Jane's choice of a husband is described, as well as the caring support she is given by Aunt Abby: "Although an invalid, she was not excluded from society. Was it strange she should seem a desirable companion, a treasure as a wife? Two young men seemed desirous of possessing her" (ch. 5, 55). The passage describing how Jane is courted by two men seems detached from the main story, because the protagonist is absent from the narrative. But on a deeper level, a parallel can be detected between Jane's fate and Frado's. Both are handicapped, Jane because she is physically disabled and Frado because of the colour of her skin. Therefore, the sentences by the omniscient narrator quoted above also implicitly evoke the protagonist's secret hopes of being desirable even though she is black. If the readers being addressed were to give an affirmative answer to the question concerning Jane, then there would also be hope for Frado.

This part of the chapter is also quite important for another reason: it reveals the domineering influence of Mrs. Bellmont on her children. She tries to push Jane into marrying a wealthy suitor, and orders her to reject the other, who is poor, but whom Jane would prefer. Although Jane cannot really protect Frado from the cruelties inflicted by her sister and mother, she nevertheless expresses her sympathy by helping Frado whenever she can, behind their backs. Jane's marriage and consequent departure from the house are felt keenly by Frado: "Thus another light disappeared from Nig's horizon" (61). Years later, towards the end of the novel (ch. 10), Jane returns home again to support her parents after Mary's sudden death, but she is unable to remain long in the oppressive atmosphere created by Mrs. Bellmont: "Jane after vain endeavors, became disgusted, weary, and perplexed, and decided that, though her mother might suffer, she could not endure her home" (ch. 10, 109).

Susan, James' wife, "was not unlike his sister Jane, who had a social, gentle, loving nature, rather *too* yielding ... His Susan had a firmness which Jane needed to complete her character ...." (ch. 5, 55). During James' illness up to the time of his death, Susan establishes a relationship with Frado, which is supported by James and Aunt Abby. Whereas Jane could protect Frado only secretly, Susan and James are sometimes more successful in preventing Mrs. Bellmont's brutality. James has become deeply religious towards the close of his life, and encourages Frado to follow his example. His and Susan's plan to take Frado back with them after his recovery is shattered when they realize that his illness is fatal. Susan treats Frado as one of the family by inviting her to James' funeral. This is the first time that she "would be allowed to mingle her grief with others" (ch. 9, 98). Years later, while at the Bellmont's on a visit with her son, Charlie, Susan encourages Frado's thirst for knowledge by giving her some books and a Bible. The impact of reading and what books mean to Frado, is conveyed in the following lines:

> Frado had emerged into womanhood, and, retaining what she had learned, in spite of the few privileges enjoyed formerly, was striving to enrich her mind. Her school-books were her constant companions, and every leisure moment was applied to them. Susan was delighted to witness her progress, and some little book from her was a reward sufficient for any task imposed, however difficult. She had her book always fastened open near her, where she could glance from toil to soul refreshment. (ch. 11, 115-116)

In this way, Susan follows her husband's example, joining Aunt Abby's efforts to help Frado to improve herself. Thus Susan also plays an important, nurturing role in Frado's life.

Another nurturing female figure, who also encourages Frado in her reading, is "a plain, poor, simple woman, who could see merit beneath a dark skin" (124). This woman is the Mrs. Walker mentioned in Allida's letter. She becomes Frado's "instructress" in the making of straw bonnets. Frado, who has been used to heavy work in and about the house, can now, for the first time, learn a trade, a trade more in keeping with a sensitive, intelligent woman such as her.[1] The nameless woman, unlike Mrs. Bellmont, is poor, but seems to be the richer in heart and mind. She even teaches her 'apprentice' "the value of useful books", which made her feel "capable of elevation" (124).

> ... [S]he felt that this book information supplied an undefined dissatisfaction she had long felt, but could not express. Every leisure moment was carefully applied to self-improvement, and a devout and Christian exterior invited confidence from the villagers. Thus, she passed months of quiet, growing in the confidence of her neighbors and new found friends. (124-125)

It can be concluded that when looking at the female characters in the novel, elements from both the Slave Narrative and Woman's Fiction can be detected. Inspite of this, there are nevertheless many instances in which there is a departure from the norm. Thus, the Woman's Novel's nurturing mother is absent. Neither Mag Smith nor Mrs. Bellmont, in their self-willed activity, remotely correspond to the loving, but passive, mother-victim image. The magnanimous and childless woman, who is the orphan's moral guide through all life's difficulties, is represented by Aunt Abby. She is one of the main nurturing female figures in the novel, who, together with James, Susan, and later in the narrative, Mrs. Walker, encourage Frado's reading, While reading is important for the heroines of Woman's Fiction, the gaining of literacy is even more so for the hero or heroine of the Slave Narrative. By introducing Frado to "book-knowledge", the nurturing women characters, Mrs. Marsh, Aunt Abby, Susan and Mrs. Walker, are the main ones responsible for Frado's mental and physical 'survival'.

Our Nig is Harriet Wilson's creation; if we consider it to be an autobiography, as Allida does, then it is clear that the narrator-author would not have been capable of putting her life story on paper without the help of the other women mentioned above. Whereas Aunt Abby

---

1 In *The Color Purple,* Celie is inspired by Shug Avery to sew pants.

and Susan seem more concerned with Frado's religious development, Mrs. Walker introduces her to "useful books". Here again, protagonist and author merge, in that the book's many epigraphs by various authors illustrate Harriet Wilson's extensive reading.

Harriet E. Wilson's "experiment" is a novel which embodies elements from both the Slave Narrative and Woman's Fiction. Faced with difficulties in finding a form for the theme of her autobiographical novel, the existence of slavery-like conditions in the North, the author creates a "new" novel. The rigid structure of the Slave Narrative, with its limits as to the representation of the slave's personal development, was inadequate. Woman's Fiction, on the other hand, with its traditional happy ending in marriage and its overly simplistic friend-foe philosophy was not entirely satisfactory either. Therefore Harriet Wilson, the first Afro-American and first black woman to publish a novel in the United States, created an autobiographical novel which portrays the development and growing up of a black girl in a white family in 19th-century Massachusetts.

The narrator's portrayal of the protagonist's trials at the mercy of her mistress and her mistress' daughter is related in accordance with the tradition of the Slave Narrative: i.e. Frado's daily work routine, her scanty meals, the punishments, her religious awakening, her gaining of literacy and, finally, her 'revolt'.

Some of the nurturing female figures, who empathize with Frado and who introduce her to 'book-knowledge' and to the Gospel, are similar to the characters appearing in Woman's Fiction. Aunt Abby, for example, represents the magnanimous mother figure and guide of the abandoned heroine; and Jane, Susan, Frado's first teacher, and the 'poor woman' (Mrs. Walker) all become the protagonist's allies and friends, either shielding her from Mrs. Bellmont's and Mary's brutality or instructing her; this group stands for the heroine's surrogate family. Frado's two antagonists, Mrs. Bellmont and Mary, are typical villainesses, who are terribly punished for their deeds by contracting some fatal illness towards the end of the novel.

Despite similarities with the form of the Slave Narrative and Women's Novels, the author had to step beyond their limits in order to find a voice of her own. This is seen in the change of narrators, the admitted omissions, the open ending, the novel's advertisement, the inclusion of the reason for writing the novel, and the writer's independence, which is mentioned in the preface and in the appendix. *Our Nig* closes a gap in African-American literary tradition by offering a bold portrayal of a black girl's development from childhood to womanhood. By telling of Frado's tribulations as well as her final 'liberation' from her mistress' yoke, the narrator-author gives a voice to

> "[t]he "other side" [which] has not been represented [before] by one who "lives there". And not many can more sensibly realize and more accurately tell the weight and the fret of the "long dull pain" than the open-eyed but hitherto voiceless Black Woman of America." (*A Voice From The South*: "Our Raison d'Etre", II)

Chapter 3

Jacobs' *Incidents in the Life of a Slave Girl*: The Slave Mother's Voice

(a) Fiction and Reality

The Slave Mother

Heard you that shriek? It rose
So wildly on the air,
It seemed as if a burdened heart
Was breaking in despair.
...
She is a mother, pale with fear,
Her boy clings to her side,
And in her kirtle vainly tries
His trembling form to hide.

He is not hers, although she bore
For him a mother's pains;
He is not hers, although her blood
Is coursing through his veins!
...
They tear him from her circling arms,
Her last and fond embrace.
Oh! never more may her sad eyes
Gaze on his mournful face.
...
Frances Ellen Watkins Harper (1854)

In 1860, the white abolitionist and writer, Lydia Maria Child, entered the copyright for *Incidents* in the District Court of the District of Massachusetts. This narrative, which combines elements of Slave Narrative and Woman's Fiction - similar to *Our Nig* - was edited by Lydia Maria Child and published in Boston in 1861; a year later it appeared in London, under the name of Linda Brent, the pseudonym for Harriet Jacobs.[1]

---

1 Linda Brent, *The Deeper Wrong: Or, Incidents in the Life of a Slave Girl, Written by Herself*, L. Maria Child, ed. London: W. Tweedie, 1862.

In the following description of *Incidents*, the biographical data on Harriet Jacobs' life are taken from Jean Fagan Yellin's essay, "Text and Contexts of Harriet Jacobs' Incidents in the Life of a Slave Girl: Written by Herself" (263-264); from *The Meridian Anthology of Early American Women Writers*, edited by Katherine M. Rogers (449-450); and from the *Heath Anthology of American Literature*, edited by Paul Lauter (Jean Fagan Yellin 1: 1723-1725).

Owing to favourable circumstances, Harriet Ann Jacobs (ca. 1813-1897) was able to spend her early childhood with both of her slave parents and her grandmother, Molly Horniblow, the latter of whom had been freed and earned her living as a well-respected baker and citizen of Edenton, North Carolina. After her mother's early death, six-year-old Harriet was taken over by her mother's benevolent mistress. Her mistress taught her to read and write; contrary to her promise, however, she did not arrange for Harriet to be freed at her death but instead had her given to her three-year-old niece, Mary Matilda Norcom. During the first six years of her childhood Harriet thus had the advantage of a sustaining family life, despite slavery's reality. Mary's father, Dr. James Norcom (the Mr. Flint of *Incidents*) began harassing Harriet sexually when she was about fourteen years old. The author gave the different persons of her narrative fictitious names (in brackets here) in order to protect her own privacy and that of others. To shield herself from the immoral advances of the white man, who after all was old enough to be her grandfather, Harriet decided to take a white lover, the lawyer Samuel Tredwell Sawyer (Mr. Sands): "It seems less degrading to give one's self, than to submit to compulsion. There is something akin to freedom in having a lover who has no control over you, except that which he gains by kindness and attachment" (84-85). He was the father of her two children, Joseph and Louisa Matilda, whom he would later buy but - contrary to his promises - never emancipate. *Incidents* contains the story of three generations of women betrayed by their mistresses: Harriet's grandmother, Harriet's mother, and Harriet herself all had been promised that they would eventually be manumitted. Harriet even had her white lover's word that he would emancipate her two children, but as the narrator of *Incidents* says, "But, alas! we all know that the memory of a faithful slave does not avail much to save her children from the auction block"

(15).[1] In order to escape Norcom's continued harassment, Harriet decided to hide in a tiny space underneath the roof of a shed that was adjoining her grandmother's house. For seven years, she was able to watch her children without anybody knowing it; she waited for a good opportunity to send her children North. Only when she knew that they were safely out of Norcom's reach did she herself escape to New York City, in 1842. There she worked as a nursemaid for the friendly wife of the editor, Nathaniel Parker Willis (the Bruces). As Harriet still was not secure from Norcom and his daughter, who continued to pursue her even in the North, Mr. Willis' second wife bought Harriet. It was in their household that Harriet wrote *Incidents*, supported by Mrs. Willis who, contrary to her husband, was 'against-slavery'. His 'pro-slavery' stance might be the reason why Willis is hardly ever mentioned in the narrative, and why Harriet Jacobs worked secretly during the night, as mentioned in Amy's statement in the Appendix: "After the labors of the day were over, she traced secretly and wearily, by the midnight lamp, a truthful record of her eventful life" (305).[2]

The narrative is Harriet Jacobs' autobiographical account of her childhood and adolescence as a slave, her long concealment in her grandmother's house, her flight to the North, and her final reunion with her two children. Comparing the events narrated in Jacobs' account with the writer's real life, it is striking how closely they agree. Jacobs had two motives for her writing project. Firstly, she wanted to fight for the abolition of slavery, for which she gained the support of Lydia Maria Child and Bishop Paine, and secondly, she needed money in order to realize her dream of sitting "with [her] children in a house of [her] own" (302).

---

1 Sojourner Truth (in *Narrative of Sojourner Truth*) and Frado (in *Our Nig*) also fall victim to white people's broken promises; in the case of the former, a promise to free her and in the case of the latter, a promise to end Mrs. Bellmont's persecutions by moving Frado into their own family.

2 Willis' attitude is revealed by the title of his account of slave life in Virginia, "Negro Happiness in Virginia" in: *The Convalescent* (1859): 410-416 (*The Slave's Narrative* 265). In "Text and Contexts", Yellin mentions that various letters from "Jacobs to Post ... (1852-early 1853?) ...." and one from "Child ... to John G. Whittier ... (1861) ...." speak of "Jacobs' relationship with Willis" ("Notes 5" in Davis & Gates 279).

(b) Slave Narrative or 'Sentimental' Novel? Formal Aspects

As the conventional structure of the Slave Narrative has already been discussed in *Mary Prince* and in *Our Nig* (Chapters 1 (b) and 2 (b) in this thesis), this chapter will include only an analysis of the formal organization of *Incidents.*

In the structure of the texts under discussion, an influence of other literary 'subgenres', such as 'Early Fiction', Captivity Narratives and African Narratives, can be detected; it will now be interesting to find out if this is also the case with *Incidents.* This is all the more important because *Incidents,* which is the last narrative from before the Civil War to be discussed, stands at the threshold between the Antebellum Era and the Woman's Era.

The title, *Incidents in the Life of a Slave Girl. Written by Herself,* already makes reference to the Slave Narrative. First, it points out that the narrative is written by the female protagonist, the "Slave Girl", herself. Second, the reader will be confronted, not with a chronological narrative of the life of a slave girl, but with 41 episodes in the life of a slave girl. The 'Incidents' are thus sketches or scenes, which - on a structural level - mirror the Slave Narrative's episodic structure.

There are two epigraphs on the title page, one written by "A Woman of North Carolina" and the other taken from the book of "Isaiah (xxxii 9)". The first is addressed to the "Northerners", and criticizes their ignorance of the degrading effect slavery has on the human being. While this epigraph condemns Northern women and men alike because of their inability to grasp the deeper significance and the consequences of the notion of slavery, the second epigraph addresses - in an imperative tone - the more privileged "daughters" of the Americas. They are called upon to overcome their unconcern and indifference: "'Rise up, ye women that are at ease! Hear *my voice,* ye careless daughters! Give ear unto *my speech*'" (my emphasis, 3). "My voice" and "my speech" - when applied to *Incidents* - can be understood as the voice of the black woman writer and her text. Thus, both epigraphs try to rouse their white audience from their torpor and to make them begin working towards the abolition of slavery.

"The Preface [written] by the Author" herself, together with the two epigraphs and the "Introduction" by a woman editor display the woman-centred structure of the narrative. At the same time, the theme of a black family, which is held together by the grandmother, is anticipated, and so is her granddaughter's ordeal in withstanding the immoral advances of her master. The opening paragraph of the author's preface stresses - as does the Slave Narrative - the veracity of her account. She further states - which is worth considering - that she has "no motive for secrecy" concerning herself.[1]

The second paragraph of the preface contains an apology concerning the author's competence to write this text; this is special, because it applies solely to women writers.[2] The reader is told that the writer was born and raised in slavery and that she lived in a Slave State for 27 years. Jacobs' task as the writer of her Slave Narrative differs from that of her male contemporaries, Douglass and William Wells Brown, who could devote themselves solely to the task of writing, editing and lecturing. Jacobs - as well as many other women writers - had to write "these pages at irregular intervals, whenever [she] could snatch an hour from household duties" (5). In addition, she has to support not only herself but also her two children.

In the last paragraph of the preface, Jacobs states that Bishop Paine has encouraged her to publish the story of her life. Her preface is extraordinary in that the women of the North are asked explicitly to empathize with "the condition of two millions of women at the South" (6). Jacobs thus anticipates the possibility of a 'sisterhood' between black and white women, by putting the responsibility for change into the hands of women.

In her "Introduction" to *Incidents,* Lydia Maria Child calls Harriet Jacobs' pseudonymous narrative an autobiography. She briefly mentions that Jacobs is highly esteemed by her employers and that the

---

1 In Chapter 2 (b) of this thesis it will be discussed how Jacobs - contrary to her above statement - manages to keep some secrecy in order to protect her privacy and her womanhood.

2 Susanna Haswell Rowson, who can be considered America's first best-selling novelist, writes in her preface to *Charlotte, A Tale of Truth* (London, 1791; America, 1795): "I shall rest satisfied in the purity of my own intention, and if I merit not applause, I feel that I dread not censure".

truth of her tale is therefore not to be questioned. Child admits to minimal revision of the text, but has "no reason for changing her lively and dramatic way of telling her own story" (7). Whereas Jacobs apologizes modestly in her preface for the shortcomings of her text, Child explains to the reader why a woman brought up in slavery can write so well. Although this seems paradoxical, it is, however, not astonishing if we bear in mind that abolitionists and fugitive slaves had to constantly fight the common assumption that Slave Narratives were false accounts made up by white Northern abolitionists in order to destroy the South. Child's last paragraph implicitly mentions the central theme of the narrative, that is, the sexual exploitation of her "sisters in bondage" (8). She states that these immoral and shady practices of the 'Peculiar Institution' should be exposed and that every woman of the North should constantly exert "her moral influence on the question of Slavery" (8).

What makes Jacobs' narrative appear similar to a Bildungsroman is its "Contents" with its 41 chapter headings, beginning with "Childhood" and ending with "Free at Last". With its 306 pages, *Incidents* is one of the longest Slave Narratives.[1] There are many narrative pauses within each chapter, in which the narrator gives explanations of the slave system. For example: "The reader probably knows that no promise or writing given to a slave is legally binding; for, according to Southern laws, a slave, *being* property, can *hold* no property" (13). Or she presents examples to corroborate her argument that, for example, not only masters but also mistresses can abuse a 'favourite' woman slave terribly: "I once saw a young slave girl dying soon after the birth of a child nearly white ... Her mistress stood by, and mocked at her like an incarnate fiend" (24).

Of the narrative's 41 chapters or episodes, there are five which do not carry the action any further, but which serve as lessons. These 'interludes' inform on the one hand the Northern readers about the 'other' side of slavery with which they are not familiar and, on the

---

1 *The History of Mary Prince* (1831, 44 pages), *The Narrative of the Life of Frederick Douglass* (1845, 124 pages), *Narrative of the Life and Escape of William Wells Brown*, (1847, approx. 50 pages), *Narrative of the Life and Adventure of Henry Bibb, an American Slave* (1849, approx. 120 pages), *Twelve Years a Slave: Narrative of Solomon Northup* (1853, approx. 81 pages).

other hand, aim at arousing the readers' sympathy for the 'slave girl' by drawing a realistic picture of slavery's degrading effect in various areas of society, such as church, family and work.

In chapter 3, "The Slaves' New Year's Day", the narrator tries to arouse the women readers' feelings by portraying the huge difference between the reader's happiness on New Year's Day and a slave mother's despair on the same day. Here Harriet Jacobs takes advantage of the reader's identification with the sorrows of the slave mother, who is on the verge of despair because her children have all been sold away from her.

In chapter 8, "What Slaves are Taught to Think of the North", the narrator writes about the lies which slaveholders spread among their slaves about the 'terrible' North and its 'horrible' citizens, and about what they might expect of freedom there. Moreover, she condemns the North - and consequently her readers -, for passing a law enabling the South to extend its power even to the North.[1] Thus the narrator very cleverly stirs up the old enmity between the South and the North, by emphasizing how the North is indeed looked down upon by the South:

> ... the northern man is not welcome south of Mason and Dixon's line, unless he suppresses every thought and feeling at variance with their "peculiar institution." Nor is it enough to be silent. The masters are not pleased, unless they obtain a greater degree of subservience than that ... When northerners go to the south to reside, they prove very apt scholars. They soon imbibe the sentiments and disposition of their neighbor, and generally go beyond their teachers. Of the two, they are proverbially the hardest masters. (69)

Similar to Harriet Wilson in *Our Nig,* Harriet Jacobs dares touch upon the sensitive taboo of the racist North, which had already been criticized by Harriet Beecher Stowe. By attacking, practically on the eve of the Civil War, the myth that the "North is humane" and the "South

1 The passing of the Fugitive Slave Law in 1850 prompted Harriet Beecher Stowe to write *Uncle Tom's Cabin,* in its composition she relied heavily on the slave's experience as related in Slave Narratives.

is evil", neither Wilson nor Jacobs seems ready to make any compromise, even in order to promote the sale of their books.

In chapter 9, "Sketches of Neighboring Slaveholders" the reader is given some examples of the extreme cruelty of masters, mistresses and overseers to their slaves, and is shown the degrading effect of slavery on blacks and whites, women and men alike. The narrator also takes the opportunity to introduce several characters who will turn up again later in the narration and in connection with the protagonist. Mr. Litch, one of the cruel slaveholders mentioned here (71-73), will appear again in "Fear of Insurrection" (chapter 12) where he is the officer in charge of searching black people's houses and huts after Nat Turner's insurrection in 1831 (100-102). The story of Charity's son, James, and his terrible end, screwed into the cotton gin after his escape from his master, is also told in "Sketches" (74-76). The readers will be reminded of this cruel murder at a crucial moment in the narration in chapter 29 "Preparation for Escape". After having waited almost seven years for a 'safe' possibility of escape, the protagonist turned down her first chance because her relatives had heard about James' awful fate after his escape (229).

By taking up previously related incidents and transferring them from a broader (historical) context to the protagonist's 'history', the narrator manages to underline slavery's dangerous unpredictability in general and Linda Brent's hazardous situation in particular. A good example of this can be seen in the context of her preparation for escape. The chapter, "Fear of Insurrection", sets the whole narrative into a historical context, that is, before and after Nat Turner's rebellion (97). Here, the narrator gives a detailed description of the anti-black violence which has even ravaged her own town, and during which many innocent blacks were killed.

The "Appendix" contains two testimonials introduced by Lydia Maria Child. The first one was written by the Quaker, Amy Post, a close friend of Harriet's, and is dated October 30th, 1859, in Rochester, New York (304-305). Similar to Pringle's testimony in the Supplement to *Mary Prince* (34-35), Amy Post asserts that the author of the book has been "a beloved inmate of [their] family nearly the whole of the year 1849" (304). She goes on to say that "her deportment indicated remarkable *delicacy of feeling* and *purity* of thought" (my emphasis, 304). Albert's *The House of Bondage*, published posthumously, also contains three prefaced testimonies praising the writer as a "devoted mother and wife", emphasizing her "angelic spirit" and her "holy influence", and considering her an "angel of mercy" (Preface, Introduction, The Author). Albert's and Jacobs' prefaces and Jacobs' appendix underline the importance of a rhetoric which diverts the reader's attention away from the actual subject-matter, that is, the woman writers' social critique, and towards the writers' female personality and flawless character.

Amy Post - similarly to Child in her introduction - evokes Linda's specific sufferings as a woman slave. She says that Linda had to be persuaded to publish her story because she felt ashamed of relating her experiences to the public: "She said, 'You know a woman can whisper her cruel wrongs in the ear of a dear friend much easier than she can record them for the world to read'" (304-305).

In the second testimonial, George W. Lowther, who is, in Child's terms, "a highly respectable colored citizen of Boston", confirms that Linda Brent's narrative "is full of living truths"; he says that he knew Linda from childhood and that he was familiar with her particular experiences (306).

Having analysed the formal aspects of *Incidents*, it can be concluded that its structure follows the tradition of the Slave Narrative. This story, however, has two features which make it outstanding: its woman-centred subject-matter and structure, and Child's 'provocative' inclusion of a testimonial given by a black person, whose 'word' would not be considered trustworthy if mentioned in the South.

(c) True Woman Versus Heroic Woman, or White Heroine Versus Black Heroine

This chapter will examine how the narrator uses elements from the Slave Narrative and Woman's Fiction in order to tell her story, and where she has to step outside of these forms in order to give an accurate portrayal of her protagonist's experience. Of the three Antebellum Narratives discussed in this thesis, *Incidents* is the longest, and of the three protagonists, Linda Brent is psychologically the most developed character. To follow Linda Brent's path from bondage to freedom, is also to observe the heroine's fictional representation. There is the further question whether the black heroine in general, and the protagonist, Linda Brent, in particular, can or cannot be compared to the white heroine in Woman's Fiction; the narrator herself felt "that the slave woman ought not to be judged by the same standard as others" (86). What other literary criteria have to be taken into account in order to obtain an accurate, non-stereotyped analysis of the black heroine?

Both the "Preface by the Author" and the "Introduction by the Editor" explicitly state that this narrative should arouse "the conscientious and reflecting women at the North ...." (8). Harriet Jacobs and Lydia Maria Child, in their appeal to their female readers to establish a sisterhood of the North and the South and of blacks and whites, wanted to take advantage of the growing number of (white) women readers in 19th-century America. Now, to get a fuller understanding of Harriet Jacobs' technique in representing and characterizing Linda Brent, as opposed to conventional white heroines, the 20th-century reader and scholar must be aware of the impact of the most popular literature produced and read by Harriet Jacobs' contemporaries. Let us first remember what were some of the most widely read books in 19th-century America and then consider the ideology of true womanhood.

Susan Warner's *The Wide, Wide World,* which was published in 1850, was a best-seller in the United States and in England. In the space of only two years, as many as fourteen editions were produced (Jane Tompkins, "Afterword" in *The Wide, Wide, World* 584). Harriet Beecher Stowe's *Uncle Tom's Cabin,* serialized in 1851-1852 in the abolitionist journal, *The National Era,* and published as a book in 1852, was also an incredible success; with more than 300,000 copies sold in one year (John William Ward, "Afterword" in *Uncle Tom's Cabin* 478-479). *The Lamplighter,* by Maria Susanna Cummins, published in 1854, enjoyed a similar popularity, selling more than a 100,000 copies in one year - to Hawthorne's despair, whose *The Scarlet Letter* sold less than 10,000 copies during his lifetime (Nina Baym, "Introduction" in *The Lamplighter* ix)! And finally, E.D.E.N. Southworth's *The Hidden Hand,* serialized in 1859 and published as a book with the subtitle, *or,*

Capitola the Madcap, in 1888, was still in print in the first decades of the 20th century (Joanne Dobson, "Introduction" in *The Hidden Hand* xl).

Women readers confronted in their daily readings with heroines and women characters such as Warner's Ellen Montgomery; Beecher Stowe's Eliza, Evangeline St. Clare (Little Eva), Topsy, Miss Marie; Cummins' Gertrude; Southworth's Mrs. Le Noir, Marah Rocke and even Capitola; as well as many others, had certain moral and social expectations which had to be observed by any writers of the 19th century if they wanted their writings to be sold. Kate Chopin's *The Awakening,* published in 1899, is a good example of a writer's and a novel's fate when literary conventions and moral and social traditions are flaunted. Chopin's heroine, Edna Pontellier, dared question marriage and motherhood, and finally committed adultery; consequently, the author was faced with social and literary ostracism.

The 'ideology of true womanhood', whose rules were imprinted upon generations of 19th-century American women, comprises four main virtues, "piety, purity, submissiveness and domesticity", which every woman had to absorb if she wanted to be accepted in society (Barbara Welter 21). The novels and their heroines mentioned above, together with women's magazines and religious literature, were a didactic means of presenting the guidelines to the innocent girl or young woman. In the chapter, "The Cult of True Womanhood", Barbara Welter discusses the "four cardinal virtues" of the 19th-century American woman, be she mother, daughter, sister or wife. The girl and adolescent were daily exposed to an ever-changing and hostile world, and hence had to be protected from evil influences in the guise of seductive suitors or masters who would try to lead her astray. Richardson's Pamela is the classic example of an innocent girl's long struggle to withstand her master's sexual advances. Innocence and piety finally triumph over despotism - hence the subtitle: "*Virtue Rewarded*" - and Pamela is thus recompensed - at the end of Vol. I and before further tests in Vol II - with her master's love and respect, and a happy ending in marriage. The 19th-century American girl and woman knew that these four virtues - and nothing less - would open the path to happiness and power in marriage and that the lack of only one of these would inevitably lead to a life of despair and loneliness -

rejected by society.[1] Mag, in *Our Nig*, who was left pregnant by her lover, or Marah Rocke, in *The Hidden Hand*, who had been unjustly accused of adultery by her husband, Major Warfield, and consequently was abandoned, are examples of a husband's or society's anger at so-called 'fallen women'. While a young woman guilty of such 'a crime' often contemplated suicide or tried to get rid of her child, as Hetty Sorel does in *Adam Bede*, the "women's magazines" in 19th-century America were replete with tales which ended in women's "madness or death" (Welter, 23).

"Religion or piety was the core of woman's virtue, the source of her strength" (Welter, 21). Only by relying on God and Providence, would there be 'triumphs' over the patient woman's 'trials'. It is remarkable that the reading of novels was considered a danger to pious young women! Instead, they were advised to read "religious biography" and "study history" (Welter, 33-34).

"The true woman's place was unquestionably by her own fireside - as daughter, sister, but most of all as wife and mother. Therefore domesticity was among the virtues most prized by the women's magazines" (Welter, 31). For the Victorian woman, the happy home was the foundation of human bliss. While husbands, brothers and sons had to face the daily dangers of an unpredictable world outside the security of the home, the wives, sisters and daughters felt it almost a religious duty to create an atmosphere of beauty, calmness, cleanliness and order to which the male members of the household would gladly return. The home symbolized a safe harbour for women and men alike, with the small difference that it was expected of the wife that she devote herself solely to the task of a patient comforter, fulfilling her husband's needs and wishes. In those times, countless children died in childhood and strange fevers could waste away the strongest adult, hence the 19th-century woman was also an experienced nurse. Of delicate health herself, she excelled in comforting the sufferers at the sickbed. Frado, for example, forgets her own sickness and weakness as James' comforter in *Our Nig*. Cassy heals Tom's wounds after he has been terribly beaten, and Miss Ophelia nurses Little Eva during her fatal illness (*Uncle Tom's Cabin*). The independent and adventurous Creole, Mary Seacole, who is anything but a representation of the

---

1 Mrs. Rowson's Charlotte is the typical example of a heroine who has to pay her loss of virtue with social ostracism and finally with death (*Charlotte*).

"True Woman", nevertheless experiences a strange motherhood during the Crimean War, nursing and feeding the wounded soldiers (chapter 19 in *Wonderful Adventures of Mrs. Seacole in Many Lands*).

The last of the four virtues, submissiveness, is probably best personified in Ellen Montgomery, whose childhood and adolescence offer a permanent lesson in self-sacrifice, humility, submissiveness, and self-abnegation. Just as children had to obey their parents, so had wives to accept their husbands' decisions - without any objections. Women's opinions and thoughts were considered inferior to men's. In this context, Barbara Welter quotes Caroline Howard Gilman who, in *Recollections of a Housekeeper* (New York, 1834), gives advice to the young bride in order to introduce her to the right order of things, without which there would be quarrelling and chaos in an otherwise happy home: "Oh, young and lovely bride, watch well the first moments when your will conflicts with his to whom God and society have given the control. Reverence his *wishes* even when you do not his *opinions*" (Welter 29). In her *Recollections of a Southern Matron* (New York, 1838), Gilman's perfect wife is supposed to

> repress a harsh answer, to confess a fault, and to stop in the midst of self-defense, in gentle submission ... Men are not unreasonable ... Their difficulties lie in not understanding the moral and physical nature of our sex. They often wound through ignorance, and are surprised at having offended ... If any habit of his annoyed me, I spoke of it once or twice, calmly, then bore it quietly. (Welter, 29-30)

Thus, Mrs. Shelby, in *Uncle Tom's Cabin,* is a good example of the above virtue. She tries in vain to convince her husband of the great wrong he inflicts on Tom and his family by selling him. Through daring to speak up to her husband and shake his conscience - nevertheless without success - she is put violently back into her place when rejoicing in Eliza's escape: "'Wife, you talk like a fool'!" (52). After her husband's death, Mrs. Shelby proves to be an apt business woman, managing her husband's estate, paying his debts, and liberating all their slaves - although during his lifetime she does not even ask about her husband's pecuniary difficulties. 19th-century white middle-class women were the queens of their homes, but were not to degrade themselves by tasks and thoughts which were solely the concern of the male world. Mr. Shelby very fittingly expresses this Victorian belief when his wife suggests helping him to "straighten matters": "Oh, ridiculous, Emily! You are the finest woman in Kentucky; but still you haven't sense to know that you don't understand business; - women never do, and never can" (274).

If they did not want to be labelled "nonwomen" or "semi-women", the only thing women could do was to submit to their husband's wishes and to comply with 19th-century values (Welter 40).

This myth of true womanhood shaped a whole century, although only the chosen few actually had the chance to enjoy a life devoted solely to their households, their husbands, children and religious duties. The Industrial Revolution in England and the United States tells another tale, one of poverty and misery among the working classes, with women and children working for sixteen hours a day in factories, under the most abominable conditions. These women did not have much time and energy left to indulge in the luxury of reading novels - if they could read at all - or creating a cozy home after the day's labour had been done. Hence the direct addressees of women's magazines, religious and persuasive literature had to be the girls and women of a white middle class and a black Northern elite. Nevertheless, these values that represented the experiences of only one class of women imprinted themselves on everything that stood for womanhood. It must be remembered that the heroine in Woman's Fiction can only overcome her poverty, loneliness and misery through her own efforts, that is by exercising patient submission on the one hand, and actively indulging in womanly goodness on the other.[1] Considering the everyday struggle of working-class women in the North and slave women in the South, it is sheer mockery to assume that they could have changed their lives - similar to the white heroine - by relying on their own efforts. Woman's Fiction therefore lacks certain features which are characteristic of a realistic representation of one of the earliest Afro-American heroines. Harriet Jacobs, however, combines elements of the two genres available to her - Slave Narrative and Woman's Fiction - but has to reach beyond them in order to represent her heroine, Linda Brent, on occasions which lie outside the experience of either the white heroine or the black hero. If the slave

---

1 See Chapter 2 (c) in this thesis.

woman or the slave heroine is to be judged according to the values and norms of 19th-century America, she will inevitably fall short.

How can the slave woman be pious if she is not allowed to read the Bible, and rarely has the possibility to practise her faith? Octavia Albert's informants relate repeated experiences in which their Catholic masters forbade their slaves to attend the American or Protestant church ("Charlotte Brooks" in *The House of Bondage* 1890, 38). Mrs. Bellmont is another example, illustrating the black heroine's paradoxical position. She threatens and ridicules Frado whenever she sees her reading the Bible, and complains to her husband: "I found her reading the Bible to-day, just as though she expected to turn pious nigger, and preach to white folks" (88). Wheras the white girl/heroine quite often has the advantage of a mother's (Mrs. Montgomery) or a surrogate mother's religious instruction, which plays a decisive role in the formation and assertion of a feminine ego, the slave girl/heroine faces a lot of discouragment if she wants to live according to the Gospel and the ten commandments. In the Slave Narrative, the gaining of religion is, therefore, an important step for the slave, a step with obstacles to overcome, thus - similar to the acquisition of literacy - preparing him/her for the long anticipated escape to freedom. The white heroine has to learn - as Ellen Montgomery does - to love God more than anybody or anything else and to patiently and unfalteringly accept the decrees of Providence. This is in contrast to the slave heroine/hero, whose finding of God opens up new horizons and encourages action. The slaves begin questioning the master's supremacy, and identify strongly with the Hebrews who managed to defy their Egyptian enslavers and - with God's help - set out to find the promised land. The black heroine's disobedience is, therefore, an important means to self-assertion and eventual liberty.

Chastity and purity are the most sacred gift of womanhood, the white heroine's 'moral dowry' to a suitor who is socially above her, her 'entrance fee' to marriage and a happy home. The slave heroine - also in contrast to the slave hero - faces a dilemma which cannot be resolved in accordance with the cult of true womanhood. The slave girl/heroine is confronted daily with her master's licentiousness, and hence has to develop virtues other than those associated with 'physical purity'. Whereas Richardson's Pamela has the possibility - at least before her imprisonment - of returning to her parents in case of emergency, slave heroines cannot so easily escape or disobey their masters. Moreover, what is considered socially unacceptable, even adulterous, for the plantation owner's wife, is unwritten law for his female slaves; they have to submit to him in order, on the one hand, to satisfy his sexual inclinations and, on the other hand, to help to increase his property. Despite their or rather, their masters' 'violation' of what is considered to be a true woman, Linda Brent and many other slave heroines such as Cassy (*Uncle Tom's Cabin*), Louisa Picquet (in *Collected Black Women's Narratives*), and Elizabeth Keckley, still manage to stay 'pure' in their readers' eyes.

Whereas the white heroine has to submit to the wishes of her parents, her protectors, her future husbands and finally to God, the slave heroine has to submit primarily to the slave system itself, with her master and her mistress as the powerful executors of its laws. Masters and mistresses are, therefore, put above the authority of parents, husband and God; the Slave Narratives are thus an extraordinary testimony to the 'Patriarchal Institution' and its corruptive effect on Christian ethics. As the slave's parental authority is eroded, family ties are prone to be severed; this is why the home does not figure in Slave Narratives authored by men (Olaudah Equiano, Frederick Douglass, William Wells Brown) and also why, paradoxically enough, there is an emphasis on home and mother-daughter relationships in Slave Narratives written by women. Here again, the white heroine's experience is totally different from that of the slave heroine, whose account ends with freedom (Mary Prince, Linda Brent) or independence (Frado), rather than with a happy marriage and a blissful home.

Having looked at 19th-century Christian and Victorian values and their impact on 19th-century literature and its readers in general, we will now trace Linda Brent's heroic path from slavery to freedom. Let us ask ourselves in what way the heroine is part of a literary tradition, and whether this same tradition entails certain limitations as to the representation of Linda Brent's search for identity. In contrast to male authored Slave Narratives, which generally depict the protagonist's quest for freedom as solitary and heroic,[1] Linda Brent in

---

1 An exception is Josiah Henson's autobiography, which does not present a solitary hero, but one who escapes successfully with his wife and children. In his introductory

her no less courageous struggle for liberty is forced to rely completely on other people for support. Narratives authored by women generally lack any representations of heroic deeds, such as fighting the master (in *Narrative of the Life of Frederick Douglass*) or spectacular escapes, as in Douglass' fictional Slave Narrative, "The Heroic Slave" (published in 1853).[1] *Incidents,* with its heroic female protagonist is, however, an exception to the rule. Jacobs was probably influenced by the well-known literary and public figures of her time, Sojourner Truth, Mary Seacole, and Eliza in *Uncle Tom's Cabin.*

Linda Brent's early childhood is depicted as happy and carefree, similar to Mary Prince's, with the difference that Linda, her brother William, and both of her parents can live under the same roof, in a comfortable home separated from their masters'. The sudden changes brought about - first, at the age of six, because of her mother's death and later at the age of eleven, by her mistress' death - makes her aware, mentally and physically, that she is a slave. Her father's death, shortly after her removal to the Flints, her new owners, renders her an orphan. Whereas Mary Prince in her narrative is brutally made an orphan by the slave system, Linda Brent's parents are no less tragically snatched away from her by sudden illness and death, a common way in Woman's Fiction of reducing the heroine to the state of an orphan, which generally initiates her trials.

If Frederick Douglass' and William Wells Brown's childhood reminiscences are compared with Brent's and Mary Prince's, it can be seen that the two men hardly know their mothers, because they have been separated from them at an early age, and that both have slaveholders as their fathers. They also speak of their mothers as victims, and of themselves as powerless onlookers to their mother's degradations and sufferings. At the very beginning of their narratives the two male child-heroes are already represented as lonely travellers on slavery's path, deprived of parental affection and connection. Linda Brent, on the other hand, begins her account by reflecting on the

---

words to "Father Henson's Story", Abraham Chapman states that it is one of the best-known Slave Narratives of the 19th century. *The Life of Josiah Henson, Formerly a Slave Now an Inhabitant of Canada* was published in Boston in 1849, republished there in 1858, and in London in 1859 (*Steal Away* 87).

1 An unabridged version of "The Heroic Slave" can be found in *Steal Away* 131-181.

impact of family-life on her future outlook on life: "... I was so fondly shielded that I never dreamed I was a piece of merchandise ...." (11-12). The beginning of the narrative depicts the wholesomeness of close family relations - which is absent in the 'master' Slave Narratives (Douglass, Brown) - and thus shows more clearly the discrepancy between the destinies of black and white families, and addresses more directly the Northern readers, who can empathize with a heroine who first experienced, harmony and love in a home of her own and then was brutally robbed of her sweet illusion.

The woman slave has to prove to the world not only that she exists, that is, that she is a human being, but also that she is 'woman'. *Incidents* adopts the structure common to the Slave Narrative, and adds an 'underlying structure' that is more suited to her narrative. The display of prowess, for example, is crucial to the narrative written by men, and as important to the establishment of a masculine ego as the Slave Narratives' opening sentence 'I was born ...', by which the slaves claim: 'but, nevertheless, and whatever might be said, I exist'. After this first step, which makes him part of mankind, he has to prove to the world, that is, to his readers, that he is worth being considered a human being. This is done through his heroic deeds, which emphasize his courage and manhood and prove him to be a worthy citizen of America. At the beginning of her narrative, Harriet Jacobs therefore, attributes the Slave Narrative's claim of prowess and courage to the male members of her heroine's family: her father who "had more of the feeling of a free man than is common among slaves", her uncle, Benjamin, and her brother, William (17). The chapter, "The Slave Who Dared To Feel Like A Man" - the title is an allusion to Douglass' Narrative - contains reference to William's courage and Benjamin's imprisonment and successful escape to the North. The beginning of Linda Brent's struggle to defend her womanhood (also mentioned in the same chapter) is thus underlined and framed by the acts of courage committed by her uncle and brother. Benjamin 'dares feel like a man' by openly challenging his master and taking his freedom. Linda Brent is also implied in the title - "The Slave Who Dared To Feel Like A Man" - because she dares to stand up for her womanhood:

> When [Flint] told me that I was made for his use, made to obey his command in *every* thing; that I was nothing but a slave, whose will must and should surrender to his, never before had my puny arm felt

> half so strong ... The war of my life had begun; and though one of God's most powerless creatures, I resolved never to be conquered. Alas, for me! (29-31)

Her father's, uncle's and brother's boldness and hate of servitude are an inspiration to Linda Brent. Their heroic example anticipates the heroine's victory over her oppressor, Flint.

The author's use of the device of an 'underlying structure' - mentioned above - denotes a conscious or unconscious break with certain norms inherent in 19th-century literature. As in the case of the heroic deed, the element is still there, but transferred to the heroine's male relatives.

In *Incidents*, the gaining of literacy is another element which lacks the significance commonly attached to it in male authored narratives. Thomas Jones, William Wells Brown and Frederick Douglass have to learn their letters one by one, by cunningly bribing white boys to reveal the cherished secret.[1] Their perseverance in learning not only prepares their escape but also authenticates their narrative, on whose front page the reader finds the author's claim: "Written by Himself". The child, Linda, is taught by her mistress "to read and spell; and for this privilege, which so rarely falls to the lot of a slave, I bless her memory" (16). Unlike Jones, Brown and Douglass, Linda becomes literate without much effort. The difference between the heroine of the Slave Narrative and the heroes mentioned above is again exemplified by Jacobs' twisting of the benefits of literacy. When Flint finds out that Linda can read, he writes her notes that are full of sexual allusions. At this point, 'literacy', instead of creating a distance between slave and master because it furthers the slave's escape, has the opposite effect as far as Linda Brent is concerned. Whenever Flint cannot talk to her or see her, he writes her notes in which he orders her to come to his office.

After the heroine's transfer of prowess to the male members of her family, which symbolizes her bold determination to stand up for her womanhood (chapter 10), suddenly - in seeming contrast to her earlier resolutions (chapter 4) - we find the heroine confessing her 'impurity': "I knew what I did, and I did it with deliberate calculation.

---

1 Thomas Jones' narrative, "How I Learned to Read and Write", was published in Canada in 1853 (*Steal Away* 66-75).

But, O, ye happy women, whose purity has been sheltered from childhood ... do not judge the poor desolate slave girl too severely!" (83). The narrator/heroine herself draws the parallel between th Slave Narrative and Woman's Fiction by addressing the white woman of the North. By confessing her desperate situation, the heroine tries to make white women understand the difference of their situation. Here again, Linda Brent goes beyond the common representation of the white heroine in Woman's Fiction, by deliberately and actively choosing a lover. This act, which can be considered an act of revolt against Flint's treatment, gives Linda Brent the power and endurance she needs to withstand him in the future.

Finally, her heroine's 'heroic' escape, disguised in men's clothes, after her seven-year 'imprisonment' in her cramped retreat, confirms the heroine's triumph over Flint's corrupting and destructive force.

In the last chapter of her narrative, "Free at Last", the narrator addresses her readers for the last time: "Reader, my story ends with freedom; not in the usual way, with marriage" (302). Thus, the narrator evokes the black slave heroine's dilemma: her account of her tribulations ends with freedom, and not with an expected marriage as, for example, in the case of Jane Eyre who can proudly say at the end of the novel: "Reader, I married him" (474). The remark addressed to Jacobs' readers is ambiguous. It can be understood as an apology for the deficiencies in her account, whose ending might not be satisfying to her white woman readers. Or it can be considered as an ironic critique of the frequency of patterns used in Woman's Novels.

It can thus be seen that, in general, *Incidents* is written in the tradition of the Slave Narrative *and* Woman's Fiction. In the instances discussed (e.g. literacy, heroism, womanhood and the black family), the narrative departs from the common pattern of the two genres, using devices which are more suitable in representing the black slave heroine's particular experience.

(d) The Black Family and the 'Peculiar Institution'

If *Incidents* is Harriet Jacobs' autobiography, an account of a slave girl's experience in slavery, it is no less an 'ode' to her mother, her grandmother and to enslaved mothers in general. The slave mother is represented not simply as a passive victim, but as a courageous woman trying to survive in a system which gives her no legal right to herself or her loved ones: her children, her husband and her other relatives. In the narrative, there are various 'incidents' which show a slave mother's fate, the worst of which is to lose all her children at once to a trader who is then going to sell them - each one separately - to the highest bidder.

In this chapter, special emphasis is put on the general fictional representation of the black family, and on the mother-figure in particular. Linda Brent introduces the reader to various mothers in her narrative: slave mothers, slaveholding mothers, manumitted black mothers in the South, and both black and white mothers in the North.

The analysis of the various mothers in Jacobs' narrative will begin with Linda Brent's grandmother, Aunt Marthy, because she is the symbol per se of the black mother. Her life story stands for the biography of generations of black mothers raised in slavery. She was born a slave, was later manumitted by her father, a planter in South Carolina, was again captured and sold back into slavery, was promised freedom by her mistress, but was sold again after her mistress' death, after having served her faithfully all her life. She was finally manumitted by her last owner, who bought her only in order to set her free (12-21). The protagonist's grandmother frames the narrative structurally as well as thematically. The narrator begins by praising her in the opening paragraph of her first chapter, and closes Linda's 'history' with the protagonist's "tender memories" of her grandmother "who lived to rejoice in [her granddaughter's] freedom" (303/302).

Aunt Marthy is the head of the family - blacks and whites alike gain nourishment physically and mentally from her impressive presence. Linda Brent's first description of her grandmother exemplifies the important role she plays within the family as well as in the narrator's life:

> I had also a great treasure in my maternal grandmother, who was a remarkable woman in many respects. ....
> To this good grandmother I was indebted for many comforts. ... and after we ceased to be children we were indebted to her for many more important services. (12-14)

There is an ambiguity, however, in Linda Brent's relationship to her grandmother. Both her grandmother and her mother represent the strong, virtuous - but not submissive! - black mother who, despite slavery, manages to live according to the moral standards applied to white women. This makes it the more difficult for Linda Brent to confide in her grandmother, because she realizes that she cannot live up to her high expectations, although Linda knows that her experience at the Flints' is different from her mother's and her grandmother's, who both had the unusual advantage of masters who respected them.

After Linda's mother dies, her grandmother and, later, her aunt, Aunt Nancy, take the position of a surrogate mother in her life. Linda's close relationship to these contrasting mother figures shapes her future life decisively. Whereas Linda's grandmother tries to make her children and grandchildren feel that their situation is God's will and that they should "pray for contentment" (28), Aunt Nancy instills Linda with courage: "When my friends tried to discourage me from running away, she always encouraged me" (218). Both mother figures are depicted as protective and strong forces that assist the heroine on her way to self-assertion and liberty, Aunt Martha by hiding her for seven years and Aunt Nancy by protecting her at the Flints' and by encouraging Linda's thirst for freedom.

The Flints, with Dr. Flint as the head of the house, represent the negative force in the narrative. The 'villain' Flint endangers the unity and harmony of Aunt Martha's family and also endangers the project of her life: to buy her children and grandchildren out of slavery. Mr. Flint acts destructively not only on Aunt Martha's family, but also on his own. He represents the licentious and corrupt slaveholder who spares neither his slaves nor his own family.

Mrs. Flint is the narrative's representative of the jealous mistress; instead of protecting Linda from her husband's advances, she makes Linda's life even more miserable:

> Mrs. Flint possessed the key to her husband's character before I was born. She might have used this knowledge to counsel and to screen the young and the innocent among her slaves; but for them she had no sympathy. (49)

Mrs. Flint is the South's image of the over-protected mistress of her husband's house, in appearance weak, spoilt, jealous, and sickly, "but her nerves were so strong, that she could sit in her easy chair and see a woman whipped, till the blood trickled from every stroke of the lash" (22).

Although the Flints endanger the unity of Aunt Martha's family, their vicious treatment at the same time strenghtens the ties within Aunt Martha's black family.

The I-narrator Brent, in giving an account of the tribulations not only of a 'favourite slave', but also of a slave mother, reveals to us the mother's voice. On the one hand, she describes one white mistress' betrayal of her female slaves (Mrs. Flint); on the other hand, Brent also depicts the love and support she gets from a slaveholder's wife, who hides Linda Brent in her own house (150-169), and thus helps her to finally escape to the North. A sisterhood between black and white women is further established in the North when the heroine experiences the support of Mr. Bruce's first wife (an Englishwoman) and, after her death, the support of his second wife (a Northern woman). Both white women, mothers themselves, can empathize with the heroine in her situation as the mother of two children, as well as being a fugitive slave in the North.

Thus we can see that the heroine, who grew up in the house of her parents and who after her parents' death enjoyed the support of her grandmother and aunt, experiences the life-saving ties within a black family, despite slavery's reality. Her surrogate mothers instill her with the courage to act, but also with the patience necesssary to endure the pains of her long concealment. The depiction of various other slave mothers who are at the mercy of their masters and mistresses foreshadows Linda Brent's decision to fight for her own and her children's liberty. However, Linda Brent does not judge only the white mistress' cruelties towards her female slaves, she also tries to empathize with them, aware that as the young wives of slaveholders they

> have romantic notions of a sunny clime, and of the flowering vines that all the year round shade a happy home. To what disappointments are they destined! The young wife soon learns that the husband in whose hands she has placed her happiness pays no regard to his marriage vows. Children of every shade of complexion play with her own fair babies, and too well she knows that they are born unto him of his own household. (56-57)

The absence, in general, of a picture of the black families and nurturing mothers after the slave's earliest childhood is, of course, closely connected with the slave's individual experience in bondage. The first two chapters of Olaudah Equiano's narrative, for example, relate the customs and manners of his native country, including his relationship to his parents, and especially to his mother, prior to his captivity. Equiano's personal experience, that is of abduction, placed a distance of thousands of kilometres between himself and his family in Africa, and simply did not allow a continuation of familial ties. Frederick Douglass and William Wells Brown, who had white fathers and who were both early separated from their slave mothers, obviously could not include any familial ties either. However, many Slave Narratives written by women such as Jackson, Delaney, Drumgoold, and Burton tell another tale by emphasising their relationship to their mothers.

In contrast to many other slave narratives, Harriet Jacobs' narrative depicts a black family's social contacts as well as its nurturing influence through several generations; it must therefore be considered an important and extraordinary document for historians and literary scholars alike.

Part Two

Woman's Era (1890-1900): Stereotype or Character?

Chapter 4

Harper's *Iola Leroy*: An Archetypal Novel?

(a) Antebellum and Postbellum America: A Transition

[Janette Alston] resolved more earnestly than ever to make the world better by her example, gladder by her presence, and to kindle the fires of her genius on the altars of universal love and truth. She had a higher and better object in all her writings than the mere acquisition of gold, or acquirement of fame. She felt that she had a high and holy mission on the battle-field of existence, that life was not given her to be frittered away in nonsense, or wasted away in trifling pursuits. She would willingly espouse an unpopular cause but not an unrighteous one. In her the down-trodden slave found an earnest advocate; the flying fugitive remembered her kindness as he stepped cautiously through our Republic, to gain his freedom in a monarchial land, having broken the chains on which the rust of centuries had gathered. Little children learned to name her with affection, the poor called her blessed, as she broke her bread to the pale lips of hunger. Her life was like a beautiful story, only it was clothed with the dignity of reality and invested with the sublimity of truth.

Frances Ellen Watkins [Harper], "The Two Offers" (1859)

The omniscient narrator of Harper's autobiographical short story "The Two Offers", published before the Civil War, voices the author's personal aim as well as her protagonist's, to commit her life wholly to the improvement of mankind. The story is addressed to a black audience and draws on two cousins' different outlooks on life. Laura Lagrange chooses her husband only because she considers him the better of two offers, and in order to escape "'the risk of being an old maid'" (289). Janette Alston tries to warn her cousin of the consequences of such a match, but she marries, nevertheless, and has to face the awful fate Janette has predicted: an unhappy marriage. "'... Is there not more intense wretchedness in an ill-assorted marriage - more utter loneliness in a loveless home, than in the lot of the old maid who accepts her earthly mission as a gift from God, ... ?'" (289). The omniscient narrator, having related Laura's lonely death, sermonizes on the importance of women's enlightenment in order to build and secure sustaining, happy homes free of the evils of intemperance. Not only woman's "affectional nature" should be developed, but all her human faculties, "because no perfect womanhood is developed by imperfect culture [and] intense love is often akin to intense suffering ...." (291). Harper's speech on "Enlightened Motherhood", given before the Brooklyn Literary Society in 1892, supplies her theoretical frame to "The Two Offers". There, Harper elaborates on the mother's central position in the home and encourages women to take part in the constructive work for the future of the black race (Frances Smith Foster 285-292). In *Iola Leroy,* Harper further develops the character merely sketched in Janette Alston by following her heroine's path from girlhood to womanhood, depicting her dedication and her growing sense of responsibility for the improvement of her race.

Although the publication of *Iola Leroy* (1892) succeeds *Megda* (1891) chronologically, there are three decisive reasons why Part Two of this thesis begins with a discussion of Harper's novel.

Firstly, the term "Woman's Era" - by which black women's activity in every field of society in the 1890s is understood - was created by Harper when addressing her audience in a speech on "Woman's Political Future" at the historic World's Congress of Representative Women in Chicago in 1893:[1]

> Through weary, wasting years men have destroyed, dashed in pieces, and overthrown, but to-day we stand on the threshold of woman's era, and woman's work is grandly constructive. In her hands are possibilities whose use or abuse must tell upon the political life of the nation, and send their influence for good or evil across the track of unborn ages. (Loewenberg and Bogin, 245)[2]

---

1 See Sewell, May Wright, ed. *World's Congress of Representative Women: A Historical Resume.* Chicago: Rand McNally, 1894. 433-37.

2 The 1890s was indeed a period of great productivity and activity for African-American women as the following list of authors and publications evidences: Katherine Davis Chapman Tillman; Mrs. A. E. Johnson; Octavia V. Rogers Albert; Emma Dunham Kelley: *Megda;* Anna Julia Cooper: *A Voice From The South;* Ida B. Wells-Barnett:

Secondly, Harper - as a public activist fighting for the abolition of slavery and against the Fugitive Slave Law before the Civil War, and afterwards for women's suffrage, against racism, against lynchings and the slow disfranchisement during Reconstruction and post-Reconstruction - can be considered an important representative and recorder of the Antebellum *and* the Postbellum Eras. Moreover, her *Poems on Miscellaneous Subjects* as well as her only novel, *Iola Leroy,* represent the transition of Afro-American fiction from the rural atmosphere of the antebellum South to the urbanity of the Harlem Renaissance.

And thirdly, Frances Ellen Watkins Harper was, after Phillis Wheatley, America's most famous and most popular black poet. Her first and only novel, *Iola Leroy,* can be considered the best-selling novel by an Afro-American writer in the 19th century, with editions published in Boston and Philadelphia and with as many as five printings within one year.

When Harper published *Iola Leroy,* she was 67 years old. Hence she could look back on an active and successful life as a writer and activist for human rights. In his introduction to the novel, William Still writes: "I confess when I first learned that Mrs. Harper was about to write 'a story' on some features of the Anglo-African race, growing out of what was once popularly known as the 'peculiar institution,' I had my doubts about the matter" (Still, "Introduction" to *Iola Leroy,* 1). Still's reservation was not unfounded because, if Harper had not succeeded in the novel, it would have been, on the one hand, a terrible blow for her personal career, and on the other hand, a proof to the world that Afro-Americans were not capable of moulding their subject

---

Southern Horrors; Amanda Smith; Mrs. N. F. Mossell: *The Work of the Afro-American Woman;* Alice Dunbar-Nelson; Emma D. Kelley-Hawkins; Olivia Ward Bush-Banks; Angelina Weld Grimké; Pauline E. Hopkins: *Contending Forces.* Moreover, at the Congress of Representative Women many of the above mentioned women gave speeches on the progress and success of black women in different fields of society. Clubs for African-American women were founded and "the first Congress of Colored Women of the United States was convened in Boston" in 1895. In "1896 the National Federation and the National League of Colored Women united in Washington, D.C., to form the National Association of Colored Women (NACW)." This was the first time in history, when black women "became nationally organized to confront the various modes of their oppression" (Hazel Carby 96).

matter into the superior form of the novel. Thus, Still unconsciously establishes a link to Phillis Wheatley, whose volume of poetry also had to weather the assumption of the blacks' artistic inferiority.

Iola Leroy, in comparison with the Slave Narrative with its explicit message addressed to a primarily white audience, also contains an implicit message which is addressed primarily to a black middle class, and only secondarily to a white readership. Harper's heroine, Iola Leroy, stands as a new ideal of black womanhood whose example should be followed, and with whom black readers (that is, black women) should be able to identify. White readers, and white women readers in particular, should be confronted with an example of black womanhood which would enable them to foster unprejudiced feelings towards their black sisters and fellow citizens. It is quite interesting to see a parallel between the Slave Narrative, with its direct appeal for the abolition of one of the most destructive institutions in the history of mankind, and Harper's novel with its no less direct appeal for equality and mutual understanding between different ethnic groups, and for religion, temperance, justice, and humanity in post-Reconstruction America.

As Harper's 'political' and private life, as well as her literary work, are intrinsically connected, a short biographical outline will be given in order to gain a fuller understanding of this extraordinary and courageous woman and her literary achievements.[1]

Frances Ellen Watkins (later, Harper) was born in 1825 to free parents in Baltimore, in the slaveholding state of Maryland. Although not a slave, her childhood was nevertheless desolate: on the one hand, because of the strict slave laws which had a destructive influence on the freeman and the bondsman alike, and on the other hand, because she became an orphan at the age of three. Having neither brother nor sister, the lonely child missed her mother's love intensely. She was adopted by an aunt and an uncle, the Rev. William Watkins, who was

---

1 For the biographical information on Harper, the following authors have been consulted: Bernard W. Bell, *The Early Afro-American Novel* pp. 57-60; Hallie Q. Brown, *Homespun Heroines* pp. 97-103; Hazel V. Carby, *Reconstructing Womanhood* pp. 62-94; Elizabeth Ammons in Paul Lauter, *Heath Anthology* 1: 1915-1944; Katherine M. Rogers, *Early American Women* pp. 497-503; and William Still, *Underground Railroad* pp. 755-80.

an activist in the abolitionist movement. Frances attended his school for free black children until she was thirteen years old. At that time, she went as a domestic servant to a family in Baltimore (the booksellers, Armstrong) in order to earn her own living (Hazel V. Carby 65).

Similarly to Phillis Wheatley, her talent as a writer was recognized and encouraged by her employers, but questioned by the literary authorities of her time: "The ability exhibited in some of her productions was so remarkable that some doubted and others denied their originality" (Hallie Q. Brown 98). At the age of sixteen, Frances Ellen Watkins published a volume of poetry, *Forest Leaves* (1845; also known as *Autumn Leaves*), which seems to be lost. Her oppressive experiences as a free black child during the time of slavery in a southern state, as well as the early influence of a household involved in the antislavery cause, decisively affected her future outlook on life and triggered her personal commitment to the 'uplift of her race'.

Frances Ellen Watkins left the South in 1850 to live in a free state, Ohio, where she taught domestic science at the Union Seminary in Columbus (later known as Wilberforce University). A few years later, she moved to Little York, Pennsylvania. The passage of the Fugitive Slave Law in 1850 contributed to Harriet Beecher Stowe's decision to write *Uncle Tom's Cabin*; similarly, the year 1853 helped to determine Frances Watkins' life.[1] Outraged and saddened by the newly inflicted injustice which was a further burden put on black people's shoulders, she now became completely involved in the antislavery struggle. She "became a friend and colleague of William Still, later famous as the author of the monumental 1872 history, *The Underground Railroad*" (Elizabeth Ammons in Paul Lauter, *Heath Anthology* 1: 1916). Through the stories told by slaves who had escaped from the South on the Underground Railroad, and through her own extensive travels in the South after the war, she gained a deeper insight into the cruelties and horrors of the slave system, and into the blacks' struggle against racism during Reconstruction, respectively. Her poetry, her shorter prose pieces, and her first and only novel are ample evidence of her assimilation of this fund of material circulating among the black population.

---

1 In 1853, Maryland passed a new law denying free blacks entry into the state, at the risk of being captured and resold into slavery.

Watkins' first antislavery speech, on "The Education and Elevation of the Colored Race" in 1854, was the beginning of her outstanding career as an antislavery lecturer travelling from state to state. In Maine, she was even employed as a full-time lecturer by the state Anti-Slavery Society. In 1860, Frances Watkins married a widower, Fenton Harper, in Cincinnati. They bought a farm outside of Columbus, from where she continued her literary and antislavery work. After the early death of Fenton Harper in 1864, his wife, because of debt, was forced to leave the farm with their daughter, Mary, and return to Philadelphia in order to make a living by teaching and lecturing. After the war, Harper was constantly involved in supporting and educating the black community, mainly in the South, but also in the North, by teaching and lecturing. Her speeches, made to both black and white audiences on temperance, black education, economic self-determination, civil rights, domestic reform, lynching, and women's suffrage, earned her the reputation of being one of the most important spokespersons of the Reconstruction and post-Reconstruction era. In a letter to a friend in 1871, Harper commented wittily on the difficulty of her task as a woman lecturer: "You would be amused to hear some of the remarks which my lectures call forth. 'She is a man,' again 'She is not colored, she is white. She is painted'" (Hallie Q. Brown 102).

Her first volume of poetry was written in her teens. Later, as an adult, she published three further volumes of poetry, all focusing on the themes of her lectures; this exemplifies the fusion between her literary work and her life work. In 1859, Frances Watkins published the first short story by a black person in the United States, "The Two Offers;" and when Harper's novel *Iola Leroy* was published in 1892, it was believed to be the first written by a black woman in the United States. This belief persisted until the re-discovery of Wilson's *Our Nig* in the 1980's.[1]

Frances Ellen Watkins Harper died in 1911 of heart disease in Philadelphia, after a long, hard, and often lonely life devoted to one

---

1 It is noteworthy that Emma Dunham Kelley published her first novel *Megda* in 1891 and her second novel, *Four Girls at Cottage City*, in 1898. Although her first novel was so popular as to be reprinted the following year, the author has not yet been included in any anthologies or biographies, and her novels have so far - with a few laudable exceptions - been omitted from bibliographies and literary histories. Chapter 6 in this thesis, will elaborate on this writer's neglect in more detail.

aim, the improvement of the condition of the black population in the South and the North of the United States.

(b) The Novel's Circular Structure

On the frontispiece of the 1893 edition of *Iola Leroy*, there is a photograph of Frances Ellen Watkins Harper. She is standing and looks directly into the eyes of the photographer, any observer, or the reader of her novel. She radiates inner contentment and confidence. The calm expression of her face and her modest demeanour reveal nothing of the fervor expressed in her speeches. The novel is lovingly dedicated to her daughter, Mary E. Harper, and has an introduction by William Still. Then follows a table of contents, listing 33 chapters. The 281-page novel concludes with a "Note" by the author, ending with her hope-inspiring poem:

> There is light beyond the darkness,
> Joy beyond the present pain;
> There is hope in God's great justice
> And the negro's rising brain.
> Though the morning seems to linger
> O'er the hill-tops far away,
> Yet the shadows bear the promise
> Of a brighter coming day.

Still's introduction and Harper's final note both express the didactic role of *Iola Leroy*. The novel should be an example and a guideline for the young and old Afro-Americans of the post-Reconstruction era, who are without any orientation. Faced with the daily humiliations of a racist and segregated South, their high hopes and aspirations have been repeatedly shattered since the Emancipation Proclamation. The gradual removal of their Civil Rights by disenfranchising the freedmen, the lynchings, and the feudal sharecropping system combine to leave them disillusioned with a system which is controlled by whites. Still addresses a black audience, "[d]oubtless the thousands of colored Sunday-schools in the South, in casting about for an interesting, moral story-book, full of practical lessons, will not be content to be without 'Iola Leroy, Or Shadows Uplifted'" (3), but Harper's "story" and "note" are clearly addressed to both a white and a black audience. Blacks and whites ought to learn something from the novel's message, the former in order to live according to the example of the 'race leaders' such as Iola, Harry, Miss Delany, or the Rev. Carmicle, and the latter in order to use all their power to support the black population in their struggle to lift themselves up from the pit of slavery.

> From threads of fact and fiction I have woven a story whose mission will not be in vain if it awaken in the hearts of our countrymen a stronger sense of justice and a more Christlike humanity in behalf of those whom the fortunes of war threw, homeless, ignorant and poor, upon the threshold of a new era. Nor will it be in vain if it inspire the children of those upon whose brows God has poured the chrism of that new era to determine that they will embrace every opportunity, develop every faculty, and use every power God has given them to rise in the scale of character and condition, and to add their quota of good citizenship to the best welfare of the nation. (282)

As already said, the introduction and note form an explicitly didactic frame to the novel. This structure is reminiscent of Harper's speeches, which are addressed to both a black and white audience and often end with the speaker's urging to face one's responsibility and work for the uplift of the race: "Let your homes be the best places where you may plant your batteries against the rum traffic. Teach your children to hate intoxicating drinks with a deadly hatred" ("The Woman's Christian Temperance Union and the Colored Woman", in Frances Smith Foster 285); or: "The work of the mothers of our race is grandly constructive. It is for us to build above the wreck and ruin of the past more stately temples of thought and action" ("Enlightened Motherhood" 292).

The narrative is generally related by an omniscient narrator and is rendered in standard English. The narrator's perspective, however, is repeatedly replaced by the characters' perspectives, in long dialogues which reveal the various controversies in Harper's America: e.g. Booker T. Washington versus Du Bois, black emigration, or female education as in the chapter, "Friends in Council" (246-261). Harper distinguishes her 'educated' characters (Marie, Iola, Harry, Robert Johnson, Miss Delany, the Rev. Carmicle, Dr. Latimer) from her "folk" characters (Thomas Anderson, Aunt Linda, Uncle Daniel) by their use of language: her "folk" characters' speech is rendered in dialect.

As the introduction and note form a circle on a level outside of the actual narrative (extra-textual level), a similar 'circle-structure' can be detected on an intra-textual level. The first chapter, "The Mystery of Market Speech and Prayer Meetings", introduces the reader to the "folk" during the Civil War, and the last chapter, "Conclusion", ends the novel with a description of the lives of the "folk", years after the Emancipation Proclamation. Whereas the heroine is absent from the first chapter, she and her newly wed husband are very much present in the last chapter.

The novel is set in both the South (North Carolina, Mississippi, Georgia) and the North (city of P__ (Pennsylvania), New England). It begins during the Civil War in the South, and ends several years after it - during Reconstruction - in the South again. There are several subplots, one of which (Iola's parents' story) is set - through the technique of retrospection - at a time "[n]early twenty years before the war" (ch. 9, 61). Here, the circular structure appears again, but this time on a contextual level, by the novel's opening and closing in the South. The importance of the characters' moves from South to North and back again will be discussed in Chapter 4 (d) of the present thesis.

To sum up, Harper's novel has a circular structure on three levels: an extra-textual, an intra-textual, and a contextual level.

(c) The Black Heroine: True Woman and Race Leader

How does Harper use the form of the romantic novel to make a 'political' statement concerning the role of blacks in general, and of black women in particular, in Reconstruction and post-Reconstruction America? Iola Leroy's development from childhood to womanhood, and from 'white' to 'black', is an exceptionally revealing characterization of a heroine.

As the novel opens in medias res, the omniscient narrator introduces her heroine in the same way, in the midst of danger and difficulties, in chapter 5, "Release of Iola Leroy". This opening is unlike those in Antebellum narratives, which generally begin with an account of the heroine's or slave's earliest childhood. In most Slave Narratives these first years in bondage are depicted in a relatively positive way. Besides the slave's first claim of existence, these positive childhood accounts are also a means of preparing for a striking contrast to the horrors which are related later in the narratives, and which are an expression of the devastating effects of slavery on the human body and mind. As shown earlier, Woman's Fiction often follows a similar pattern, in that the heroine, say, in *The Wide, Wide World*, is initially presented as a happy child, and this is then contrasted with her lonely and difficult life at her aunt's.

The reader is first introduced to Iola Leroy through the perspective of Thomas Anderson, a fellow slave who belongs to the same master and who would like to rescue her from the clutches of her licentious master by escaping with her to the Union army.

> "[B]ut dere's a mighty putty young gal dere at Marse Tom's ... Dey tells me dey's been sellin' her all ober de kentry; but dat she's a reg'lar spitfire; dey can't lead nor dribe her. ...
> "But ef you seed dem putty white han's ob hern you'd never tink she kept her own house, let 'lone anybody else's. ... My! but she's putty. Beautiful long hair comes way down her back; putty blue eyes, an' jis' ez white ez anybody's in dis place. ... I heerd Marse Tom talkin' 'bout her las' night to his brudder; tellin' him she war mighty airish, but he meant to break her in." (38)

In the above quotation, several important facts are mentioned by the admiring Thomas Anderson. The young, beautiful and 'white' heroine has been sold several times. Her virtue is at siege, but she has not been 'broken in' yet. She has a strong will, and so far has been resisting her enemies (her masters) successfully. Although she has nobody to protect her, she does not seem to be completely at the mercy of her masters. The fact that Iola Leroy has been sold all over the country proves that she has been able to actively prevent her former masters' licentious advances (rape). And in the narrator's own words:

Her "selfish master ... had tried in vain to drag her down to his own low level of sin and shame" (38-39).

Through the perspective of a fellow slave, the reader meets a heroine with a beautiful white face, white hands, blue eyes, and beautiful long hair who, similar to the white heroines in Woman's Fiction, has to defend her innocence. Thomas Anderson, "just as black as black can be", but nevertheless "brave", "noblehearted", and "true" (44), is contrasted with his master of the same name (Marse Tom), who has a white skin but a 'black' soul, and to whom Iola Leroy hisses, red with anger after he has tried to put his arm round her waist (in Anderson's words), "'I'll die fust'" (41).

Although Iola Leroy has been described by the slave Thomas Anderson as a "spitfire", and by her master as "airish", the white General of the Union Army - the narrator informs us - is much "impressed by her modest demeanor, and surprised to see the refinement and beauty she possessed" (39). In the following passage Harper manages to mix her abolitionist message with the General's thoughts:

> Could it be possible that this young and beautiful girl had been a chattel, with no power to protect herself from the highest insults that lawless brutality could inflict upon innocent and defenseless womanhood? Could he ever again glory in his American citizenship, when any white man, no matter how coarse, cruel, or brutal, could buy or sell her for the basest purposes? (39)

Once out of danger, Iola Leroy displays all the attributes of true womanhood. She is "full of tender earnestness", her "voice [is] strangely sympathetic", and she is gentle (39/40). As a nurse in the Union hospital, Iola Leroy holds, on the one hand, a 'true' woman's typical place in nursing - instead of children or a husband - the wounded and helpless soldiers

The first impressions the reader gets of the novel's heroine, through her fellow slave's as well as the General's perspective, is that of a 'white' woman of genteel background reduced to bondage. At that point of the narrative, the reader can only guess about her former life, and that she must have experienced some - to the reader unknown -

anguish "... as if some great sorrow had bound her heart in loving compassion to every sufferer ...." (40).

The solution to the riddle, that is, the reason for the protagonist's deep sorrow, is given in chapters 9 to 12, where we get to know her parentage: a white father and a black mother (who at one time was the slave of Iola's father). In these chapters, the omniscient narrator sketches Iola Leroy's development from childhood to early adolescence, and indicates intelligently that Iola Leroy's sorrows stem from the fact that slavery, white and male supremacy, and white injustice have reduced her to her present state. In that way, Harper manages to refute the common assumption that the mulatto is destined to sadness and ill luck because of blood admixture, which means that a drop of black blood would have a negative effect on the human being. But although the heroine's representation had to be shaped according to a set of given criteria, Harper, still manages to insert or add her personal view of True Womanhood. A black intellectual herself, she perceptibly modifies the image of True Womanhood so that it might fit her almost white heroine. From the very beginning, for example, it is made quite clear that Iola Leroy is virtuous, intelligent, and refined, not because of her white blood but in spite of it.

It can be argued that Harper wanted to express an important message through her heroine, Iola Leroy, and did not depict her as almost white simply because she had to succumb to the literary pressure of her time. By introducing the important topics of 'amalgamation' and of 'passing for white' - which she could not have done so effectively if it had not been for her white-skinned heroes with whom both blacks and whites can identify - Harper clearly defines the mulatto's role as a race leader, thus as belonging to a chosen elite who fight in the ranks of the black population for the uplifting of the race.

As Harper's *Iola Leroy* stands in the tradition of the abolitionist novel, it is not surprising that the 19th-century reader could then, and the 20th-century reader still can, detect some parallels with Harriet Beecher Stowe's fair heroes and heroines, and William Wells Brown's almost white mulatto character Clotel (named Clotelle in his 1864 and 1867 versions). Some scholars, such as Sterling Brown and Hugh Gloster, too harshly and too quickly rejected *Iola Leroy*'s merit, simply because they refused to see more in Harper's novel than an imitation of Brown's: "There is little question about the source of *Iola Leroy*: it is almost wholly the product of reading Brown's *Clotelle* " (Gloster, 30).[1] Moreover, in *The Negro Novel in America*, Robert Bone falsely concludes:

> ... *Iola Leroy* lacks the urgency of other protest novels of the 1890's. The explanation is not far to seek: Mrs. Harper was one of the foremost Abolitionist poets of the 1850's, but she was sixty-seven years old when *Iola Leroy* was published. She was separated from the other novelists of this period by a full generation; her social consciousness, formed during the Abolitionist struggle, did not encompass the post-Reconstruction repression. (32)

Harper's 'lack of overt protest' in *Iola Leroy* is definitely not due to her age, because in her poems and speeches she openly and fervently criticises the failure of Reconstruction. However, Harper's representation of an almost white heroine of genteel background, barely resembling the post-Reconstruction reality of an average black woman, has to be understood in a double, inter-dependent context. Firstly, the author's choice of the form of the romance novel limited her interpretation of her heroine, because Harper had to move within and conform to its traditional frame. Secondly, the author had to create a heroine who had utterly absorbed the ideal of the cult of True Womanhood, by which her 19th-century readers judged themselves as well as the heroines they wanted to identify with. Bone's, Brown's and Gloster's criticisms derive from a failure to take into account social history, literary history, and traditions, that is to say, both the text *and* context. Barbara Christian in her paper, "The Uses of History" (165-170) - given at National Women's Studies Association Conference in 1983 - speaks about the absolute "need to establish the historical origins and context of a literature ...." in order to fully appreciate and understand it:

> In attempting to understand Afro-American women's literature, especially that of the novel, it is practically impossible to ignore its historical roots. I believe (quite unfashionably) that this is true for all

---

1 Sterling A. Brown, Arthur P. Davis, and Ulysses Lee, eds. *The Negro Caravan: Writings by American Negroes.* 1941. Rpt. New York: Arno and The New York Times, 1970. p. 139.

> literary traditions. In addition, the need to establish the historical origins and context of a literature that emerges from groups of people considered to be marginal or despised is even more critical to its understanding and appreciation. For such literature comes out of needs that are scarcely literary in the esoteric meaning that this society attributes to art. Such literature is not only the product of the individual writer's desire to express herself or to create beauty (though these are significant aspects), but also to affect the historical moment - that is, to help to create social change. Nor is this desire a question of the individual writer's perceived intentions of choice. Because the conditions that determine literary worth are also historical, those peoples who are not seen as part of History of Literature must struggle to insist upon their own totality, their own significance in their time. Thus the nineteenth century Afro-American women writers (terms that were contradictory in that time) *were* seen through historical images, whether they wanted to be or not. They *had* to respond to the images of their race and sex that challenged their ability to even perceive of themselves as creators of literature. (*Black Feminist Criticism* 165/6)

Although art - and this applies to everything which deserves this label - should be timeless, in that it should hold truths which represent mankind's innermost feelings, a novel like Harper's cannot be discussed without including its historical context in the analysis. This would include, for example, the political debates which shook the America of the 1890s and of the turn of the century.

By giving her characters a voice, as in the case of Eugene Leroy and his cousin, Alfred Lorraine, Harper displays the two contradictory points of view of the question of slavery. The narrator's description of Iola's father as a "young, vivacious, impulsive, and undisciplined" man leads one to expect a bad end (61). In the two cousins' characters, Harper shows the double-consciousness of the South; one of them is careless, against slavery but not really outspoken about it (similar to St. Clare in *Uncle Tom's Cabin*), the other one is calculating, pro-slavery, believing in the inferiority of the black race and consequently in the supremacy of the white. Lorraine's reaction to his cousin's decision to marry a black woman, who was formerly his slave, foreshadows the catastrophe: "'I would rather follow you to the grave [than to your wedding],' replied Lorraine, hotly, while an expression of ineffable scorn passed over his cold, proud face" (72).

Chapter 10, "Shadows in the Home", is a flashback giving an insight into Iola's happy and carefree childhood before her 'awakening': "Into that quiet and beautiful home three children were born, unconscious of the doom suspended over their heads" (76). Similarly to the first happy reminiscences of the slave's early childhood days in the Slave Narrative authored by women, the child Iola does not yet foresee what everybody around her knows. The three children live a sheltered life on the plantation, but as they are still small they do not seem to notice their isolation from other white children.

Marie Leroy, their mother, is also depicted - according to the ideal of True Womanhood - as a beautiful and almost white woman. Although she has been manumitted by her husband, and as mistress of a plantation owns slaves herself, she still feels and suffers for the misery of her race. Therefore she tries to persuade her husband to free their slaves. It is this love for her people which Iola and Harry have 'inherited' from their mother, but this love can be fully developed only when they finally know their real parentage and origin. Their mother could neither achieve the manumission of their slaves, because her husband's "hands [were] tied by law and custom ... [and] public opinion" (78), nor persuade him to believe in her "sad forebodings" after her terrible dream: "One night I dreamt that you were dead, that the lawyers entered the house, seized our property, and remanded us to slavery" (80). Her dream foretells the tragedy which will befall the family because her husband's "ear was too dull to catch the sound; his vision was too blurred to read the signs of the times" (78).

Marie Leroy serves as Harper's 'porte-parole' in her appeal for the liberty of every human being and in her decisive rejection of caste prejudice (76-84). She is decidedly her husband's superior where argumentation on the subject of slavery is concerned. Her husband's death a few years later and her children's fate of being sold as slaves, prove her to be a black Cassandra who has not been listened to:

> "My dear husband, you may be perfectly right, but are you not preparing our children for a fearful awakening? Are you not acting on the plan, 'After me the deluge?'" "Not at all, Marie. I want our

> children to grow up without having their self-respect crushed in the bud." (84)

By describing the singular fate of the Leroys, Harper evokes the problem of a whole nation, and by portraying Iola and Harry, her fair protagonists, she tries to prove that it is not amalgamation which is the cause of their sorrows, but that slavery and a white man's betrayal (Lorraine's) stand at the beginning of their trials.

Only after Iola Leroy has realized her new situation and accepted her roots, that is, her 'black' mother, can she fully understand the slaves' position, whereas before her 'awakening' she had stated, in a discussion with her classmates:

> "Slavery can't be wrong ... for my father is a slave-holder, and my mother is as good to our servants as she can be. My father often tells her that she spoils them, and lets them run over her. I never saw my father strike one of them. I love my mammy as much as I do my own mother, and I believe she loves us just as if we were her own children. ... Our slaves do not want their freedom. They would not take it if we gave it to them. ... My father says the slaves would be very well contented if no one put wrong notions in their heads" (ch. 12, "School-Girl Notions" 97-98)

Harper structures her characters' discussions similarly to her own speeches. First it is Iola who speaks - she "being a Southern girl and a slave-holder's daughter, always defended slavery when it was under discussion" (97) - after which Harper refutes the heroine's arguments by giving the floor to her 'abolitionist' classmates. In the above quotation, Iola Leroy adopts the argumentation typical of an idyllic and idealized Old South, with caring masters and mistresses and contented slaves, as depicted in Thomas Nelson Page's *In Ole Virginia* (1887) and Joel Chandler Harris' Uncle Remus Tales.[1] Although Iola has the last word in the discussion by jokingly inviting her friends to New

---

1 Iola's words particularly echo Old Sam, Marse Chan's faithful slave and body-servant, who unquestioningly and admiringly glorifies the Antebellum South with its aristocracy: "'Dem wuz good ole times, marster - de bes' Sam ever see! Dey wuz, in fac'! Niggers didn' hed nothin' 't all to do - jes' hed to 'ten' to de feedin' an' cleanin' de hosses, ...'" ("Marse Chan" in: Page's *In Ole Virginia* 10).

Orleans: "I think one winter in the South would cure you of your Abolitionism" (99), Harper soon refutes Iola's words by melodramatically introducing Louis Bastine, Alfred Lorraine's unscrupulous attorney, who has arrived in order to trick Iola back to the South and into slavery.

An account of a similar tragedy, involving two girls whom Bastine's friend knew, apart from foreshadowing Iola's possible fate, highlights the black woman's situation in slavery: she is sold as an 'object' to be used and abused by white men. These two girls did not survive the fact that they were black and reduced to slavery. Thus there seem to be only two given possibilities: a death in innocence, or a life in sin.

Eugene Leroy's decision that their children, Iola, Harry, and Gracie, should not know of their black blood is a mistake. This is underlined several times by the narrator. By not revealing their children's roots, the parents bring about their crisis, as symbolized by Gracie's death and Harry's long illness. Gracie has to die because she cannot face her new life: "... a lovely vision, too bright for earth's dull cares and weary, wasting pain" (96). Harper has her pass away in a beautiful deathbed scene reminiscent of Eva Clare's innocent death in *Uncle Tom's Cabin*. Harry, who has been informed in the North through a letter from Iola, falls dangerously ill because of the shocking news. Iola is the strongest and the most heroic of them all. Because of her sick mother and her dying sister, she only has a couple of minutes to recover from this terrible blow:

> Almost wild with agony, Iola paced the floor, as the fearful truth broke in crushing anguish upon her mind. Then bursting into a paroxysm of tears succeeded by peals of hysterical laughter, said: - "I used to say that slavery is right. I didn't know what I was talking about." Then growing calmer, she said, "Mother, who is at the bottom of this downright robbery?" (105/6)

Harper's depiction of her heroine in this trying situation lacks realism. Iola's quick adaptation to her new situation seems too ideal to be true, but on the other hand it befits a heroine who has to live and act according to the code of True Womanhood.

However, if it is considered that Woman's Fiction has only two possible paths for her assaulted heroines to tread, namely death in innocence or a long, patient struggle for survival, Iola has already passed her first test, that is, she, unlike her sister Gracie, triumphs over death. Iola also passes her second test successfully, that is, she triumphs over her licentious masters by remaining innocent and pure. This heroic act proves the heroine to be a True Woman. Her invincibility in matters of chastity is the key to success in everything the future has in store for her. This is a motif which will be taken up again by Iola's mother in the 'conversazione', when she says that "[we] must instill into our young people that the true strength of a race means purity in women and uprightness in men ...." (254). Here, Harper clearly refutes the Southern stereotype of the unchaste black woman; Iola's purity contrasts her with the white men's lust for their black female slaves.

After Iola's dreadful 'awakening' to her blackness and her real origin, Harper's heroine stands on the threshold of a new era, *her* new era, to which she has been introduced by her mother, who told her of her black roots. Although the 'awakening' is a shock to Iola, it is also a chance, because it triggers the heroine's development.

The earlier chapter, "School-Girl Notions", introduced the reader to a rather conceited girl who was trapped in a world of illusion and deceit. Only when Iola knows as much as the reader does about her, can she really grasp the slaves' reality and feel for them, as she is now one of them. Furthermore, only when she knows of her roots is she able to seek and find nurturing help among her people. After her husband's death, Iola's mother can finally break her silence and take her place - which she has always wanted to hold - as a mediator between the black world and her children. Thus she is the first to refer her daughter to her people in the hour of despair and danger: "'Some of the most beautiful lessons of faith and trust I have ever learned were from among our lowly people in their humble cabins'" (107).

The great mental and physical change Iola has undergone since her separation from her family after her father's and Gracie's deaths is best revealed at the Methodist Conference, where her brother does not recognize her, and at the breakfast table the following morning, as they all sit happily reunited.

> Near him sat two ladies, one fair, the other considerably darker. There was something in the fairer one that reminded him forcibly of his sister, but she was much older and graver than he imagined his sister to be. (193)
> ...
> The next morning, as they sat at the breakfast-table, Marie said: -
> "My dear child, you are so changed I do not think I would have known you if I had met you in the street!"
> "And I," said Harry, "can hardly realize that you are our own Iola, whom I recognized as sister a half dozen years ago."
> "Am I so changed?" asked Iola, as a faint sigh escaped her lips.
> "Why, Iola," said Harry, "you used to be the most harum-scarum girl I ever knew - laughing, dancing, and singing from morning until night." (195)

Iola's 'school-girl notions' and the above breakfast scene are instances in which the reader is given full insight into Iola's character before her 'awakening'. By letting her characters, Harry and Marie, speak about Iola, Harper again underlines her heroine's change from a happy and somewhat superficial 'white' girl to a mature and serious 'black' heroine who has "passed through a fiery ordeal of suffering" (195) As it has already been mentioned, the first and most important step towards change was the heroine's acceptance of her fate, otherwise she would have succumbed to the first shock, as in the case of Gracie. The second trial she had to go through was the defence of her innocence and purity, which on a secondary level is symbolical of a defence of womanhood per se. Iola's experience in slavery and as a nurse at the Union hospital made her further empathize with those who still suffered, or had suffered, in slavery and for those who were wounded or died because they fought for the abolition of it. A further and no less decisive step was Iola's rejection of Dr. Gresham, her white suitor. Although she loved him, she could not accept his offer of marriage because this meant that she would have to 'pass for white' and thus would not be able to serve her 'race'. Harper, in her depiction of a heroine who rejects a white suitor and a life of ease and luxury, definitely goes beyond Brown's representation of his heroines, Clotel, Mary (*Clotel*, 1853), and even Clotelle (*Clotelle* 1864/1867). Neither in American nor English 19th-century woman's literature is there a similar representation of a heroine who sacrifices her personal happiness in order to be able to "do something of lasting service" for her people (262). There are four reasons why Iola finds the strength to refuse the man she loves. Firstly, she "intends ... to cast [her] lot with the freed people as a "helper, teacher and friend" (114). Secondly, she wants to find her mother, the hope of which has helped her to endure all her trials. Thirdly, she believes that, because of the whites' colour prejudice, there is an insurmountable barrier between blacks and whites. And fourthly, she has realized that, because of her fate, she has become more and more aware of the injustice inflicted on blacks, and is therefore more capable of supporting the cause of her fellow-sufferers:

> The intense horror and agony I felt when I was first told the story are over. Thoughts and purposes have come to me in the shadow I should never have learned in the sunshine. I am constantly rousing myself up to suffer and be strong. ... I have passed through a fiery ordeal, but this ministry of suffering will not be in vain. I feel that my mind has matured beyond my years. I am a wonder to myself. It seems as if years had been compressed into a few short months. (114)

Only the heroine's personal history and her conscious knowledge of it can bind her to the history of all blacks. Iola's growing awareness of her origin thus has a nurturing, healing, and strengthening effect on her.

As a nurse in the hospital and as a teacher of the freedmen's children, Harper's heroine proves to be an independent woman who can look after herself and earn her own living. Similarly to the white heroines in Woman's Fiction, who as orphans at one point in their lives have only themselves and their good characters to rely on, and thus have to build up nurturing relationships to replace the lack of a family, Harper's black heroine also has to go through a phase of loneliness: Thomas Anderson, her only friend, dies during the war, and Dr. Gresham's offer cannot be accepted. After having found her family, that is her mother and her brother, as well as an uncle, Robert Johnson, and his mother (Iola's grandmother), Iola Leroy ventures North with her uncle. A few weeks later, she says to him:

> "Uncle Robert, ... I have a theory that every woman ought to know how to earn her own living. I believe that a great amount of sin and misery springs from the weakness and inefficiency of women." (Harper, 205)

This opening of the chapter, "Northern Experience" - with Iola's theory concerning the origin of women's weakness and inefficiency - is highly reminiscent of Louisa May Alcott's own life as well as of her most feminist heroine, Christie Devon in *Work: A Story of Experience* (1872).[1]

Both Harper's black heroine and Alcott's white heroine have to go through the humiliating experience of looking for work and of being rejected, the former because of race prejudice and the latter because of social prejudice. Harper and Alcott are both exceptional in their depiction of two rather independent women characters, and it is quite obvious that both authors added an alternative to Woman's Fiction. Harper did it by portraying a black and independent woman whose main aim in life is the 'uplift of her race', and who 'per chance' found a black husband with a similar background and the same aim. Alcott did it by showing a white woman who wants to go beyond the prospect of being simply a farmer's wife in a little village, and who wants to experience something new and to lead an independent and worthy life. Louisa May Alcott's Christie Devon also rejects a life of ease and luxury (as Mr. Fletcher's wife) in order to do something for mankind.

The chapter, "Friends in Council", reveals the heroine's project for the uplift of the race - which is also Harper's. Iola Leroy wants to become a teacher of domestic science among her people. In a paper on the "Education of Mothers", she presents the project at the 'conversazione', an intellectual gathering of some leading figures of the time for the discussion of questions relevant to the race ("Friends

---

1 In 1862 Alcott enlisted as a nurse in a Civil War army hospital in order to find new experience and to be independent (Elaine Showalter, "Introduction", in *Alternative Alcott*). Christie Devon, similarly to Iola Leroy, declares one day to her startled aunt: "'Aunt Betsey, there's going to be a new Declaration of Independence. ... I mean that, being of age, I'm going to take care of myself, and not be a burden any longer'" (Louisa May Alcott 239).

in Council"). Marie Leroy, as the representative of the race's mothers at the 'conversazione', aptly summarizes the need for such a training:

> "You know," said Mrs. Leroy, "that after the war we were thrown upon the nation a homeless race to be gathered into homes, and a legally unmarried race to be taught the sacredness of the marriage relation. .... [As] Sir Galahad [says]: -
>
> 'My strength is the strength of ten,
> Because my heart is pure.'
>
> And where this is wanting neither wealth nor culture can make up the deficiency." (253/4)

At the end of the novel, Iola Leroy has become a teacher of domestic science among her people in the South. Thus closes the circle which opened with Iola's mother's instruction to her daughter to turn for comfort and solace to her own people in the cabins - at the beginning of her 'awakening'. The heroine is now able to 'invest' the nurturing influence she received from her mother and her surrogate family (Thomas Anderson, Aunt Linda, Uncle Daniel) in the education of her own people, among them the young mothers of the race.

The roles Harper assigns to her mulatto characters (Iola, Harry and Dr. Latimer) make it obvious that the author sees them as an elite who should function as race leaders. However, her black characters (the Rev. Carmicle and Miss Delany) about whom it is especially pointed out that they have no white blood in their veins, have an even better formal education than the heroes, Iola and Harry. The Rev. Carmicle and Miss Delany (a teacher herself) can, although they are no heroes in Harper's fictional world, be considered race leaders as well. If 20th-century scholars want to understand Harper's deliberate use of colour in her novel, this is a crucial point. Her characters, Iola, Harry and Dr. Latimer, all could have passed for white, but they decided to reject riches and social position in order to take their place among their people "as their teacher, friend, and adviser" (263). Harper is also aware of the colour prejudice among blacks, when she makes Lucille say in response to Harry's proposal "'your mother may not prefer me for a daughter. You know, Harry, complexional prejudices are not confined to white people'" (278).

Finally, it can be stated that Harper utterly revolutionized Woman's Fiction in America by presenting her 19th-century audience with a married heroine who, instead of devoting her life only to her husband, as in the case of Jane Eyre, continues teaching among her people even after marriage! Here, Harper's heroine Iola Leroy goes beyond the Janette Alston of "The Two Offers", who could not yet envisage both a life of duty as a teacher of her people *and* marriage.[1]

Fiction and reality fuse when Iola mentions to Dr. Latimer, her black suitor, that she would like to write a book as a guideline for blacks. Thus, Harper's own life and projects - as a teacher, lecturer, adviser, wife, mother, and writer herself - are reflected in her heroine's words and in her character as a whole. This vision of a heroine who "would like to do something of lasting service for the race" (be it the writing of a novel or any other project helping blacks) stands at the center of the novel. It is the recurrent motif around which the whole text revolves, and on which the argument is built:

> "Why not ... write a good, strong book which would be helpful to them? I think there is an amount of dormant talent among us, and a large field from which to gather materials for such a book."
> "I would do it, willingly, if I could; but one needs both leisure and money to make a successful book. There is material among us for the broadest comedies and the deepest tragedies, but, besides money and leisure, it needs patience, perseverance, courage, and the hand of an artist to weave it into the literature of the country."
> "Miss Leroy, you have a large and rich experience; you possess a vivid imagination and glowing fancy. Write, out of the fullness of your heart, a book to inspire men and women with a deeper sense of justice and humanity." ...
> "But who believes any good can come out of the black Nazareth?"
> "Miss Leroy, out of the race must come its own thinkers and writers. Authors belonging to the white race have written good racial books, for which I am deeply grateful, but it seems to be almost impossible for a white man to put himself completely in our

1 Although all of the Brontë sisters' heroines harbour a wish to go on with their respective occupations after marriage, only Frances Henri in *The Professor* manages to do so.

> place. No man can feel the iron which enters another man's soul." (262/3)

In conclusion, it must be emphasized that Harper wants to stress the importance of her mulatto characters' place among their people as their moral and political guides. But in order to become race leaders, her heroine and hero first have to accept their black parentage. When they are aware of their origin, they can build up their personalities and are able to gain strength and confidence among their own people. Only then will they be capable of channeling all their energy into the 'uplift of the race'.

Harper's message is quite clear: only when you accept your blackness can you help your people. 'Passing for white' might be easier, but you lose the chance of your individual growth, as well as the strength which is needed among your own people.

Although Harper had to make certain concessions to the form of the 'sentimental' novel and to the charisma of her heroine, as prescribed by the cult of True Womanhood, she nevertheless moves beyond certain limits by depicting an independent black woman who chooses duty to her people over 'romance', and work over leisure.

(d) The Black Community: A Search for Mothers

Phillis Wheatley, the first Afro-American poet, can be seen as a prototype in her endeavour to restore her disrupted family ties in a metaphorical way, by subtly intertwining her African experience (her parents' sun-worship)[1] with her American and Christian reality. In her case, there was no hope of ever finding her parents, or people of her own tribe, or in returning to her *motherland*, Africa. Thus, freedom is a recurrent metaphor in her poetry, and is one of her primary subjects.

---

1 See: Shields' essay "Phillis Wheatley's Struggle for Freedom in her Poetry and Prose" (in Phillis Wheatley 240-245); and Margaretta Odell, *Memoir and Poems of Phillis Wheatley; A Native African and a Slave. Also, Poems by a Slave* (3d ed., 1838; reprint Miami, Fla.: Mnemosyne, 1969), 12.

The poem, "To the Right Honourable William, Earl of Dartmouth, His Majesty's Principal Secretary of State for North America, &c.", is an eloquent example of the way in which Wheatley transposes her personal bondage - and that of all blacks - to New England, which suffers under England's "iron chain" and "[t]yranny" (Phillis Wheatley 73-75). Metaphorically equating New England's bondage with her own, she also connects the New World to her African mother country.

The motif of the restoration of disrupted families reappears again in Woman's Fiction and in Afro-American Literature. It is characteristic for the heroines in Woman's Fiction to restore their severed family ties by searching for a surrogate family; it is equally characteristic of 19th-century Afro-American Woman's Literature to show a heroine trying to restore her family ties by searching for her kin, who have been scattered all over the country as a result of slavery.

At the centre of Harper's only novel we find, on the one hand, Iola Leroy's growing awareness of her roots, her people, and her own responsibility towards them and, on the other hand, the importance of re-structuring a strong and supportive black community.

In a way which is reminiscent of the Slave Narrative authored by women, Harper opens her novel by introducing the reader to a small slave community at the time of the Civil War. All of them - with the exception of Uncle Daniel and Aunt Katie, who are husband and wife - have been cruelly separated either from their partners, children, or parents, by force of slavery. Their religious meetings and reunions at night show a certain harmony and common feeling, which is a substitute for their lack of family. Uncle Daniel, Aunt Katie, and Uncle Ben, who after the War is sent to Congress to be a representative of his people, are father and mother figures. That the other slaves call them aunt and uncle underlines a wish to restore some kind of family relationship.

Harper then contrasts this slave community with the whites' 'community'. The reader gets to know the respective masters or mistresses (the white 'community') of each slave as seen through the slave's perspective. Thus, the slave's individual experience is in the foreground when he recounts to his fellow-slaves, in the manner of the Slave Narrative, the cruelties inflicted upon him by his master or mistress. Using this narrative technique, Harper not only gives a voice to black people in order to re-tell their experiences in their own words, but also, at the same time, refutes the repeatedly used stereotype of the contented slave of the Plantation School, as, for example, when Robert Johnson claims that not even the best master can compensate for a slave's freedom:

> "I ain't got nothing 'gainst my ole Miss, except she sold my mother [Iola's grandmother] from me. And a boy ain't nothin' without his mother. I forgive her, but I never forget her, and never expect to. But if she were the best woman on earth I would rather have my freedom than belong to her." (17/18)

Her characters' judgment of their owners' intemperance, licentiousness, or cruelty towards their slaves exemplifies the slaves' high moral standing, and thus Harper places them above their owners. The white 'community' is depicted as endangered by intemperate, violent, and licentious husbands who bring disharmony to the home. The Civil War further destroys the white community, or what is left of it. Thus Harper rejects the common argument of the Southern patriarch who fervently defends the system in stating that black people need the help and support of a superior race, that is the whites. Harper quite effectively shows that blacks have been successfully looking after themselves since they got their freedom.

The chapters, "Searching For Lost Ones" and "Striking Contrasts", show the former slave community of the first four chapters again after the War. The freedmen are depicted as better off than the whites not only mentally but also materially. The former masters and mistresses have been reduced to poverty, and some of the mistresses have been deserted by their husbands, or their husbands and sons have been killed in the war. Gundover and his family, who treated their slaves (and above all Iola Leroy) in a terrible way, all have to face - in the fashion of 19th-century Woman's Fiction - an awful death. The 'bad' characters thus have to pay for the deeds committed during life, with a death in agony:

> Gundover had died soon after the surrender. Frank Anderson had grown reckless and drank himself to death. His brother Tom [Iola's master] had been killed in battle. Their mother, who was Gundover's daughter, had died insane. Their father had also passed away. ... As Robert passed leisurely along, delighted with the evidences of thrift and industry which constantly met his eye, he stopped to admire

> [Aunt Linda's] garden filled with beautiful flowers, clambering vines, and rustic adornments. (153)
> ...
> After [Aunt Linda] had set the table she stood looking in silent admiration, chuckling to herself: "Ole Mistus can't set sich a table as dat. She ought'er be yere to see it. Specs 'twould make her mouf water. Well, I mus' let bygones be bygones. But dis yere freedom's mighty good." (164)
> ...
> "Ole Gundover's overseer war my marster, an' he used ter lib in dis bery house. I'se fixed it up sence I'se got it. Now I'se better off dan he is, 'cause he tuck to drink, an' all his frens is gone, an he's in de pore-house." (173/174)

At the beginning of the novel, the heroine, Iola Leroy, is shown as worse off than all the other black characters. Having been educated in the North, away from her family, and ignorant of her real origin, she has not been able to build up strong and supportive relationships like, for example, Robert Johnson, Thomas Anderson, Uncle Daniel, and Aunt Linda, who all had the black slave community for nurturing support. She has been uprooted, both physically and mentally, by living in the North, away from her family, and by not knowing her real origin. She lacks both family and surrogate family. Only when she finds a friend, first in Thomas Anderson and later in Robert Johnson, does her desperate and lonely situation improve.

She can only leave the South and go North again, when her severed familial ties are restored in the South, that is after having found her mother, her brother, Harry, an unsuspected uncle, and a grandmother, as well as friends such as Aunt Linda and Miss Delany, Harry's future wife.

The slave's move from South to North is a recurrent motive in the Slave Narrative, and symbolizes the slave's path from bondage to freedom. Twentieth century Afro-American Literature also uses this metaphor to describe the blacks' escape from a South full of impediments (racism) to the development of black people, to a hopefully freer North (see Wright's *Black Boy* and *American Hunger*, Ellison's *Invisible Man*, Morrison's *The Bluest Eye*). Iola Leroy, however, ultimately moves in the opposite direction.

At the very beginning, the heroine moves from the South to the North. She has to leave the South and her black mother because her father does not want his children to experience the negative influence of slavery's reality. In the North, and ignorant of the fact that her mother is black, Iola Leroy holds her father's conviction that slavery is not evil, and that the slaves do not really want their freedom. The North's colour prejudice as experienced by a black student at her college, demonstrates that the 'free' North is not simply a paradise for blacks. This incident, which Iola relates in one of her letters to her parents, foreshadows the heroine's personal encounter with the North's colour prejudice, when years later, she is looking for a job in the North. By the heroine's move from South to North, Harper shows Iola to be figuratively orphaned, in that she is alienated from her motherland, the South, as well as from her people, the black community. Therefore, in discussions with her young abolitionist friends at college, she is not able to really understand the cause of the slave.

Her second move is from the North back to the South. Only when reunited with her mother in the South, and when strengthened by her comforting advice to look for help among the "lowly people in the cabins", can Iola overcome her death wish, which would free her from her sufferings, similarly to Gracie. The trip back to the South enables the heroine to find her lost family members and to find new black friends. By describing the character's urge to restore broken family ties - first expressed in the Slave Narrative - Harper stresses the importance of the mother-child relationship. Robert Johnson tries to find his long lost mother. Iola also searches for her beloved mother. The importance of the mother-daughter relationship is further underlined when Iola rejects Dr. Gresham with the following words:

> "When the war is over I intend to search the country for my mother. Doctor, were you to give me a palace-like home, with velvet carpets to hush my tread, and magnificence to surround my way, I should miss her voice amid all other tones, her presence amid every scene. Oh, you do not know how hungry my heart is for my mother! Were I to marry you I would carry an aching heart into your home and dim its brightness. I have resolved never to marry until I have found my mother. ... I have pledged my life to that resolve, and I believe time and patience will reward me." (117/118)

Only when Iola has found her mother, her brother, and other people belonging to the black community will she be able to look for herself. The familial background and the new-found friends give her the strength, support, and necessary self-confidence to venture forth.

Iola's third move is again from the South to the North. The second time in the North, she is together with her uncle and her grandmother. Thus she is still among her relatives, and has their full support. Eventually her mother joins her, and her brother and Miss Delany visit them in the North, so that the whole family is reunited in the North. In the North, and free of obligations towards her family, Iola rejects Dr. Gresham for the second time. Although Iola experiences colour prejudice when trying to find work in the North, she does not despair. Her uncle and her grandmother, as well as the new found black friends, strengthen her conviction that she wants to consecrate her whole life and all her energy to the uplift of her people. The two reunions with black America's leading people (in the chapters: "Open Questions' and "Friends in Council") depict a utopian society anticipating Du Bois' theory of an intellectual elite mentioned in his article, "The Talented Tenth" (in Booker T. Washington, *The Negro Problem*).[1] The North which Harper envisions is not Wright's, Ann Petry's, Ellison's, nor Baldwin's destructive North. Hers is a slightly idealized North, with a growing community of black intellectuals.

Iola's last move is again Southward. There she settles down, together with her husband, in the midst of her reunited family and a prospering black community of well-to-do freedmen. The South of the final chapter is similar to Harper's North, an idealized South focusing on a black community which lives in harmony and which has little contact with the white population. Harper's final picture of a peaceful South, with hard-working blacks who rely on themselves for their mutual support, anticipates Zora Neale Hurston's *Their Eyes Were Watching God*, and also Alice Walker's *The Color Purple*. The 'folk'

---

1 Du Bois' essay was published in 1903, although he had already described the thoughts - concerning the necessity of an intellectual elite leading the masses - in his Harvard years. These ideas can be found in his manuscripts from 1894: "Harvard and the South"; "The Afro-American"; The True Meaning of an University", (MS, 1894 and quoted in Meier, *Negro Thought* 304). Thus, it can be maintained that Harper's representation of black leadership in *Iola Leroy* foreshadows Du Bois' 'Talented Tenth' (Carby, *Reconstructing* 84).

characters of the first chapter are reunited again in the last, and form a whole together with the returned intellectual characters.

In conclusion, it can be said that Harper sees the restoration of the black community and the restoration of sound families as the centre for her characters' personal enlightenment. Iola Leroy starts developing in a positive way only when reunited with her mother. That Harper relocates her harmonious black community back in the South shows her deep belief that every individual should work and prosper where he or she is most needed, and that the black intellectual elite should combine forces with the 'folk' for the uplifting of the whole black population, South *and* North.

Iola Leroy is indeed an archetypal novel, because it touches upon arguments, theories, motifs, and subjects which can be considered the foundation of the Afro-American experience, and which are unique to Afro-American literature. The novel's 'universal' thrust can also be re-experienced when reading our contemporary Afro-American women writers (Paule Marshall, Maya Angelou, Toni Morrison, Alice Walker, Gloria Naylor).

Chapter 5

Hopkins' *Contending Forces:* Assimilation or Protest?

(a) Biographical Remarks

The Negro race, like all races, is going to be saved by its exceptional men. The problem of education, then, among Negroes must first of all deal with the Talented Tenth; it is the problem of developing the Best of this race that they may guide the Mass away from the contamination and death of the Worst, in their own and other races. Now the training of men is a difficult and intricate task. Its technique is a matter for educational experts, but its object is for the vision of seers. If we make money the object of man-training, we shall develop money-makers but not necessarily men; if we make technical skill the object of education, we may possess artisans but not, in nature, men. Men we shall have only as we make manhood the object of the work of the schools - intelligence, broad sympathy, knowledge of the world that was and is, and of the relation of men to it - this is the curriculum of that Higher Education which must underlie true life. On this foundation we may build bread winning, skill of hand and quickness of brain, with never a fear lest the child and man mistake the means of living for the object of life.

W. E. Burghardt Du Bois, "The Talented Tenth" (1903)

Although the turn of the century was and still is widely considered to be the age of Washington and Du Bois, their influence on writers such as Harper and Hopkins should not be overestimated, nor should the productions of the latter two be viewed solely within the heated debate of those two male race leaders. As mentioned in Chapter 4 (d) of this thesis, Harper had already anticipated Du Bois' 'Talented Tenth' through her representation, in her novel *Iola Leroy,* of race leaders such as Iola, Harry, Miss Delany, Dr. Latimer and Rev. Carmicle. Moreover, both Harper and Hopkins were strongly influenced by the great political and literary activity of black women during the Woman's Era, in particular by Anna Julia Cooper's *A Voice from the South* (1892) and Ida Wells-Barnett's *Southern Horrors: Lynch Law in*

All Its Forms (1892). Hopkins can actually be considered the most productive writer of the turn of the century.

The decade opens with the publication of Harper's *Iola Leroy* (1892) and closes with the publication of Pauline E. Hopkins' *Contending Forces. A Romance Illustrative of Negro Life North and South* (1900).

Pauline E. Hopkins was born in Portland, Maine in 1859. During her childhood she moved to Boston with her parents, Sarah Allen and Northrup Hopkins. Both her father and, later, her stepfather were from Virginia; her mother, however, came from an old New England family. It is this New England heritage which finds expression in her fiction, which is centred around Boston with its long history of abolition. As a young and promising writer of fifteen, and a student of the famous Girls High School in Boston, Hopkins won a prize of ten dollars in gold for the best essay on the "Evils of Intemperance and Their Remedy" in a contest financed by William Wells Brown (Jane Campbell on Hopkins, in *Dictionary of Literary Biography*, 183).[1] After graduating from High School, she started a career in writing and the theatre, and by the age of twenty-one had already created and produced her first musical drama, *Slaves' Escape: Or, The Underground Railroad* (1880), playing a major role herself. Owing to this initial success, followed by many other successful performances together with her family - the Hopkins Colored Troubadours - she gained a reputation as "Boston's Favorite Soprano" (Penelope L. Bullock 106; Jane Campbell in Lauter, *Heath Anthology* 2: 172). As Hopkins could not rely solely on writing for a living, she also worked as a stenographer and public lecturer. In the 1890s she worked as a clerk, first for Republican politicians and later for the Massachusetts Bureau of Statistics.

The year 1900 was decisive for Hopkins' career as a writer both of fiction and nonfiction. She published her first and best-known novel, *Contending Forces*, as well as the short story, "The Mystery Within Us",[2] which appeared in the first issue of the *Colored American*

---

1 The undated essay can be found in the "Pauline E. Hopkins papers at Fisk University Library, Nashville" (Carby, *Reconstructing* "Notes" 4., 191).

2 *Colored American Magazine* 1 (May 1900): 14-18; this short story, as well as "Talma Gordon," "General Washington, A Christmas Story," "A Dash for Liberty," "Bro'r Abr'm Jimson's Wedding, A Christmas Story," "The Test of Manhood, A

Magazine, of which she was a founding member (James P. Draper, *Black Literature: Criticism* 1024).[1] At the same time as the foundation of the *Colored American Magazine*, Walter Wallace and his associates founded the Colored Co-operative Publishing Company, which published both the *Colored American Magazine* and *Contending Forces*. When the second issue of the magazine appeared, Hopkins was already "listed as editor of the Women's Department", and in 1903 she was promoted to the position of literary editor (Jane Campbell, *DLB* 188). From 1900 to 1904 she contributed innumerable articles on politics and society, two biographical series, "Famous Women of the Negro Race" and "Famous Men of the Negro Race",[2] along with many short stories and three serialized novels,[3] sometimes using her mother's

---

Christmas Story," and "As the Lord Lives, He is One of Our Mother's Children," were all published in the *Colored American Magazine* between May 1900 and Nov. 1903; they can also be found in the 1991 volume of the Schomburg Library, *Short Fiction By Black Women, 1900-1920*, edited by Elizabeth Ammons.

1 The journal's main aim and high ambitions, as well as Hopkins' great influence on it, are well expressed in the editorial statement in the first issue:

> American citizens of color, have long realized that for them there exists no monthly magazine, distinctively devoted to their interests and to the development of Afro-American art and literature. ... The Colored American Magazine ... offer[s] the colored people of the United States, a medium through which they can demonstrate their ability and tastes, in fiction, poetry, and art, as well as in the arena of historical, social and economic literature. Above all it aspires to develop and intensify the bonds of that racial brotherhood, which alone can enable a people, to assert their racial rights as men, and demand their privilege as citizens. ... A vast and almost unexplored treasury of biography, history, adventure, tradition, folk lore poetry and song, the accumulation of centuries of such experiences as have never befallen any other people lies open to us and to you. (Quoted in Hazel Carby, *Reconstructing* 122-123; see: "Editorial and Publishers' Announcements," *Colored American Magazine* 1 (May 1900): 60-64).

2 These biographical series featured well-known black people such as Mrs. Jasper, Sojourner Truth, Harriet Tubman, Fanny Jackson Coppin, Frances E. W. Harper, William Wells Brown, Frederick Douglass, Charles Lenox Remond, and John Jasper (Jane Campbell, *DLB* 189; see: *Colored American Magazine* 4-5 (1901-1902); 2-5 (1901-1902)).

3 The three novels were serialized between March 1901 and November 1903: "Hagar's Daughter, A Story of Southern Caste Prejudice," "Winona. A Tale of Negro

maiden name, Sarah Allen, as a pen name. It is not quite clear why Pauline Hopkins chose to use a pseudonym, but she was probably reluctant to appear as one of the major contributors to the journal (Jane Campbell, *Dictionary of Literary Biography 187*). Hazel Carby states in *Reconstructing* that the extent of Hopkins' influence on the magazine is difficult to estimate, but argues that a "textual analysis" of the contributions to the magazine would suggest that Hopkins played a major role in the life of the journal until 1904 (122). At this time, because of great financial difficulties, the journal was moved from Boston to New York; editorial control passed to Fred R. Moore, who was a great admirer of Booker T. Washington and his "philosophy that Negroes should try to improve their status in America through self-help and economic enterprise" (Penelope L. Bullock 114). The magazine's first four years in Boston had been marked by mainly literary contributions, but its change of editors, sponsors and location in 1904 was accompanied by a change to a policy highly reminiscent of Booker T. Washington: the magazine now contained descriptions of business enterprises owned by blacks, and public figures, both black and white, presented their "views on the subject of industrial education" (Penelope L. Bullock 115). Given the editorial statement of the first issue published in Boston in 1900, we can understand that Pauline Hopkins did not appreciate this shift away from intellectual and literary fields to economic ones. Consequently, she left the *Colored American Magazine* in 1904 and began to write for the *Voice of the Negro*.[1] In 1916, Pauline Hopkins and Walter Wallace issued the *New Era Magazine: An Illustrated Monthly Devoted to the World-Wide Interests of the Colored Race* in Boston (Penelope L. Bullock 115).[2]

In 1930 Hopkins was working for the Massachusetts Institute of Technology. On 13th August of that year she died suddenly and tragically when "the liniment-saturated flannel bandages she was wearing to relieve the neuritis she suffered were ignited by an oil stove in her room" (Jane Campbell, *DLB* 189).

Life in the South and Southwest," "Of One Blood. Or, the Hidden Self" (Jane Campbell, *DLB* 182).

1 In 1905 Hopkins published in this journal "a sociocultural survey series called 'The Dark Races of the Twentieth Century'" (Jane Campbell, *DLB* 189).

2 In 1916 Hopkins' last published work appeared in *New Era*: A novella entitled "Topsy Templeton" (Jane Campbell, *DLB* 189).

In common with all the authors discussed in this thesis, Pauline Hopkins is a tragic example of a gifted writer who was neglected both by her contemporaries and has been ignored by the critics until very recently. Claudia Tate, in her paper, "Pauline Hopkins: Our Literary Foremother", states that it is easier to "cite the few works in which she is mentioned than to refer to the many which fail to mention her at all" (54). In Part Three of this thesis, Hopkins' critical reception or rather, 'non-reception' will be discussed in detail.

(b) Romance or Political Novel?

The novel's title and subtitle, *Contending Forces: A Romance Illustrative of Negro Life North and South,* anticipate not only the way the characters are caught between two opposing poles (e.g. North - South, Du Bois - Washington, political action - disfranchisement and servitude, white - black, good - evil) but also the author's difficult task of trying to give a 'true' representation of black people's lives while feeling hampered in her endeavour because of the form she had to choose. Thus there is a constant tug-of-war between the form of the romance and the black characters' portrayal within it. As we have seen in the earlier chapters of this thesis, Harriet Wilson, Harriet Jacobs, and Frances Ellen Watkins Harper all had to struggle with the restrictions that were imposed on them by the form they had chosen. This phenomenon even surfaces in the illustrations by R. Emmet Owen - on the novel's frontispiece as well as by the ones dispersed throughout the novel - where the characters are repeatedly depicted as white or 'almost white'. These illustrations are not always consistent with the narrative, in that they portray all the main characters as fair-skinned. In the narrative, however, William's and Dora's complexions are described as being the color of an almond shell and of a delicate brown, respectively.

Emerson' s epigraph on the title page, "'The civility of no race can be perfect whilst another race is degraded'", already indicates the novel's political stance. In the 1850s Emerson was a fervent advocate of abolition, and the epigraph was still strikingly valid 50 years later, at the turn of the century, when the abolition of slavery was seen to be only a first step towards the solution to the race problem. The failure of Reconstruction, followed by the blacks' experiences during post-Reconstruction with its mob rule and lynch laws, disenfranchisement, segregation, colour prejudice, and destructive sharecropping system make the black population realize resignedly that, in reality, it was the South that had won the war. As Northern politicians and former abolitionists slowly but surely withdrew their support of the blacks' cause, the old dichotomy between the strong and obstinate South and the yielding North was again becoming firmly established. It required the efforts of writers such as Harper, Hopkins, Wells-Barnett, and Cooper, together with political leaders such as Washington and Du Bois, plus the Harlem Renaissance, and a Civil Rights Movement with a non-violent leader such as Martin Luther King, to finally demolish, in the 1950s and 1960s, the South's stronghold of racism.

Further evidence of the novel's political tone is offered by Hopkins' dedication:

To the Friends of Humanity Everywhere
I offer this humble tribute
written by
one of a proscribed race. (7)

The author of *Contending Forces* not only affirms here that she is black, but also summarizes in one word what it means not to be white in American society, namely, social and economic ostracism.

In the first paragraph of the preface, the author states that this "little romance", or "fiction", should help "to raise the stigma of degradation from my race" (13). Thus, by using the form of the romance, Hopkins tries to achieve a political, ethical, and social goal, that is to present her people in a more realistic light. Whereas Woman's Fiction tried to be a model to individuals, especially women, focusing on the heroine's personal change which would open up to her vast and unforeseen possibilities, Hopkins boldly maintains that her romance should influence a wider circle of people in order to change people's social behaviour towards blacks. Hopkins, therefore, goes beyond Woman's Fiction by emphasizing not only the protagonist's own responsibility, independent of social and economical forces, but also the individual's struggle to find a place within a highly prejudiced society, that is, the responsibility is to be shared by the heroine, the characters around her and, most importantly, society as well (i.e. Hopkins' contemporaries and her readers). It is interesting to note that Hopkins does not apologize for her "daring venture" (the writing of her romance) - as do Harriet Wilson and Harriet Jacobs.

It is also noteworthy that it is not only the black race who should profit by this romance, but "the world at large" as well. Thus Hopkins stands in the tradition of women writers such as Wilson, Jacobs, and Harper who tried to instruct their white readers by giving them a different picture of black people in general, and of black women in particular:[1]

> Fiction is of great value to any people as a preserver of manners and customs - religious, political and social. It is a record of growth and development from generation to generation. *No one will do this for us; we must ourselves develop the men and women who will faithfully portray the inmost thoughts and feelings of the Negro with all the fire and romance which lie dormant in our history,* and, as yet, unrecognized by writers of the Anglo-Saxon race. (13-14)

Here again, Hopkins mentions the importance of fiction as a recorder of social history, and she argues like Dr. Latimer that "out of the race must come its own thinkers and writers" (Harper, *Iola Leroy* 263). Hopkins states quite clearly in her preface that her novel is at the same time both romance and political novel. She argues that in the South, lynch law, mob rule, and concubinage, as well as the sexual exploitation of black women, are part of the blacks' reality, whereas in the North, the blacks have an equally difficult struggle to find a job, earn a living, and get a decent education. It is Hopkins' wish to bring

---

1 This picture is strikingly at odds with, for example, the 'happy mammies' depicted in the fiction of the Plantation School, the minstrel shows, or in films such as *Gone With the Wind* (by Margaret Mitchell 1936). *Gone With the Wind* is a perfect example of how the Plantation School influenced fiction and moving pictures far into the 20th century. This monumental film became history, and for a long time it had stood, all over the world, as a symbol of the American Civil War as perceived by 'Southern' whites. With the release of the movies *Roots* (the novel of the same name was written by Alex Palmer Haley, 1976) and *The Color Purple* a different, more realistic, picture of America's history has been presented, including the blacks' experience, too.

the South's "anarchy" into the light of day by telling "an impartial story, leaving it to the reader to draw conclusions" (15).

> I have presented both sides of the dark picture - lynching and concubinage - truthfully and without vituperation, pleading for that justice of heart and mind for my people which the Anglo-Saxon in America never withholds from suffering humanity. (15)

Hopkins' penultimate paragraph ends most interestingly on a conciliatory note. She probably tries here to touch her white audience's pride by drawing on their 'innate' sense of justice, even if reality has so far proven to be otherwise. At the same time, the author calls upon her white readers to use their influence in order to lift the weight of prejudice off the black race. Thus the work of Hopkins, together with that of Mary Prince, Jacobs, Wilson, and Harper, can be considered 'littérature engagée' that has been effectively produced by many American writers and by some French writers such as Jean-Paul Sartre, Albert Camus, and Claire Etcherelli.[1]

Contending Forces has 22 chapters, each chapter with an epigraph - similarly to Harriet Wilson's *Our Nig* - that underlines the various events in the narrative. Whittier, Cowper, Shakespeare, Gray, Emerson, Tennyson, Goldsmith, and Longfellow serve as her source, proving her to be widely read in both American and English literature. As already pointed out in Part One of this thesis, Cowper was a favourite among abolitionists; his poetry adorned many Slave Narratives. Emerson and Whittier were both impassioned advocates of the abolition of slavery and therefore good examples of "the Anglo-Saxon in America [who] never withholds [justice of heart and mind] from suffering humanity" (15).

---

1 With her novel *Elise ou la vraie vie,* Claire Etcherelli received the Prix Fémina in 1967. She also belongs to the category of the 'unrecognized' women writers. Simone de Beauvoir says about her novel "Une admirable et tragique histoire d'amour entre un Algérien et une Française. Et surtout, quelqu'un: quelqu'un qui parle avec une voix d'une inoubliable justesse" (cover, *Elise ou la vraie vie,* Editions Denoël, 1967).

Hopkins' novel, like Harper's, spans the period of several decades connecting the Antebellum Era with the Postbellum. But whereas *Iola Leroy* begins in medias res, i.e. at the height of the Civil War, and only later comments retrospectively on Iola's parents and on her own childhood long before the war, the first four chapters (i.e. the subplot) in *Contending Forces* are set in Bermuda (ch. 1) and North Carolina (chs. 2-4) several decades before the Civil War. Before the main characters of the subplot - the Montforts (Charles, Grace, and their two sons, Charles, Jr. and Jesse)[1] - are introduced, an omniscient narrator instructs the reader about "the romantic history of the emancipation of the slaves in the islands" (18).[2] The whole novel is related by this omniscient narrator, who often comments on political and moral questions by means of lengthy intrusions. In Chapter 4, for example, before relating the family's tragedy, the narrator - anticipating the Montfort catastrophe - moralizes on the fate which can befall people if they do not act according to "the natural laws of humanity:"

> Nature avenges herself upon us for every law violated in the mad rush for wealth or position or personal comfort where the rights of others of the human family are not respected. If Charles Montfort had been contented to accept the rulings of the English Parliament, and had allowed his human property to come under the new laws just made for its government, although poorer in the end, he would have spared himself and family all the horrors which were to follow his selfish flight to save that property. (65)

---

1 Charles, Jr.'s and Jesse Montfort's descendants - William and Dora Smith, and Charles Montfort-Withington - play a major role in the main plot of the novel.

2 Mary Prince's slave narrative does not depict slavery in such a romantic way as Hopkins. Quite the contrary! Prince states that the West Indies exceeded all the other slave states in brutality towards their slaves. Hopkins does not, however, want to extenuate the evil of slavery by representing Bermuda and the Montforts in even a slightly romantic light. The melodramatic subplot of the first four chapters serves as a fictitious means of contrasting the 'mild' West Indies - because under British rule - with harsh North Carolina - because under Southern American rule. This is, of course, as unrealistic as Hopkins' statement in her preface that the Anglo-Saxon in America would always act justly towards those deserving compassion.

Montfort does not stay in Bermuda, because he is afraid of losing all his money with the emancipation of his slaves. He is not one of the cruel slave holders, but he wants to decide for himself just when to emancipate his slaves, and consequently he moves his property and family to North Carolina. The villain, Anson Pollock, because of his passionate love for Grace Montfort, incites "the committee on public safety" (53), of which he is the leader, to raid the Montfort family mansion.[1] Charles Montfort's violation of "the natural law of humanity" causes his and his wife's destruction; his two sons will subsequently be sold into slavery.

The main action takes place first in Boston and later in New Orleans, several generations after the Montfort tragedy, towards the end of the century. Whereas the subplot is set within a more or less white society, the main plot is firmly set within Boston's black society, with Ma Smith's lodging-house at its centre. The second to last chapter, "After Many Days", connects the subplot to the main action by melodramatically revealing the Smiths' link to the English aristocracy, in the person of Charles Montfort-Withington, who is a Member of Parliament. Whereas Jesse Montfort, after his escape from slavery, married his rescuer's daughter - of whose several children Ma Smith was one - Charles Montfort, Jr. followed his owner and rescuer to England, marrying his daughter there. His son, Charles Montfort-Withington, is thus a direct descendant of Jesse's brother Charles Jr. and is therefore, Ma Smith's cousin.

It takes rather extraordinary coincidences to finally unveil the complicated family relations and restore the severed ties among the Montfort descendants. Charles Montfort, Jr.'s English rescuer in chapter 4, as well as his own son Charles Montfort-Withington, the Member of Parliament, are representatives of the just and humane Anglo-Saxons, who in England, early supported abolitionism. Hopkins shows not only that each of the individual families, white or black, can be traced back to a common experience - the history of slavery - as in the case of the Montforts and the Pollocks, but also that their experience involves the Anglo-Saxon world.

---

1 The John Pollock Langley of the main plot is a descendant of the "villainous and unscrupulous" Anson Pollock of the subplot (381).

In conclusion, it can be stated that *Contending Forces* combines the romance, with its melodramatic plotline, virtuous heroines, noble heroes, impudent villains, strange coincidences, supernatural events, and highly emotional love scenes, with a political novel bearing a moral, social, ethical, and humanitarian message.

(c) Sappho's Two Identities

In this chapter there will be a discussion of Hopkins' use of her heroine's double identity to refute the common assumption, which black women constantly had to fight against, that black women were not as chaste as white women and that, therefore, white men were naturally entitled to take advantage of their 'moral weakness'.

Sappho Clark, the heroine of *Contending Forces,* figures in the main plot, but she is connected to the subplot through a fate similar to that of Grace Montfort. Because Anson Pollock wants to possess his friend's wife, Grace, he kills her husband and sells their children into slavery. Finally, Grace Montfort commits suicide so as not to become Pollock's concubine. Mabelle Beaubean - which is Sappho Clark's former name - has been sexually victimized by her white uncle, her father's half brother, who first raped her and then placed her in a brothel. Mr. Beaubean, her father, after telling his half brother that he will seek justice in the Federal courts, is burnt alive in his house the following night, together with his family. Mabelle Beaubean, rescued by her foster brother, Lycurgus Sawyer, is the only survivor. He places the desperate girl in a convent, where she is supposed to have died in childbirth.

Hopkins' *Contending Forces* and magazine novels "Hagar's Daughter" and "Of One Blood", like Jacobs' *Incidents* and Harper's *Iola Leroy,* all revolve about the theme of the black woman's victimization by white men. Whereas the Slave Narratives authored by men, and also the first Afro-American novel *Clotel,* portray women in terms of their victimization only (Clotel throws herself into the Potomac in order to escape being taken captive), the authors mentioned above go beyond those representations and show the heroine's successful struggle to shape her life according to her own wishes - as, for example, Linda Brent, who takes a white lover in order to prevent sexual harassment by her owner.

The reader first learns of Sappho's real identity (Mabelle Beaubean) only in chapter 14, "Luke Sawyer Speaks to the League", when The American Colored League is holding a meeting to discuss a recent case of lynching in the South. Three decisive reasons make Luke Sawyer one of the most important minor characters in the story. Firstly, he reveals Sappho's real identity. Secondly, by relating his own personal history as well as hers, he refutes the myth of the black rapist. As one of Hopkins' spokespersons, he shows the link between lynchings and the whites' economical interests, as exemplified in the case of his father, who was a well-to-do businessman and had to die solely for that reason. In the case of the Beaubeans, who were destroyed because of one man's selfish lust, the reason for lynching is ascribed to another source - the white rapist. And thirdly, Luke Sawyer clearly advocates a Du Boisean stance (also taken by Will Smith and Sappho Clark) by calling for action, courage, justice, brotherly affiliation, and self-respect; this is opposed to the Washingtonian stance (taken by Dr. Arthur Lewis, Dora Smith, and John Langley), embodying the policy of contentment, conservatism, and acceptance of the lack of vote and rule for the black race, in which Sawyer sees the black man's destruction.

The reader is first introduced to the new lodger (Sappho) by Dora Smith, who tells her mother about her in the first chapter of the main plot: "She's too beautiful for that dreary back room. ... she has the best of references. Father Andrew gives her the best of characters ...." (ch. 5, 81). Dora further informs her mother that the new lodger has a typewriter, and earns a good living with it working at home. Dora continues:

> "But really, ma, you won't be able to keep from loving her; she has the sweetest and saddest face I ever saw. I have read of the woman with a story written on her face, but I never believed it anything but a fairy tale. You'll believe me when you see her and talk with her." (89)

After Dora's introduction of their new lodger, the omniscient narrator adds further details:

> Tall and fair, with hair of a golden cast, aquiline nose, rosebud mouth, soft brown eyes veiled by long, dark lashes which swept her cheek, just now covered with a delicate rose flush, ... a combination of queen rose and lily in one. (107)

Here we are presented with an almost white heroine of outstanding beauty and noble traits of character. Sappho is depicted as a virtuous and independent woman working for her own living. Because of the North's colour prejudice, however, she has to take her work home. Hopkins combines fiction and reality when she elaborates - by means of direct authorial address - on the blacks' difficulties in securing a job: "... the poor Negro finds himself banned in almost every kind of employment" (83). From the very beginning, Hopkins creates suspense around Sappho's person. Her face expresses a sadness which suggests a secret the reader feels provoked to unveil. Although, she excels the women and men around her, the main characters are all depicted as people of noble character - with the exception of John Langley: "... to a reader of character, the strong manhood and honesty of purpose which existed in Will Smith were lacking in John Langley" (90). If she wants to be socially accepted as a True Woman, however, and not be considered an outcast, Sappho must keep her former life secret. Little bits of information concerning it (her mother comes from New Orleans, Sappho has some beautiful embroidery) lead the reader along the complicated plotline to the solution of the riddle in chapter 14, "Luke Sawyer Speaks to the League". There, the link between Mabelle and Sappho's life is established when Sappho faints after hearing her own story.

Both Iola Leroy's and Sappho Clark's personal stories are representative of the crimes committed on women during slavery and the Reconstruction and post-Reconstruction Eras. Both women are depicted as refined, fair-skinned beauties of virtuous character. Iola Leroy, however, manages to stay 'pure' and 'innocent' in the midst of the degradation around her, whereas Sappho - whose story seems more realistic - could not avoid being sexually abused, similarly to thousands of women during and after slavery. Hopkins definitely goes beyond Harper's *Iola Leroy* in the depiction of her heroine, Sappho. Hopkins' novel is more dangerous for the reputation of black women than Harper's, because she depicts a heroine who - because of her past experience - cannot easily embody the cult of True Womanhood.

Sappho turns out to be a 'fallen' woman, but her perfect manners, genteel bearing, and absolute reserve when, for example, she is intruded upon in her room, first by William, who only wants to light her fire, and later by John Langley, attest that she is a True Woman despite the fact that she has a child. Hence, Hopkins expands the concept of True Womanhood by adding to the description of her heroine's spotless character the political implications of her fate as an unmarried mother. Hopkins shows, therefore, that slavery and Southern racist propaganda are the source of the black woman's reputation for lacking in virtue. By voicing through William Smith the clever argument that the mulatto population is proof enough that whites have had unlawful contacts with black women, Hopkins defends black womanhood in general, and Sappho's in particular (299-230).

In her discussion with Dora on the question of women's virtue, Sappho reveals that she is not absolutely sure that she could not all the same be made responsible for her terrible fate (her sin) at the hands of her white rapist. Through Dora's arguments, which appease Sappho's tortured conscience, Hopkins further informs the reader how virtue, True Womanhood, and chastity have to be viewed by the True Christian:

> "Then you are not one of those who think that a woman should be condemned to eternal banishment for the sake of one misstep?"
>
> "Not I, indeed; I have always felt a great curiosity to know the reason why each individual woman loses character and standing in the eyes of the world. I believe that we would hang our heads in shame at having the temerity to judge a fallen sister, could we but know the circumstances attending many such cases. And, after all we may do or say," continued the girl softly, "the best of us, who have lived the purest lives on earth that mortal can conceive, find at last that our only hope lies in the words of that text - 'This man receiveth sinners.'" (100-101)

Hopkins' Sappho, like the poetess of Lesbos, is greatly admired by all who are acquainted with her. Even Dora, who usually does not have close women friends, feels attracted by her beauty and her intelligence:

> There was a great fascination for her about the quiet, self-possessed woman. She did not, as a rule, care much for girl friendships, holding that a close intimacy between two of the same sex was more than likely to end disastrously for one or the other. But Sappho Clark seemed to fill a long-felt want in her life, and she had from the first a perfect trust in the beautiful girl. (97-98)

The two women develop a strong and long-lasting friendship which cannot be destroyed even by John Langley's impudent passion for Sappho. In the chapter, "Friendship", Hopkins combines two important points. On the one hand, the author shows the friendship developing between Dora and Sappho, who are discussing love, men, and politics, and on the other hand she elaborates didactically, through her spokesperson Sappho, why it is so essential for the blacks to have the franchise:

> "... If we lose the franchise, at the same time we shall lose the respect of all other citizens. Temporizing will not benefit us; rather, it will leave us branded as cowards, not worthy a freeman's respect - an alien people, without a country and without a home." (125)

The reader is confronted with two women characters who are completely opposed to each other. Dora, as a representative of 'domesticity,' believes men to be her superiors, and therefore has no opinion of her own insofar as politics is concerned: "'I am willing to confess that the subject is a little deep for me, ... I'm not the least bit of a politician, and I generally accept whatever the men tell me as right; .... '" (125). She simply accepts what her friend, Dr. Lewis, tells her. But she nevertheless admires Sappho for her independence in general and her outspokenness on the import of suffrage. The significance of their friendship is best exemplified, at the end of the novel, when Dora names her daughter after Sappho.

John Langley's insult towards Sappho triggers her decision to leave Boston. His proposal to take her as a concubine connects her past - an experience in the South with a white man - with her present - an experience at the hands of a black man in Boston. This is the second time - the first was when listening to Luke Sawyer's story - that Sappho is directly and brutally confronted with her own 'history'. The first time, she reacted by fainting, which reflects her symbolical death as Mabelle Beaubean, whereas this time she realizes that she cannot keep her past a secret any longer. Her letter to Will Smith, in which she tells him of her real identity and of John's indecent proposal, are a further step towards the climax at the end of the novel, when the two lovers are reunited. After reading Sappho's revealing letter, William's thoughts are related by the omniscient narrator: "God of heaven! how could he bear to think that his beautiful Sappho - his pure girl-love, had been subjected to such brutality!" (330). For Will, Dora, and their mother, Sappho is as pure as before, and her whole past 'history' is seen only in the light of Luke Sawyer's account: Sappho's brutal rape by a white man, and the subsequent destruction of her family by an infuriated mob. Thus Hopkins manages to remove the blame of rape from the victimized black woman by revealing that a white man is the cause of all her miseries.

The final step in bringing the two lovers even closer to "their desired haven" - as the title of the last chapter promises - is Sappho's acceptance of her child, Alphonse (ch. 22). After writing her letter to Will and while still in Boston, she decides to take Alphonse back to the South and never to leave him again. Thus Sappho finally accepts her long rejected motherhood, gaining from this the fortitude necessary to endure her present loss:

> Now she felt that her losses could not be paid, but in the years which followed she learned to value the strong, chastening influence of her present sorrow, and the force of character it developed, fitting her perfectly for the place she was to occupy in carrying comfort and hope to the women of her race. (347)

In a melodramatic scene in New Orleans, the two lovers are finally reunited three years after Sappho's flight from Boston. John Langley, however, who cannot escape the Pollocks' heritage, meets a different destiny at the end of the novel. Similarly to his ancestor, Anson Pollock, who destroyed the Montfort family because he could not control his jealous and selfish passion, John Langley disturbs the Smiths' harmony with his blind passion for Sappho. His selfish behaviour provokes Sappho's flight from Boston, ends his friendship with William Smith, and makes Dora Smith break off her engagement with him. However, his destructiveness does not, finally prevent the family's happiness, nor does he have to die a villain. Towards the close of his life, he shows remorse for his deeds, and finally acknowledges his mother:

> He thought of his newly found mother, whom he had been ashamed to acknowledge. His sight failed, his limbs lost their feeling, his heart was nearly pulseless - it was death. "O God! receive my soul. Dear, dear mother" - The child of sunny climes folded himself more closely in his blankets for the last time, and slept to wake no more on earth. So the dawn of Easter Sunday found him. That undisciplined soul went forth to wander in celestial spheres, there to continue the salutary lessons begun on earth, under the guidance of God's angels, who minister to the needs of the immortal soul. (400-401)

At the end of the novel, then, the constructive forces win out over the destructive ones as the villain, Langley, dies in loneliness, far from civilization. Thus everything which has been predicted by Mrs. Frances, the seer, has come true.

It can be concluded that Hopkins' heroine, Sappho, like Iola Leroy, has to go through a certain period of suffering and development which finally results in her acceptance of her past life and of motherhood. The novel's last scene shows the newly-wed couple, William and Sappho, together with Alphonse, Dora and Dr. Lewis, their daughter, Sappho, and Ma Smith on a ship bound for Europe to visit their recently-found relative, Mr. Montfort-Withington. This trip is highly metaphorical. It symbolizes, on the one hand, the slave's quest for his dispersed family members and, on the other hand, the link between the New World and the Old World, of the present with the past.

Sappho's two identities have merged into a wholesome single one as she decided to accept her past and her motherhood. She is a True Woman, greatly resembling her fellow-sisters of Woman's Fiction at the end of the novel. The last scene, however, does not show her in her cosy home in the midst of her friends, her surrogate family. On the contrary, the heroine is presented on the move, for similarly to Iola Leroy, Sappho plans to join forces with her husband in "... the establishment of a school which should embrace every known department of science, where the Negro youth of ability and genius could enter without money and without price" (386). Thus, the novel ends on a harmonious note, not only with the characters at last happily joined, but also as concerns black politics and black leadership in general: the two couples joining in one family, the Lewises represent the Washingtons and the Smiths the Du Boises.

It is noteworthy that Hopkins - although clearly advocating Du Bois' policy through, her spokespersons Sappho and William and in her articles published in the *American Colored Magazine* - at the end of *Contending Forces* predicts a utopian future which promises that the two leaders with their two different programmes do not necessarily have to compete with each other, but that the work of both could offer a wholesome uplift of the black population.

(d) The Self-Sufficient Black Community

In *Contending Forces,* Hopkins shows us the workings of a self-sufficient, more or less harmonious black community, through the example of Ma Smith's lodging-house and the black church.

In the chapter, "Ma Smith's Lodging-House", the reader is introduced to all of the main characters in the novel: Ma Smith (the owner of the boarding-house) and her two children, Dora Smith (Dora Grace Montfort Smith) and William Smith (William Jesse Montfort Smith),[1] Dora's fiancé, the villain John Langley (John Pollock Langley), and Sappho Clark. The Smith's family history is partly revealed by an omniscient narrator. Most of the characters are either owners of or lodgers in the boarding-house. It is a centre of action, where people fall in love (Sappho and William), where Sappho is abused by John, who threatens to expose her false identity, where important decisions are made (Sappho decides to leave the boarding house and Will (William), the man she loves; Dora decides to marry Dr. Lewis), where crucial letters are read (Sappho's, and Will's from Bermuda), where engagements are broken off (Dora and John's) and where family

---

1 Dora and William Smith's full names - mentioned only once in chapter 5, p. 83 - reveal their family connection with the Montforts of the subplot.

connections are revealed (Mr. Montfort-Withington's visit and life-story).

The lodging-house is representative of the black Bostonian community of the 1890s. Dora and Will's mother wants to make her home and parlour a centre where people can meet, enjoy music together, and discuss the important political issues of the day. Whereas the Northern black community depicted in *Iola Leroy* is made up only of black intellectuals, Hopkins' black community is a conglomerate of black people of mixed backgrounds and achievements. On the one hand, the boarding-house shelters an intellectual elite consisting of the lawyer and politician John Langley, the 'politician' and race leader William Smith, the manager of the boarding house, Dora Smith, who stands for the intelligent, pleasant house-wife, and Sappho, who is a representative of the independent, well-bred, and well-educated black woman who believes in the Du Boisean approach to solving the problems of lynching and of building up the blacks' self-esteem (ch. 7 "Friendship"). This group of young people represents the Postbellum generation. On the other hand, there are the two ex-slaves, Mrs. Ophelia Davis and Mrs. Sarah Ann White, representing the Antebellum generation. They are industrious, honest, shrewd black working women who have known each other for a long time, as they were the slaves of the same owner before the emancipation.

It is noteworthy that the black father seems to be physically absent from the black community depicted in *Contending Forces*. Ma Smith, Mrs. Willis, and Mrs. Davis are all widows, and Sappho has no husband either. For Mrs. Smith, motherhood and commitment to the Baptist church are recompense enough. Mrs. Willis stands as a representative of the women's club movement, and can be considered a feminist of the Old Guard:

> Money, the sinews of living and social standing, she did not possess upon her husband's death. Therefore she was forced to begin a weary pilgrimage - a hunt for the means to help her breast the social tide. The best opening, she decided after looking carefully about her, was in the great cause of the evolution of true womanhood in the work of the "Woman Question" as embodied in marriage and suffrage. (ch. 8, 146)

The sewing-circle, with Mrs. Willis as the leading figure, represents the beginning of the women's club movement. It shows women of all ages sewing together and at the same time discussing questions concerning blacks in general and black women in particular. Mrs. Willis is an authority on any subject, political or moral. The black women's "Sewing-Circle" is later contrasted with "The Canterbury Club Dinner", where only men are invited to talk about the latest event which shook the South: the lynch law. William Smith, John Langley, and Dr. Lewis are the only blacks present at the club meeting. They have been invited because they have gained a reputation as race leaders of rare intelligence, and therefore should impart their views on the race problem (ch. 17). Hopkins' women characters are active, intelligent and interested not only in the building up of a home for themselves but also in working together within their community for the improvement of the blacks.

It can be concluded that in *Iola Leroy* a black community had first to be created, whereas in *Contending Forces* Hopkins shows a microcosm of a well-to-do black community centred around a black family's lodging-house and the church to which they all belong. Although the villain is not absent in Hopkins' world - as pictured in *Contending Forces* -, the good forces eventually triumph over the destructive ones. In that way, Hopkins presents the reader with a utopian society which should inspire black people, and with which they should be able to identify.

In *Contending Forces,* as well as in her later magazine novels, Hopkins clearly reveals her preoccupation with genealogy, miscegenation, mysticism, black social history, and politics. Consequently, *Contending Forces* combines elements from the political novel, protest novel, didactic novel, romance, and fictional history. Upon hearing the term 'protest novel,' the 20th-century reader might immediately be reminded of Wright's *Native Son,* and hence probably feels that Hopkins' novel lacks somewhat in protest. Hopkins, however, is quite outspoken in her condemnation of the lynch law, women's sexual exploitation, slavery and social injustice. Her characters voice the political debates of her time, which makes her fiction an important socio-historical document. Thus, neither *Contending Forces* nor her later stories can be viewed as an acceptance of conformity with any political or formal standards. Moreover, her fiction is deeply rooted in the belief that blacks and whites have a common heritage which reaches beyond America's boundaries, to Europe in the case of *Contending Forces* and to Ethiopia in "Of One Blood". Therefore Hopkins' heroines and heroes know themselves truly only when their family relations are unveiled by coincidences which reveal that the races are inseparably connected through miscegenation:

> But who shall judge the handiwork of God, the Great Craftsman! Caste prejudice, race pride, boundless wealth, scintillating intellects refined by all the arts of the intellectual world, are but puppets in His hand, for His promises stand, and He will prove His words, "Of one blood have I made all races of men." (Hopkins, "Of One Blood" in *The Magazine Novels* 621)

Chapter 6

Kelley's *Megda*: Black Characters, or White?

(a) An Unrecognized Writer

If before sin had cast its deepest shadows or sorrow had distilled its bitterest tears, it was true that it was not good for man to be alone, it is no less true, since the shadows have deepened and life's sorrows have increased, that *the world has need of all the spiritual aid that woman can give for the social advancement and moral development of the human race.* The tendency of the present age, with its restlessness, religious upheavals, failures, blunders, and crimes, is toward broader freedom, and increase of knowledge, the emancipation of thought, and a recognition of the brotherhood of man; in this movement woman, as the companion of man, must be a sharer. So close is the bond between man and woman that you can not raise one without lifting the other. The world can not move without woman's sharing in the movement, and to help give a right impetus to that movement is woman's highest privilege. (Emphasis mine)

Frances Ellen Watkins Harper, "Woman's Political Future" (1893)

That Emma Dunham Kelley has been included in the Schomburg Library is a decisive step towards the discovery of this writer of the Woman's Era, and towards a (re-)evaluation of her novels, *Megda* (1891) and *Four Girls at Cottage City* (1898). The following discussion will show in what way Kelley, offering a spiritual message, can be considered to be as valuable an author and chronicler of Afro-American culture and life as writers like Harper and Hopkins, who sounded a more explicitly political note in their works.

The consistent omission of Kelley's name, and the titles of her novels, from bibliographies, anthologies, biographies, and literary histories is indeed striking. Why is this black woman writer virtually absent from the literary canon? Why is she omitted even from the *Dictionary of Literary Biography*? Is it due to her writing in the subgenre of 'girl's fiction' or did she simply fall victim to the 20th-century critics, who for decades considered only those novels as true representations of the black experience that expressed 'protest' in the way Richard Wright's *Native Son* (1940) and Ann Petry's *Street* (1946) did? They condemned any black novelist for conforming to white standards unless his or her work clearly articulated the black hero's or heroine's alienation at the hands of a white, racist society. Both the white critics and the white publishers have been the arbiters of the black writer's success or - what is more likely - his or her fall into oblivion:

> As many Afro-American authors themselves remark, the question of audience has long plagued blacks, and has been compounded by the fact that most major publishers are white and their readership white. When these publishers think it advisable to print the works of black authors, they anticipate images of black life that accord with the prevailing cultural stereotypes - anything from the obsequious darky of the 1880s to the raging militant of the 1960s. [Up to the 1980s] only the rare white publisher has recognized or encouraged artistic independence in black writers. (Margolies and Bakish xi)

Zora Neale Hurston, Paule Marshall, Toni Morrison, Alice Walker, and Gloria Naylor were the first women authors who actually dared question this kind of biased criticism, by publishing novels that were not primarily emphasizing white racism.[1] Like *Iola Leroy* and *Contending Forces,* their novels are centred around predominantly

---

1 Zora Neale Hurston, for one, who published her work in the 1930s and 1940s, died in poverty and obscurity after a life committed wholly to the survival of her people's cultural heritage. Hurston was novelist, folklorist, and anthropologist in one person (see: Robert E. Hemenway's biography, *Zora Neale Hurston: A Literary Biography,* 1977 and Alice Walker's anthology of Hurston's work, *I Love Myself When I Am Laughing ... : A Zora Neale Hurston Reader,* 1979). Hemenway's and Walker's works retrieved Hurston from oblivion and gave her her rightful place in American literature. Alice Walker further increased Hurston's popularity by calling her her literary ancestor (see Walker's two essays: "Zora Neale Hurston: A Cautionary Tale and a Partisan View" and "Looking For Zora"). Hurston's best books, *Mules and Men* and *Their Eyes Were Watching God* , in which she focusses on folklore, black life, herself, and the Southern black community, record and transmit a wholesome black cultural heritage.

black communities. Our contemporary black women writers create fictional worlds that are defined by their black characters, not simply by 'typical' black characters who exist and react only in relation to white racism.

When first published in 1891, *Megda* was very popular, so much that it had to be reprinted in 1892;[1] it is therefore an error to call *Iola Leroy* (1892) either the first novel of the 1890s or (as Gloster maintains, in *Negro Voices* 30) the first novel published by a black woman in America after the Civil War.[2]

Emma Dunham Kelley's highly spiritual message, her representation of her heroines' comfortable middle-class status, her "preoccupation with skin color and [her] studied avoidance of any mention of race" might also have been responsible for the novel's being so neglected (source: see footnote 1). Although *Megda* "presents a number of problems to anyone trying to place it within the tradition of Afro-American women's fiction", as Molly Hite argues in her introduction to *Megda* (xxvii), it is nevertheless a novel by a writer of the Woman's Era. If scholars interpret the novel and its heroine, Megda, only from a 20th-century feminist perspective, they will conclude, falsely, that Megda does not undergo a development simply because she becomes a contented Reverend's wife instead of a teacher or an actress. Here again, as already maintained in earlier chapters of this thesis, it is important to evaluate the novel within its 19th-century socio-historical context. If overt social protest seems to be absent from *Megda*'s fictional world, it does not necessarily follow that it does not exist on another, deeper level. Thus one should not focus only on Megda's conversion at the end of the novel, to the Protestant doctrine of personal salvation. It is more important to look at her development from adolescence to womanhood, within her community and as a significant member of it.

Finally, if this Christian Bildungsroman focusing on girls is full of contradictions, its discussion and analysis can be considered the more

---

1 Molly Hite, in her introduction to *Megda* (xxvii).

2 Amelia E. Johnson's text *Clarence and Corinne; Or, God's Way* (1890) can be considered the first novel by a black woman in America after the Civil War! Neither Margolies and Bakish nor Watson include it in their studies. Jackson maintains in *A History of Afro-American Literature* that "... *Clarence and Corinne* becomes the first novel by a Negro writer to concentrate on whites, and not on blacks" (vol. 1, 391).

enlightening because it reflects in some way or other the difficult and contradictory aspects of Kelley's America of the 1890s, "the nadir" of Afro-American history (Rayford Logan in Carole McAlpine 10). Harper's speech on "Woman's Political Future" at the historic World's Congress of Representative Women in Chicago in 1893, in which she states that "... the world has need of all the *spiritual aid* that woman can give for the social advancement and moral development of the human race. ..." unmistakably places writers like Kelley within the tradition of Afro-American Women's Fiction (Loewenberg and Bogin 244, and see also the epigraph of this chapter, emphasis mine).

(b) From Woman's Fiction to Girl's Fiction

Megda and *Four Girls at Cottage City* can both be classified as "girl's fiction". Nina Baym argues that Louisa May Alcott's publication of *Little Women* in 1868 sparked a change in the women's writing tradition, from "limit-breaking woman's fiction" to "limit-enforcing girl's fiction" (*Woman's Fiction* 279/296).

Unlike *Iola Leroy* and *Contending Forces, Megda* has neither a preface nor a note appended to the novel, nor an epigraph adorning the front page, which might reveal something about the author's life, work, or aspirations.[1] Emma Dunham Kelley's photograph on the frontispiece and the dedication to her mother are the only pieces of extra-textual information about the author:[2]

---

1 Kelley's later novel, *Four Girls at Cottage City*, has an author's preface in which the book's evangelistic mission and female audience are mentioned explicitly: "If any discontented one, after reading the life of Charlotte Hood, will say to herself, 'I am thankful it is as well with me as it is', the Mission of this book will have been fulfilled" (5). Moreover, this later book is dedicated not to her mother but to "dear Aunt Lottie whom I have often and truly called my 'second mother' (3).

2 Even if Kelley leaves her readers in the dark concerning her characters' racial origins, they know that the novel's author is an Afro-American woman with dark eyes, brown hair, and fair skin. Kelley's photograph indeed greatly resembles the narrator's description of Megda. As we do not know any more about the author's life than that she published her two novels in Boston and, therefore, probably lived in or near Boston, we

> With deepest joy and thankfulness I dedicate this volume to my widowed mother to whose patient love and unwearied devotion during years of hard struggle and self-sacrifice I owe all that I am and all that hope holds before me in the future. The Author. (5)

Even more interesting, however, than knowing that Kelley had a widowed mother and felt so greatly indebted to her, is the simple fact that the novel is dedicated to her mother. Kelley, similarly to Harper who dedicated *Iola Leroy,* to her daughter, belongs to a tradition of Afro-American Women's Literature that stresses the mother-daughter relationship. Kelley's matrifocal novel constitutes a link to the Antebellum Era with its Slave Narratives authored by women (e.g. Mary Prince's and Harriet Jacobs'), and their specific celebration of their mothers and grandmother respectively, without whom they would have remained weak and voiceless. Moreover, the dedication mirrors in some way the novel's main focus on the development of daughters, who are in turn going to be mothers of daughters.

The novel has 25 chapters, all of which are set in a small Northern town, probably close to Boston, with the exception of ch. 20 "A Visit", which relates the girls' one-week holiday at Cottage City, and part of the final chapter, which shows Megda and Arthur at "Maude's summer home [...] at Yonkers" (384). Molly Hite, in her introduction to *Megda,* states that Henry Louis Gates, Jr., has identified Cottage City as modeled on Oak Bluffs, "a summer resort of the Massachusetts black bourgeoisie since the late nineteenth century ...." (xxx). The action, which spans a period of about twelve years, centres on a group of young middle-class women - in a Baptist community - on the threshold of full womanhood.[1]

---

can only speculate whether Megda is an autobiographical novel. However, the repeated narratorial intrusions on behalf of Megda reveal the author's partiality towards her heroine, and also her fear that the readers might see Megda in the wrong light as for example, on the evening of her performance in a scene from Macbeth: "She looked pale, but oh, so girlishly sweet and pure" (ch. 11 "The Entertainment" 152). Here, the narrator explicitly mentions Megda's pure character because her acting is considered sinful by the Baptist community.

1 The heroine, Meg (short for Megda) is about 18 years old at the beginning of the novel, and at the end about 30.

The novel describes Megda's development, which finally leads to her conversion to Christianity, followed by her marriage to the town's minister (the Reverend Arthur Stanley); the story is told by an omniscient (1st-person) narrator who is particularly fond of Megda. Therefore there are frequent intrusions (more than twenty) where the narrator wants to highlight, excuse, or condemn a character's behaviour. Kelley's didactic intention is further underlined by recurrent questions to the reader and by lengthy narratorial disquisitions:

> Now, I had no idea of writing a love-story when I began, nor have I any idea of making it into one now; I am giving the facts of the case, and no more. If I put more sentiment than wisdom in it, pardon me; it is the fault of the age we live in. Yet a little sentiment now and then, has never been known to hurt anybody; it is only when it is carried to extreme that it is objectionable, and then - it but verifies the old adage - "Extremes are dangerous." (272)

(c) The Heroine's Conversion

As already mentioned in the introduction of this chapter, colour - especially the white one - plays a crucial role in the description and even the characterization of Megda and her school friends. By the device of colour, Kelley achieves two important objectives. Firstly, colour is used to tell the reader - and this seems to be very important in this novel - that most of the characters have skin that is not white, but dazzling white. And secondly, it underlines the characters' individual steps towards their experiences in conversion to Christianity.

Meg and all her classmates - except Ruth Dean and Maude Leonard - are described and by implication, as being extremely fair-skinned. Ruth Dean's "dark" and Maude Leonard's "rich" skin colour constitute a great contrast to the other girls' complexion. Ruth, who is extremely good in the Christian sense of the word, comes from a poor family, whereas Maude, who is a liar and a hypocrite, comes from a very rich one. Accordingly, Ruth is depicted by the narrator as a "small, slight" girl with a "dark face", "dark beautiful eyes with a dreamy, far-away look", and "dark, work-worn hands", her dress is "neat" but "shabby" (75); Maude is described as having "large black eyes and raven hair" (171), and a "rich color in her dark cheek" (77). Thus it cannot be argued that Kelley uses colour in order to point out the characters' social differences. Another example to support this reading is Hal Randal, Megda's brother, whose skin colour is described as brown: "Hal took [Meg's white hand] in his own strong, brown one" (32). Moreover, in the novel, skin colour never says anything about the 'goodness' or 'badness' of a character. It is rather that Kelley wants to illustrate the characters' inner changes by changing the colour or the expression of their faces. Thus colour in Kelley's novel is used as a metaphor, on the one hand representing the characters' inner self and on the other hand, revealing his or her individual change.

Maude, who is the first to leave the little community shortly after graduation from high school, is a good example which would bear closer examination:

> The first link was broken in the golden chain. But Maude had no regretful feelings; and as she moved down the aisle leaning proudly on her husband's arm, her face expressed nothing but joy and happiness.
> And so she passed from among them, to enter a life of social pleasure and excitement, and from that night until years after, she was literally lost to them. (301)

She returns only after her death, to be buried in her home town. A highly melodramatic death-bed scene shows Maude, deprived of beauty, money, health, and husband: "The great, black eyes opened slowly, and looked up in [Megda's] face. All color was gone from the thin face; it was white enough now" (388). At the beginning of the novel, Maude's "rich colour" symbolizes her material privileges and her careless character, and when in the novel's final chapter, her face is white enough, that means that she has repented of all her sins (i.e. of a life of pleasure, luxury and excitement) and is therefore purified, as white is the colour of purity and chastity. Here, Maude's white skin stands for personal change and heavenly salvation.

Ethel Lawton is the second girl to leave the community, but unlike Maude, her 'departure' is an involuntary one. Both girls leave the community on their respective wedding days, Maude in order to "enter a life of social pleasure and excitement" (301), and the angelic Ethel in order to 'enter the gates of heaven'; "Ethel was dying the death, as she had lived the life, of a Christian" (339).[1] Ethel, the first girl in Megda's class to be converted, is the leader of the town's prayer meetings, "the 'Young People's Christian Endeavor'" (186). She is described as "tall and fair-haired" with "a fair sweet face" (10/11). She is the only child of rich parents and, similarly to Ruth, is the personification of goodness and purity; this is demonstrated by her skin which is not only white, but transparent. The description of Ethel's face varies only slightly from "white as a snowdrop", "almost transparent" (108), "pale and refined" (130), "white as the driven snow" (224) to "white as the pillow" shortly before her death (337). She has to die in order to make place for Megda, whom she asks on her deathbed to promise to go on with her (Ethel's) religious work (373).

The heroine herself has difficulties in finding her faith; this is due to her wilful nature, a false idea of Christianity, and hence her harsh attitude to 'sinners' like Maude and 'weak' people like her friend, Laurie. She has to realize, painfully, that all her friends 'leave her', one after the other, to be converted. She stands between the angelic Ethel, whose goodness she knows she can never equal, and the hypocritical Maude, whom she despises. Megda's special position within the small community of her friends is further exemplified by the narrator's description of her. The heroine's "golden-brown hair" (158) is contrasted with Ethel's, Laurie's, and Dell's "golden" hair. Megda is depicted with "lovely dark eyes" (9), a pale face and "full lips" (157). "Her face [is] not beautiful only fair and sweet and girlish" (26). It is repeatedly mentioned that Megda is extremely proud of the whiteness of her delicate and small hands. She is not described as a beauty, but the

---

1 In the novel's final chapter, Maude's death-bed scene is contrasted to Ethel's (ch. 25), thus exemplifying the antagonism between the two characters. This contrast is a didactic means of showing the difference between a True Christian's quiet and fearless death and that of a person who during her life has not thought much about God and eternity: "[Megda] had never seen anyone die but Ethel, but alas! Maude's death-bed was vastly different from what Ethel's had been" (387).

narrator always makes sure that her white face and hands - a sign of purity and inner beauty - are stressed whenever Megda is mentioned in the novel.

The opening chapter of the novel begins in medias res, introducing the reader to the heroine, Megda Randal (Meg), and her best girl-friend, Laurie Ray, who are in the middle of a discussion of the recent conversion of two of their classmates (Ethel Lawton and Maude Leonard). These four girls, who are in their late teens, are the novel's main characters. Ethel, Laurie, and Maude - although she is Megda's greatest enemy - will have a decisive influence on Megda's life and her final conversion to Christianity. The first chapter not only introduces us to Megda's appearance and lovable personality but also anticipates the hidden qualities that will lead to her conversion at the end of the novel. Ethel, who underwent conversion shortly before, reads in Megda's palm the following signs concerning her future:

> "I see," began Ethel in a low, earnest voice, that belied the smile on her face, "a happy, merry, laughing girl. She is happy, she is merry, she is laughing; but under all the happiness, all the merriment, all the laughter, runs a vein of deep, earnest feeling; a wish to be good, to be true, to be noble. ... [S]ome day it will make itself known to her and fill her whole being so that she will know no peace and happiness until the longing is satisfied, and she proves herself worthy of the noble feelings and lofty desires that her nature has been endowed with. ... She has a great capability for making friends; all who know her love her. For this reason, and also because it is her nature to be light-hearted and gay, she is apt to forget that the good Father who has endowed her with these blessings - this bright, happy nature, this faculty for making friends, the rare accomplishments of mind and body - will one day demand them all from her hands with the question, 'What have you done with the talents I gave you?' She does not mean to be careless, she is irreverent, she has great respect for old age. She is only a little thoughtless, a little carried away by her own light-heartedness. She has yet to learn the sad lesson of Life, perhaps she will learn it with many tears and bitter heart-aches; perhaps her soul will draw to its Maker through a deep appreciation of His mercies to her. But whether by smiles or by tears, by sorrow or

> by happiness, this dear heart will be laid at the feet of the crucified One. It must be given to the Father of all mercies." (13-15)

Ethel's 'sermon' foretells the experiences which her friend, Megda, will have to pass through in order to become a true Christian, and summarizes the development the heroine undergoes in the novel. Both Ethel and Arthur Stanley, the town's young minister,[1] are Megda's mediators on her way to find her faith. They voice the belief that in life one has to rely wholly on God and has to cultivate one's own individual talents in order to contribute to God's work and to do something for mankind:

> "... You have talents; some day God will ask you to give an account of them. When a person is rich, we expect more from him, where money is concerned, than we do from a poor person. It is just so with God. ... to those He gives the most, He expects the most from." (181-183)

What Kelley demands of her heroine in 1891 is the same as what Maria Stewart - who as early as the 1830s was probably the first American-born woman to deliver fiery public speeches - demanded of her racially mixed audiences. In their study on *Black Women in Nineteenth-Century America,* Loewenberg and Bogin maintain that

> Mrs. Stewart laid heavy burdens of duty upon the members of her audiences. Women were particularly obligated to strengthen the black community by making full use of their own inner resources. Individual initiative was to be nurtured as an instrument for ethnic advance. White women and white men were entreated to recognize the aspirations of blacks, to uphold their right to equality. While she passionately desired the abolition of slavery, she was not unmindful of the plight of the free black for whose spiritual emancipation from poverty and prejudice no effort was too great. Employment in various occupations, not only in menial work, and all the rights of citizenship were essential steps toward equality for those already free. But to the "fair daughters of

---

1 See his 'sermon' to Megda (ch. 12, 181-183).

> Africa" she addresses some of her most stirring words. She called upon them to lift their minds above the "load of iron pots and kettles," to develop a spirit of independence in order to rise above the level of servant drudgery and attain full human potential. External change was not enough: she exhorted blacks to the moral regeneration that would merit divine aid in their righteous cause. (183-184)

Although Maria Stewart's message is more direct than hers, Kelley nevertheless strikes a similar note with her focus on Megda's talents, which should be cultivated for a greater cause. Although race is never mentioned in the novel, the novel's spiritual message, and the fact that it was written by an Afro-American woman in the 1890s, implies the blacks' cause: fighting for equality, tolerance and acceptance in an increasingly racist and prejudiced environment. Kelley's social message also becomes clear when Ethel reproves Megda for believing that wealth is the ultimate path to happiness. At the end of the novel, Maude's example speaks for itself by showing the consequences of a selfish life consumed in thoughtless pursuit of pleasures.

Megda is presented before her conversion as a good-hearted, lovable, but wilful adolescent with rather innovative ideas, great talents, and set opinions on human character and on the equality between the sexes. In a discussion with her brother, Hal, Megda argues:

> I do admire character in a man or woman; I make no distinction between the two sexes. There is no reason why a woman should not possess character as well as a man. I hold that there is more real moral character in a woman's little finger than in a man's whole body. ... I will speak of men and women collectively now, not individually, putting woman where she ought always to be put - on a basis with man. (60)

At the end of the novel, Megda marries Arthur Stanley; she had first lost him to Ethel because of her wilfulness and finally regained him, but only as second choice, after Ethel's death. Giving up teaching, along with her ambition to do something with her elocutionary talents, Megda finds a new field of activity as wife, mother of three children - including Maude's - and as an important member of her community.

Megda is greatly committed to her religious work, which Ethel begged her to go on with after her death: "[Megda's] life was filled up with work - noble work - in her home and in the world outside. Beloved by everybody, ... Meg's heart was filled full of gratitude to her Heavenly Father, and with tender pity for all His suffering children" (394). Although she is 'only' a minister's wife and not a minister herself - despite her gifts as a speaker - it has to be stated that she is her husband's equal. Here again, "we late-twentieth-century readers must be ever mindful that our notions of sexual equality differ greatly from those of the late-nineteenth-century writers" (Claudia Tate in *Domestic Allegories,* 121).

To sum up, it can be asserted that the heroine undergoes the development which is possible within the limits of Woman's Fiction: she becomes a minister's wife. The narrator, however, still underlines that Megda is not yet 'perfect', which means, that she has not quite overcome her former traits of wilfulness, temper, pride, and independence. Moreover, Kelley's narrator undermines her own discourse by saying that Arthur might be able to "banish all signs of temper, pride and wilfulness" in his wife (376), but not in his daughter, Ethel, "a veritable miniature of Meg", who "reigns queen over all, even her grave, dignified papa" (377). Thus Meg's character traits live on in her daughter, little Ethel, and this leaves room for speculation as to whether Ethel will have the possibility of developing the talents that her mother could not, such as elocution, acting, and teaching.

(d) A Lesson for Whites and Blacks: The Perfect Community

As depicted in *Megda,* the community is matrifocal like the one in *Contending Forces,* which symbolizes, on the one hand, women's self-reliance and, on the other hand, the fatherless families which were all too common during the time of slavery. The fatherless family is also a recurrent motive in 20th-century Afro-American literature. There are few male characters of any importance in the novel; apart from the adolescent girls' male friends, whom they eventually marry, there are

Judge Lawton (Ethel's father), Arthur Stanley (the minister), Augustus Belmont (Maude's unstable, intemperate husband), and Mr. Leonard (Maude's father).

Megda, with its special focus on women characters, religion and domesticity, also stands in the tradition of Woman's Fiction. Although Megda and Ruth grow up without fathers, the Lawtons lose their daughter, Ethel, and Laurie is orphaned when her parents die in a train accident, it is only Maude who seems to suffer extremely - at the hands of an intemperate husband and also because she has no faith. She is the only character who leaves the community and with it its nurturing and regenerative power. But because Maude escapes from the extant social control with its strict moral code, her life is doomed to failure. Megda also makes a journey, albeit a short one, away from the protection of the community. It is at Cottage City, where she stays with her friends, Laurie and Dell, that she comes to realize her weakness when she exposes herself to the temptation of dancing - a temptation which she cannot withstand. On her way back to their home-town, Megda reaches her conclusion, as she says to herself, "'Darling Laurie, ... What a lesson you have taught me! You have taught me the meaning of that prayer, 'Lead us not into temptation'" (298). This trip away from home brings Megda closer to her friend, Laurie, and makes her even more aware that she has to put all her faith in Jesus and should not try to rely on her own strength.

The middle-class community as described by Kelley is powerful, protective, and nurturing for the various members - poor or rich - within it. Apart from the unexpected deaths of some of its members, nothing seems to be able to shake its harmony. But even death is accepted as God's will, which cannot and should not be questioned. Although for a 20th-century reader, this novel seems to be extremely 'limit-enforcing', it nevertheless shows that the community's strength lies in the people's high moral code and their belief in God's justice, which do not consider riches or colour but only an individual's merits. Personal talent has to give way to the greater goal, that of human salvation, which will then further the (black) community's cause, too.

In *Megda* there are various smaller 'communities' which make up the larger community of the town. Thus Megda moves from her family to the group of school friends, and then back to her family to found a family of her own, but where this family is still strongly connected with the others in the community.

The novel's climax is reached in the very last chapter, as Megda holds the dying Maude, her former enemy, in her arms and asks for forgiveness because of her hard and haughty treatment of her. It is the second time, after her conversion experience, that Megda submits completely, relying fully on God's help. Thus she is able to pray for Maude in order to help her to repent her sins and to be accepted in heaven. After Maude's death, little Maude, her daughter, returns home with her new fosterparents, the Stanleys, in order to fill the place her mother has left in the community:

> She was three years old, and had her mother's rich, dark beauty, except her eyes, which were large and bright, but a deep blue, and the lashes were long and curly; but Meg could see even then that there was pride and temper in every line and feature. (389)

It can be seen in conclusion, that Kelley presents the perfect workings of a (black) community to the reader. She wants to emphasize that her heroine's development is closely connected to the (black) community. Without the help of its members, Megda could not have experienced religious conversion, and thus could not have been 'saved', and in turn could not have encouraged other people's salvation. Throughout the novel, the (black) community is depicted as a very strong and positive force which has its strict moral codes but which is interested in the well-being of all of its members, be they rich, poor, faithless or faithful. By portraying an ideal community such as *Megda*'s, Kelley wants to underline the connection between a community's deep immersion within the Christian tradition and racial uplift. Her (black) readers should thus be inspired and encouraged by Megda and her friends to set similar examples of Christian friendship and spiritual salvation within their communities. However, "[c]hronic racial despair seems to have caused the demise of idealized domesticity in black women's fiction, as those authors in the prime of life (like Kelley-Hawkins, Johnson, and Tillman) ceased publishing it" (Claudia Tate in *Domestic Allegories* 228).

Part Three

A Critical Reception: Biased Critics?

So widespread was the debate over "the nature of the African" between 1730 and 1830 that not until the Harlem Renaissance would the work of black writers be as extensively reviewed as it was in the eighteenth century. Phillis Wheatley's list of reviewers includes Voltaire, Thomas Jefferson, George Washington, Samuel Rush, and James Beatty [sic], to list only a few. Francis Williams's work was analyzed by no less than David Hume and Immanuel Kant. Hegel, writing in the *Philosophy of History* in 1813, used the absence of writing of Africans as the sign of their innate inferiority. The list of commentators is extensive, amounting to a "Who's Who" of the French, English, and American Enlightenment.

Henry Louis Gates, *The Signifying Monkey* (1988)

This chapter will outline the 'major' direction in criticsm relating to the six black women writers addressed in this thesis, beginning with a discussion of the general reception of works by Afro-Americans in the eighteenth century and in 19th-century Antebellum America.[1] These early Afro-American women writers have been omitted in countless anthologies, bibliographies, biographies, and literary histories, and so it will be easy to mention the relatively few scholars who do include them in their studies.

In *The Signifying Monkey*, Henry Louis Gates maintains that since the 17th century Europeans and Americans had asked themselves if the African race was able to create works of art. It was commonly believed that if the black race did produce a 'black Plato', then the claim of their innate inferiority would be refuted for ever. The Age of Enlightenment, with its foundation in the Cartesian philosophy which puts reason above any other human characteristics and thus proves the difference between the animal and the human

1 The publication dates mentioned in this chapter always refer to a book s first publication, while the page references refer to the edition listed in the bibliography.

species ('Je pense, donc je suis'), considered writing "the visible sign of reason". Therefore the works of the first black "speaking subjects", such as Phillis Wheatley, Francis Williams, Jacobus Capitein, Wilhelm Amo, and Ignatius Sancho were widely reviewed in the eighteenth century. Phillis Wheatley, for example, was reviewed by some of the most illustrious representatives of the Enlightenment (129). In his *Philosophy of History* (1813), Hegel argues that the absence of literature by Africans proves their inferiority. This view demonstrates that the Age of Enlightenment overestimated cultures with a long written tradition and did not value the richness of Africa's oral tradition. These philosophical arguments of the Enlightenment combined with the religious (e.g. Thornton Stringfellow) and literary ones (Plantation School) of 19th-century America helped corroborate the claim that blacks were inferior and their situation as slaves therefore justified.[1]

With the publication of thousands of slave narratives from 1760 to 1865, the slaves managed to demonstrate their humanity and their intellectual capacities. In the first chapter of *The Slave's Narrative,* Davis and Gates reprint a selection of the numerous reviews of slave narratives in order to show that slave narratives were widely and enthusiastically read in Antebellum America ("Written By Themselves: Views and Reviews, 1750-1861" 3-34). Davis and Gates maintain that a great number of reviews appeared in "anti-slavery newspapers, such as *The Liberator,* edited by William Lloyd Garrison in Boston between 1831 and 1865" (3). These reviews have in common that they all - like the slave narratives with their prefaces and supplements - attest that the accounts are true and that the slaves wrote them themselves.

In his introduction to *Six Women's Slave Narratives,* William L. Andrews examines the major themes and forms of six slave narratives, that are common to most Afro-American women's autobiographies from the 19th and early 20th centuries. He claims that the "ability of black women to recover in the darkness of past

---

1 Chapter 1 (c) of this thesis discusses different texts which give an insight into the 'proslavery thought' in the Antebellum South. Thornton Stringfellow's essay on slavery's providential character, can be found in Drew Gilpin Faust's anthology, *The Ideology of Slavery: Proslavery Thought in the Antebellum South, 1830-1860.*

oppression the light for a better day unites female slaves narrators from Mary Prince to Annie Burton in a heroic literary sisterhood" (xlii). Moreover, he maintains that Mary Prince's "verbal and physical resistance to her sadistic master and mistress" emphasizes the black woman's strength to *actively* resist injustice. This portrait of a black woman who is not 'simply' depicted as a passive victim, greatly influenced the American tradition of black women's autobiography (xxx). *The History of Mary Prince* has been included in the *The Classic Slave Narratives* (1987), a collection edited by Henry Louis Gates (183-242), in The Schomburg Library (1988), and an excerpt of it in Busby's international anthology *Daughters of Africa* (1992: 27-30). In *Subjects of Slavery, Agents of Change* (1992), Kari J. Winter compares female Gothic novels with female Slave Narratives, such as: *The History of Mary Prince, A Narrative of the Life and Travels of Mrs. Nancy Prince, Incidents, Louisa Picquet,* and *Memoir of Old Elizabeth.* Winter states that "Mary Prince insightfully analyzes how black and white women often shared a common bondage as well as the ways in which white women often tyrannized black women" (91). She concludes her study by saying that "[t]he women who wrote Gothic novels and slave narratives ... recognized that they were struggling for a type of liberation that they would never attain in their lifetimes. ... Nonetheless, the authors kept alive visions of a better world and celebrated moments of ecstasy in the present world ...." (148).

Henry Louis Gates re-discovered *Our Nig* at the University Place Bookshop in New York City, in 1981. In 1983, he reprinted the 1859 edition of *Our Nig* with an "Introduction", and "Notes" by himself, and a "Chronology of Harriet E. Adams Wilson" by David Ames Curtis. In his introduction, Gates includes a list of the historians, bibliographers, and literary historians, who overlooked Wilson in their studies. He says that only few scholars actually mention *Our Nig* and relate it to a black woman (xxxi-xxxiv). Gates' and Curtis' research proves that Wilson was indeed black and the author of *Our Nig*. In their essay "Establishing the Identity of the Author of Our Nig", David A. Curtis and Henry Louis Gates recount their efforts to establish the novel's authenticity (1990). In *A History of Afro-American Literature* (1989), Blyden Jackson consecrates one chapter to Harriet E. Wilson (343-363). An excerpt of *Our Nig* is included in Busby's international anthology *Daughters of Africa* (58-66). In her essay "Down & Out &

Black in Boston", Margo Jefferson argues that Wilson's text is part 'drama', part 'declaration', and part 'documentary' (1983). In her paper "Adding Color and Contour to Early American Self-Portraitures: Autobiographical Writings of Afro-American Women", Frances Smith Foster examines the works of three 'free' black women in Antebellum America: Jarena Lee, Nancy Prince, and Harriet Wilson (1985). Foster maintains that these and other narratives of "early Afro-American women vary widely, but in each case they shed new light upon our too dimly perceived history. They offer new forms, new modes, new styles to our rigid definitions of literature" (in Pryse and Spillers, *Conjuring* 37). In his study, *Amalgamation! Race, Sex, and Rhetoric in the Nineteenth-Century American Novel,* published in 1985, James Kinney states that *Our Nig* - by treating the subject of amalgamation detached from "the limiting context of slavery" - presents "some interesting variations foreshadowing later works, on the treatment of miscegenation in novels published between 1850 and 1865" (100). Moreover, Kinney appends a chronological list of novels of miscegenation from 1792-1914 to his study (235-240). In *The Afro-American Novel and Its Tradition* (1987), Bernard W. Bell underlines that Wilson's novel combines "the sophistication and sentimentality of the Euro-American literary tradition" as well as "the Afro-American oral tradition and slave narratives". This confirms that elements from both traditions helped to create and develop the "early Afro-American novel" (50). In *Reconstructing Womanhood* (1987), Hazel V. Carby challenges Gates' claim that *Our Nig* can be considered the first novel by a black writer because of its use of elements and conventions of sentimental novels. She states that these conventions can also be found in various other Slave Narratives and argues that Wilson's work is rather "an allegory of a slave narrative, a 'slave' narrative set in the 'free' North" (43). In her essay "'Our Nig' and the She-Devil: New Information about Harriet Wilson and the 'Bellmont' Family" (1993), Barbara A. White presents her latest discoveries about Wilson and the "Bellmont" family. She states that Wilson was not serving "the Samuel Boyleses but the Nehemiah Haywards, an established Milford farming family" (22). White's research on the Hayward family reveals that there is a close similarity between them and the 'Bellmonts'. Thus she concludes that *Our Nig* can be considered "autobiographical fiction" (44).[1] Eva Lennox Birch underlines the importance of Wilson's novel because it established a tradition: "Undoubtedly Our Nig raises questions about racism, sexism, and religious experience which become dominant preoccupations in the literature of black American women writers in the twentieth century" (*Black American Women's Writing* 24). Comparing Frado with Morrison's Pecola Breedlove (*The Bluest Eye*) and Walker's Celie (*The Color Purple*), Birch argues that "the black woman-child had been persuaded that her unworthiness and her ugliness were mutually inescapable" (23).

The anonymous review of Jacobs' *Incidents*, in *The Anti-Slavery Advocate* (No. 53, Vol. 2 (1 May 1861), 1), is probably the first 'critique' of her narrative.[2] The reviewer states that she or he is "acquainted with the writer" and has "great confidence in her truthfulness and integrity" (Davis and Gates 32). In *The Slave Community* (1972), John W. Blassingame, however, questions the veracity of Jacobs' tale. He argues that in some of the fictional slave narratives, "the major character may have been a real fugitive, but the narrative of his life is probably false" (233). He maintains that "the work is not credible" because it is "too orderly" and because "too many of the major characters meet providentially after years of separation" (234). As a historian focussing on 'simple' facts, Blassingame neither takes into account the writer's freedom in arranging her tale nor her particular situation as a woman slave. In 'Text and Context of Harriet Jacobs' *Incidents in the Life of a Slave Girl: Written by Herself* ", Jean Fagan Yellin restores the long questioned authenticity of Jacobs' Slave Narrative, "by the discovery of a cache of her letters" (i.e. the correspondence between Jacobs and Child), and thus refutes the arguments of those scholars who have questioned the validity of the account (262).[3] Yellin sees Jacobs' text as

---

1 For further reference: see Lauter, *Heath Anthology* (vol. 1, 2628-2637), Harris, *DLB* (vol. 50, 268-271), Draper, *Black Literature: Criticism* (vol. 3, 1975-1983).

2 The review is included in Davis and Gates' study (32-34).

3 In her "Notes", Yellin lists both the scholars who have accepted the authenticity of Jacobs' narrative: Vernon Loggins, Marion W. Starling, *The Slave Narrative* (212-220), Charles Nichols, Gilbert Osofsky, Stanley Feldstein, as well as the ones who have denied it: Blassingame, Sterling A. Brown, Arthur P. Davis and Ulysses Lee, Arna Bontemps (note 2, 278).

"at once the plea of an erring American female, the heroic recital of a valiant black slave mother, and a woman's vindication of her life" (263). In *Women and Sisters* (1989), she holds that by 'reinventing womanhood', Jacobs challenges patriarchal and racist definitions of true womanhood (77-96). In *Reconstructing Womanhood,* Hazel Carby heavily criticizes scholars such as Blassingame who do not consider texts by women "credible because they deviate from the conventions of male-authored texts" (46). Furthermore, Carby believes that "Jacobs's attempt to develop a framework in which to discuss the social, political, and economic consequences of black womanhood prefigured the concerns of black women intellectuals after emancipation" (61). In her essay "Green-eyed Monsters of the Slaveocracy: Jealous Mistresses in Two Slave Narratives", Minrose C. Gwin discusses the problematic relationship beween the woman slave and the white plantation mistress in general and Linda Brent and Mrs. Flint in particular. She asserts that in writing about a white woman "who transferred [her] jealous rage ... to [her], Jacobs [...] evoke[s] the autobiographical process as an avenue toward understanding and order" (50). In her essay "'Loopholes of Retreat': Architecture and Ideology in Harriet Jacobs's *Incidents in the Life of a Slave Girl* ", Valerie Smith demonstrates that each time Linda Brent is 'enclosed' she is actually gaining power to plan her own and her children's escape (212-226). In her study *Black American Women's Writing* (1994), Eva Lennox Birch maintains that "slave narratives also reveal that maternal bonding could be emotionally catastrophic for women whose children could be sold away from them" and continues by stressing that in the case of slave mothers like Linda Brent "the enforced sundering of maternal ties intensified the bonding, particularly between mothers and daughters, through whom family history is traditionally passed on" (15). A summary of *Incidents* was published in Child's *The Freedmen's Book* in 1865. *Incidents* has been included in *The Classic Slave Narratives* (333-515), and in The Schomburg Library with an introduction by Valerie Smith. In 1987, Jean Fagan Yellin edited *Incidents* with an introduction, illustrations, a chronology of Jacobs' life, part of her correspondence, and notes. In *A History of Afro-American Literature,* Jackson claims that "[i]n justice to *Incidents,* it must be said that Jacobs manages, with all of her attention to her problems with white men, also to testify on other aspects of slavery. Like Northup, she was a good observer, and so, although her role as a black Pamela invests her narrative with its major distinction, her story may be read with profit solely as a thoughtful slave's picture of what slavery had meant to her" (156). Passages from Jacobs' Slave Narrative have been included in the following anthologies: Judith Fetterley, *Provisions* (279-305); Mary Helen Washington, *Invented Lives* (16-70); Jean Fagan Yellin in *Heath Anthology* (1: 1723-1751); and Katherine M. Rogers, *The Meridian Anthology* (449-470). Busby's *Daughters of Africa* includes the same extract which appeared in Child's *The Freedmen's Book* (69-74).

The great literary productivity of black women during the Woman's Era proves that, for black intellectuals such as Harper, Hopkins, and Kelley, the publication of their works was comparatively easier than for the black writers of the Antebellum period, who obviously wrote and published under much harder conditions. If we take into account that *Megda* was so popular that it had to be reprinted in 1892, one year only after its publication, that *Iola Leroy* was the best-selling novel of an Afro-American writer prior to the 20th century, and that *Contending Forces* was Hopkins' most important publication, it is indeed striking that so little is known about these black women writers.[1] Although there are more references in scholarly works to these later writers than to those of the Antebellum Era, the critical neglect of their novels, none the less, mirrors the virtual absence, until recent years, of black women writers in general from the African-American literary canon.

Criticism on Harper is more concerned with her poetry than with her only novel or her short stories. However, there are some brief 'analyses' of *Iola Leroy* which more often than not rather display the scholar's prejudice vis-à-vis this black woman novelist than his critical judgement of her work. In *The Negro Genius* (1937), Benjamin Brawley thus states that: "... [m]atter that in the hands of ... Jane Austen would have been sufficient for a book is often rushed over in a page. ... As a whole the book is hardly more than an interesting experiment" (120). In *Negro Voices in American Fiction* (1948), Hugh M. Gloster knows that there "is little question about the source of *Iola Leroy*: it is almost wholly the product of reading Brown's *Clotelle*" (30). In *The Negro Novel in America* (1958), Robert Bone attributes Harper's lack of

---

1 The Schomburg Center for Research in Black Culture, which is a division of The New York Public Library, was not able to trace the size of these editions.

protest to her age: "She was separated from the other novelists of this period by a full generation; her social consciousness, formed during the Abolitionist struggle, did not encompass the post-Reconstruction repression" (32). In his critical study of more than a century of black literature, *The Way of the New World* (1975), Addison Gayle, Jr., omitting Wilson, Jacobs and Hopkins, claims that it is due to the small number of novels written by blacks (*Clotel, The Garies and Their Friends, Blake*) "that sentiments, ideas, and beliefs contrary to those of others never received an honest hearing. How *disastrous* this was for Blacks ... can be seen in the case of ... Harper" (my emphasis, 26).

The 1980s, which started off with Barbara Christian's *Black Women Novelists*, can be regarded as the beginning of a more serious consideration of Harper's novel. Christian proves that Harper's characterization of Iola Leroy tries to refute common stereotypes. Moreover, she shows Harper's belief that women along with men should use their intellect and energy for the improvement of the black race (19-34). In *Prologue* (1985), Watson gives a summary of the novel and analyzes Harper's vision of racial equality. Bell, *The Afro-American Novel* (1987), maintains that *Iola Leroy* continues in the tradition of the abolitionist novels but presents more complex images of black women, "the black family and the roles blacks played in liberating themselves" (57-60). Hazel Carby concludes her chapter "'Of Lasting Service for the Race': The Work of Frances Ellen Watkins Harper" by underlining the importance of the inclusion of her novel in the literary canon: "Its dismissal or neglect by feminist or Afro-American literary critics leaves each tradition impoverished by its absence" (*Reconstructing Womanhood* 94). In her elaborate study *Domestic Allegories of Political Desire: The Black Heroine's Text at the Turn of the Century* (1992), Claudia Tate discusses *Iola Leroy*. And finally, in her study *Black American Women's Writing*, Birch asserts that "[u]sing the sentimental novel as a vehicle in the knowledge that this mode of address was assured of a large white femal audience, Harper enables the reader to confront the consequences of racism" (28).

The first biographical essay on Frances E. W. Harper is included in William Still's *The Underground Railroad*, which was published in 1872 (755-780). He is considered the main source on Harper. Still also wrote the introduction to the 1893 edition of *Iola Leroy*, in which he praises her novel as "the crowning effort of her long and valuable services in the cause of humanity" (3). Later, a biographical sketch of

Harper was incorporated in Hallie Q. Brown's *Homespun Heroines* (1926). She describes Harper's career as a lecturer and her abolitionist work with the Underground Railroad. In 1988 the Schomburg Library published two volumes by Harper: *Complete Poems of Frances E. W. Harper,* and *Iola Leroy,* with an introduction by Frances Smith Foster. In her introduction, Foster claims that *Iola Leroy* is an important work which "represents the transition from the antebellum period to the Harlem Renaissance and links Afro-American fiction to women's fiction" (xxxvii). In 1990 Foster edited *A Brighter Coming Day* which comprises - in four parts covering the period from 1853 to 1911 - Harper's letters, speeches, essays, and fiction. It is a valuable work for those who are interested in comparing her speeches with her fiction. Mary Helen Washington considers Harper and Hopkins as 'forerunners' and includes excerpts from *Iola Leroy* and *Contending Forces* in her anthology, *Invented Lives.* Her bibliographic notes give a good overview of each author's critical reception. In *A History of Afro-American Literature,* Jackson dedicates a whole chapter to Frances Ellen Watkins Harper (265-292). Harper is also represented in the *Heath Anthology* (Elizabeth Ammons 1: 1915-1944), in the *DLB* (vol. 50, 164-173), in *Black Literature: Criticism* (vol. 2, 975-985), and in Busby's *Daughters of Africa* (81-89).

Although Pauline E. Hopkins was a writer, a publisher, and an editor, criticism on her work is sparse. However, if her work is discussed at all, criticism is mostly limited to her novel. Gloster asserts confidently that "*Contending Forces,* like *Iola Leroy* ... is characterized by the usual exaggerations of its genre. Perhaps the best comment that may be made about the book is that it provides interesting sidelights on the struggles of a middle-class Negro family for education, employment, and social adjustment in post-bellum Boston" (34). Robert A. Bone, *The Negro Novel in America,* devotes only a few paragraphs to Hopkins, criticizing her 'belief' in "the myth of the Anglo-Saxon superiority" (19). Ann Allen Shockley's essay, "Pauline Hopkins: A Biographical Excursion into Obscurity" (*Phylon* 33 (1972): 22-26), is the first piece of criticism which treats Hopkins seriously. Judith R. Berzon, *Neither White Nor Black* (1978), gives a short comment on Du Bois' influence on Hopkins. In her afterword to the 1978 edition of *Contending Forces* (Southern Illinois University Press 403-409), Gwendolyn Brooks condemns Harper's assimilationist philosophy. In her essay "Pauline Hopkins: Our Literary Foremother" (1985), Claudia Tate analyses in what way Hopkins uses 19th-century literary conventions to represent the blacks' cause. Tate further states that "Hopkins and her contemporaries firmly believed that knowledge would eliminate social injustice of all kinds and improve the quality of human life" (64). In her study *Domestic Allegories of Political Desire,* she discusses *Contending Forces* and *The Magazine Novels* in comparison with other novels written by black women writers during the 1890s. In *Reconstructing Womanhood,* Hazel Carby consecrates a whole chapter to Hopkins' *Contending Forces* and work for the *Colored American Magazine,* and one chapter to her *Magazine Fiction*. Carby argues that "*Contending Forces* was the most detailed exploration of the parameters of black womanhood and of the patriarchal limitations of black manhood in Hopkins' fiction" (144). The Schomburg Library published two volumes of Hopkins' fiction: *Contending Forces* with an introduction by Richard Yarborough and *The Magazine Novels of Pauline Hopkins* in 1988. She is also included in the *Heath Anthology* (Jane Campbell 2: 172-191) and in Busby's international anthology *Daughters of Africa* (127-135). For further information on her see *DLB* (vol. 50, 182-189), and *Black Literature: Criticism* (vol. 2, 1023-1037).

The consistent omission of Kelley's name, and the titles of her two novels, from bibliographies, anthologies, biographies, and literary histories is astonishing. Emma Dunham Kelley is not even included in the *Dictionary of Literary Biography*. Many scholars have considered *Iola Leroy* erroneously as either the first novel of the 1890s or as the first novel published by a black woman in America after the Civil War. Gloster, for example, argues falsely in *Negro Voices* that "[*Iola Leroy*] was the first novel published by an American Negro after the Civil War ...." (30). In contrast, Edward Margolies and David Bakish's bibliography, *Afro-American Fiction, 1853-1976* (1979), Hazel V. Carby's work, *Reconstructing Womanhood* (1987), Elizabeth Ammons' *Conflicting Stories* (1992), and Frances Smith Foster's *Written by Herself* (1993) all list *Megda*'s title but omit *Four Girls at Cottage City*. Carole McAlpine Watson's study, *Prologue: The Novels of Black American Women, 1891-1965* (1985), even adds a short summary of the novel (142-143). By analysing the novels written by black women between 1891 and 1920, Watson concludes that these novels all concentrate more or less on "religious behaviour and values". It is the novelists' concern to show to their readers the relationship between their characters' faith and the "social and political uplift of American blacks". She further claims that Kelley's *Megda* and Amelia Johnson's *The Hazeley Family* are the only novels of the Woman's Era that do not incorporate any social or political messages but focus only on the spiritual uplift of the individual soul (10). The Schomburg Library is the first collection that incorporates Kelley's novels and, to my knowledge, Margolies and Bakish, Watson, Carby, Jackson, Ammons, and Foster are so far the only scholars who have included Kelley's name in their studies. In her introduction to the Schomburg Library edition of *Megda,* Molly Hite asserts that even if the novel does not include any social and/or political issues, it is nevertheless a novel by a black woman of the Woman's Era. She concludes by arguing that the novel - although it does not question white middle-class values - is an important and interesting document because "it also incorporates tensions over issues of race and gender" (xxxvii). In *Domestic Allegories of Political Desire* (1992), Claudia Tate discusses "eleven extant domestic novels - about courtship, marriage, and family formation - written by African-American women during the decade of the 1890s and the first years of the twentieth century ...." (4). The following novels are the focus of her study: *Iola Leroy, Contending Forces,* "Hagar's Daughter", "Winona", "Of One Blood", *Clarence and Corinne, The Hazeley Family, Megda, Four Girls at Cottage City,* and Katherine D. Tillman's *Beryl Weston's Ambition* and *Clancy Street*.

Finally, it can be concluded that the 1970s brought about a distinct change in the critics' consideration and judgement of these early black women writers. They tried to analyse the works of black women within a historical and social context. Moreover, they were interested in finding a continuity within the Afro-American tradition by introducing the works of these black women into the African-American literary canon. The short list of the text's literary reception reveals that the discussion has only begun. More black women authors have to be retrieved and re-evaluated in order to complete the picture of the African-American literary tradition.

I have now taken up my pen to introduce to the notice of the public, a book containing productions of an interesting young authoress. The occasion is one relatively of importance, and certainly of great interest to myself. ... The best way to do justice to young writers is to weigh their thoughts without so strict a regard to their style as we should pay in the case of elder writers. ... My authoress has a taste for poetry. And this is much to the advantage of any one who makes an effort in this difficult part of literature. The opinion has too far prevailed, that the talent for poetry is *exclusively* the legacy of nature. ... There is no doubt that the talent for poetry is in a high degree *attainable*. My authoress has evinced her belief in this position. She is willing to be judged by the candid, and even to run the hazards of being severely dealt with by the critic, in order to accomplish something for the credit of her people. She has done well by what nature has done for her, in trying what art will add. The fact is, this is the only way to show the fallacy of that stupid theory, that *nature has done nothing but fit us for slaves, and that art cannot unfit us for slavery*! ... her success will, relatively, be our own. A mutual effort is the legitimate way to secure mutual success. Egypt, Greece, and Rome, successively, gave their own authors success, and by a very natural consequence, the reputation which they secured to their authors became their own. The history of the arts and sciences is the history of individuals, of individual nations. When Egypt was a school for the world, all the Egyptians were not teachers of the arts and sciences. The Romans were not all Ciceros, nor were the Greeks all Homers, or Platos. But as Greece had a Plato why may we not have a Platoess?

James W. C. Pennington, introduction to Ann Plato's volume of essays (1841)

Part Four

Conclusions:
From the Antebellum Era to the Woman's Era: A Development

I am not alone in believing that the great American story of the future is to spring from the lives of colored people. Where in just the mere everyday life can you match the humour, the geniality, the pathos, the tragedy even, that is to be found in ours. Some day a genius white or black is coming and he is going to see us, seize upon us, take us just as we are, no more no less, and make himself immortal through us.

Angelina Weld Grimké

The Decision to Write: From Dependence to Independence

Only America's 'Peculiar Institution' could bring forth a literature such as the Slave Narrative. Slave narrators, women and men alike, had in common that they wrote in order to inform the world - their white readers in the United States and in England - about the horrors slavery had inflicted upon them. But the Slave Narrative did not only inform, it also urged the reader to become active in the abolitionist movement, and thus it can be considered a literature of propaganda and protest. For the first time in history, the slaves had a voice of their own, by which, on the one hand, they could affirm, their existence and consequently their humanity, and on the other hand could refute the claim that blacks could not write. An estimated number of at least 6000 extant narratives - beginning with Briton Hammon's in 1760 - underline the historical impact of the abolitionist movement.[1] Their audience was clearly white and middle-class, and so were the sponsors, the abolitionists. Although the slave narrators were greatly influenced by their abolitionist friends - this is exemplified by the Slave Narrative's rigid pattern, common to all narratives - some slave narrators nevertheless found ways to keep their individual identity.

---

1 This number probably includes the dictated narratives collected in the 1930s by the Federal Writers' Project.

Slave Narratives were used as a political weapon in promoting the abolitionists' cause. By describing in minute detail the slaves' miserable lives and their immense suffering, the abolitionists hoped to stir their readers' feelings. In most cases, the slave narrators were supported in their endeavours to publicize their particular experiences in slavery. They shared the abolitionists' belief that their story was an important testimony in proving to the world that slaves were human beings, and therefore deserved to be treated as human beings.

Mary Prince - in 1831 the first black woman to author a Slave Narrative - told her life story to an amanuensis, "a lady", who happened to reside in the house of the English abolitionist, Thomas Pringle, where Mary Prince was working as a domestic servant after leaving the Woods' house in England. Thus the narrative was first dictated to the lady and then "pruned into its present state" by Pringle before publishing it (Mary Prince, Preface iii). Mary Prince had two motives for undertaking her project. First, in order to provoke action for the abolition of slavery, she wanted to show to England and its citizens what slavery was like in the British Colonies. And second, she wanted to make her case public in such a way that her former masters, the Woods, would be publicly forced to manumit her; for although Prince was 'free' in England, she was nevertheless partly 'bound', because she could not return to her husband or her friends without the risk of being thrown back into the state of cattle slavery. Mary Prince was thus 'bound' in a triple way: by British law, which accepted slavery in its colonies; by the Woods who obstinately refused Prince's manumission; and also partly by Pringle, on whom she was financially dependent because of his roles as her employer and as editor of her Slave Narrative.

Harriet Jacobs is similar to Mary Prince, to the extent that she was also supported by abolitionists (Lydia Maria Child, Amy Post and Bishop Paine) in recording her experiences. But whereas Mary Prince addressed a mixed, English middle-class audience, Jacobs tried to elicit the empathy of white middle-class women living in the North of the United States. Of all the Slave Narratives, *Incidents in the Life of a Slave Girl* is the one which best describes the woman's particular trials in slavery. Jacobs' narrative can therefore be considered specific, as it adopts a clearly woman-centred subject matter. By breaking the taboo on the discussion of the female slave's 'rape' at the hands of her white master, the idyllic notion - as promoted by the Plantation School - of a love relationship between the white master and his beautiful mulatto slave was questioned. Jacobs had first to be convinced and then repeatedly urged to publish her most personal experiences of slavery. Although she was reluctant to publish an account of the life she was ashamed of, she nevertheless knew that it would be important for the "two millions of women at the South, still in bondage, suffering what [she] suffered, and most of them far worse" (Jacobs 6).

Although free, Jacobs (Linda Brent), like Prince, was not yet independent. She was a nurse in Nathaniel Parker Willis' family (the Bruces in the narrative); Mrs. Willis had bought her from her former masters, the Norcoms (the Flints in the narrative) and had then manumitted her. Jacobs' motive for embarking on the project of writing her narrative is primarily an abolitionist one, and only on a second level is it a personal one. She probably also needed money in order to realize the dream of her life, as stated in the words of Linda Brent: to "sit with my children in a home of my own. ... But God so orders circumstances as to keep me with my friend Mrs. Bruce. Love, duty, gratitude, also bind me to her side" (Jacobs 302).

Harriet Wilson's motive for embarking on her "experiment" of writing a novel - the first novel published in America by a black woman - was not an abolitionist one. What makes her unique among the writers of the Antebellum Era is that her main reason for writing the novel was to raise money in order to support herself and her sickly child. She hoped that the sale of her book would secure her an income so as to prevent the child's premature death. She seems to have been absolutely independent of an editor, as she published the novel herself. Moreover, neither her preface nor her appendix give any hint that Wilson's text was "pruned into its present shape" - as was admitted by Mary Prince's editor, Thomas Pringle, - or that it was slightly revised, as was done by Harriet Jacobs' editor, Lydia Maria Child. Wilson exposed the existence of racism in the North of the United States prior to the Civil War, questioned the veracity of her 'fugitive slave' husband, and showed the limits to the friendliness of abolitionists "who did n't want slaves at the South, nor niggers in their own houses, North", thus confirming that Harriet Wilson must have been independent of the abolitionist discussions of her time (Harriet Wilson

129). A further and most interesting point is that Harriet Wilson, unlike Mary Prince and Harriet Jacobs, addressed her "colored brethren" and in that way actively changed the focus from a primarily white readership to a black one.

The Woman's Era novels in general, and *Iola Leroy, Contending Forces,* and *Megda* in particular, also all address a primarily black middle-class readership. This change from a white, Northern, middle-class audience - as addressed by the Slave Narrative - to a black, middle-class audience - as addressed by the Woman's Era novels - marks a further step towards the black woman author's increasing development of independence. Although the Antebellum Era and the Woman's Era both produced didactical texts - the former to instruct white readers, and the latter to convey to white and black readers alike a positive image of black life by "rais[ing] the stigma of degradation from [the black] race" - it is noteworthy that the black women authors of the 1890s wrote explicitly for a black audience (of black women), and, in the case of Kelley, for an audience of women (Pauline E. Hopkins 13).

Frances E. W. Harper, Pauline E. Hopkins, and Emma Dunham Kelley, in comparison to Mary Prince, Harriet Wilson, and Harriet Jacobs, had the advantage of a more or less solid formal education. The three of them published more literary works than just the novels discussed here, but neither Harper nor Hopkins could live off her writing.[1] Harper had to support herself by teaching, lecturing, and writing, and Hopkins, as a clerk and writer. In addition, Harper and Hopkins were important public figures who were greatly involved in 'the uplift of the race', Harper as an antislavery lecturer before the Civil War and after it, as a teacher in the black communities of the South, and Hopkins as a writer and major contributor to the *Colored American Magazine,* of which she was a founding member. They believed that blacks had to be taught and guided by a black elite who should be able to instill in the black population a feeling of pride and self-esteem. Both writers considered fiction to be a powerful and effective means of instructing the black masses. Harper's and Hopkins' novels, and even Kelley's - although it seems to lack in protest - had a common goal: they wanted to portray characters with whom blacks were able to identify. Although *Iola Leroy* and *Contending Forces* are

1 Nothing has been recorded about Kelley's life.

novels published during the post-Reconstruction period, they nevertheless follow the tradition of the black abolitionist novel. Their mission had evolved from the abolition of slavery to the 'abolition' of mob law, racism, segregation, and disenfranchisement. Kelley follows a different, but no less effective, path in order to do something of 'lasting service for the race'. Whereas Harper and Hopkins saw the blacks' weapon against racism in the black population's political, moral, and formal education, Kelley believed that only the salvation of the individual soul would finally bring happiness to the people. Her view is consistent with the 19th-century argument that by the elevation of the spirit, the problems of racism and injustice could be diminished or even eliminated.

After the many thousands of Slave Narratives, by which the ex-slaves refuted for the first time the claim that blacks could not produce literature, Harper's novel, *Iola Leroy*, marks a milestone in the African-American tradition. It was also written to prove to white America that blacks were capable of creating works of art such as the novel. Phillis Wheatley, the slave narrators of the Antebellum Era, and the novelists of the Woman's Era are therefore connected by one and the same experience. They all demonstrated to the world that the black race could create poetry and fiction.

For the writers of both Eras, then, the decision to write was triggered by the wish to refute the common assumption of black people's inferiority. The writers of both Eras wanted to project a better image, more realistic than that of the Plantation School, of black life prior to the Civil War and during Reconstruction and post-Reconstruction. Whereas the Antebellum writers were still highly dependent either on their abolitionist sponsors or on the political and/or formal implications of the Slave Narrative, the writers of the Woman's Era enjoyed greater independence and freedom of expression, as they were not bound to any particular movement.

The Choice of Form: From the Slave Narrative to the Novel

The Slave Narrative had a rigid form, and hence did not leave much scope for the narrator's expression, outside of the text's usual structure, which begins with the slaves' account of their birthplace, their connection with the master's family, and their daily routine, continues with their gaining of religion and literacy, and finally describes their escape. This tripartite structure of the Slave Narrative is not an invention of the American slave. In form, content, and structure it closely resembles the Captivity Narratives written by the Puritans, thus demonstrating the abolitionists' influence on the authors. Harriet Wilson, however, did not choose to follow the pattern of the Slave Narrative for her Bildungsroman of a black girl, but took the more ambitious form of the novel, the 'sentimental' novel. But Frado's experiences as an indentured servant in a Northern household correspond more to the life of a slave in the South than to that of a 'sentimental' heroine. That is, Wilson combined elements from the Slave Narrative with elements from the sentimental novel. So did Harriet Jacobs. She chose the pattern of the Slave Narrative, adding elements from the sentimental novel. Thus both authors must have felt that they could not fully represent their heroines within the limitations of one form. Their conscious or unconscious decision to go beyond one given form, by adding elements from another, also underlines the authors' increasing liberty with form and anticipates the novels written during the Woman's Era.

Harper's, Hopkins', and Kelley's novels are all influenced by the tradition of Woman's Fiction as defined by Nina Baym. Harper and Hopkins, however, continued by developing the abolitionist 'propaganda' and 'protest' inherent in the Slave Narrative, and going beyond it in the settings of their respective novels: the America of Reconstruction (*Iola Leroy*) and of post-Reconstruction (*Contending Forces*). Furthermore, both novels constitute a link between the Antebellum Era and the Woman's Era, as they open before the Civil War and consequently describe the devastating influence of slavery on their black *and* white characters for generations. Although all three writers - above all, Kelley - seem to adapt themselves largely to a given norm, the widely read Woman's Fiction, there are nevertheless subversive elements within each text which reveal the authors' conscious or subconscious undermining of the form used. These nonconforming elements can best be seen when the heroines' individual developments are discussed. By choosing the form of girl's fiction, Kelley, of all the Woman's Era writers, seems to be the one who conforms most to the norms of white America: purity, piety, domesticity, morality, and a clear notion of good and evil. But it is exactly this 'conformity' on a formal level, the absence of any mention of race, and her preoccupation with colour and with her characters' salvation, which demonstrate how Kelley breaks away from the 'political novel' as produced by Harper and Hopkins to continue in the tradition of the Spiritual Narratives of authors such as Maria W. Stewart (1835), Jarena Lee (1849), and Julia A. J. Foote (1886) (in *Spiritual Narratives*). Although her Christian Bildungsroman follows the tradition of white western culture and religion with its typical white-black imagery, Kelley nevertheless creates a setting which can be seen as representative of any middle-class society in either Europe or the United States.

The development from the Slave Narrative to the novel of the 1890s expresses the black woman writer's wish to enlarge the possibilities for her representation of black characters and black life. The black women writers' combination of more than one form, fusing elements from different literary genres, as it were, shows the creative force of a young literary tradition. Furthermore, it affirms, on the one hand, its common roots in a unique experience and, on the other hand, its foundation in western culture, history and literature.

The Heroine's Quest: From Liberty to Happiness

In the Slave Narratives, the heroes or heroines undergo a physical and psychological development which, however, is limited, due to the tripartite structure of the Slave Narrative with its traditional South-North move. The author's scope for characterizing the heroes or heroines is therefore confined within a rigid pattern. None the less, *The History of Mary Prince, Incidents,* and many other narratives published by black women such as Jackson, Delaney, Drumgoold, and Burton slightly modify the narrative's classic structure. This is due to the fact that the experiences of women in slavery were obviously different from those of men. Therefore women slave narrators, instead of concentrating on the slave's 'heroic escape', describe instead the support they received from their mothers, grandmothers, other relatives, fellow slaves, and even white women, on their way to freedom. Whereas the Slave Narratives authored by men follow the slave's solitary journey to freedom, those written by women focus more on the woman slave's specific trials in slavery, including motherhood, licentious masters, their own sale, the sale of their children, and the sale of their mothers. The climax of these narratives is not the slave's escape, but rather the reunion of loved ones.

Mary Prince does not escape at all, she simply walks off. Linda Brent only escapes 'heroically' after she has been in hiding for seven years. Her two children, whom she would have had to leave in bondage, prevent her from fleeing. But all three Antebellum heroines do eventually gain their freedom: Mary Prince as she touches English soil, and then leaves the Woods' house; Frado, when she finally finds the courage to leave the Bellmonts; and Linda Brent, when she is bought and manumitted by Mrs. Bruce, her employer in the North. Although all three heroines undergo a physical and mental journey from bondage to self-assertion to liberty, Linda Brent's is the most traditional one. Hers is a physical journey from the Southern slave states to the 'free' North. The Slave Narrative's ultimate goal is liberty, therefore all of the Antebellum Era's heroines discussed in this thesis move in this direction. *Our Nig* and *Incidents,* however, do not end simply with the protagonists' long awaited freedom; they also anticipate the traditional ending of the sentimental novel: Wilson by opening the novel's final chapter with Frado's marriage which, however, - two paragraphs later - turns out to be a failure, and Linda Brent by comparing her lot to that of white heroines: "Reader my story ends with freedom; not in the usual way, with marriage" (302). Although, in their quest for freedom, Mary Prince, Frado, and Linda Brent have become more and more self-confident, they are still far removed from the white heroine's happiness in the midst of her friends at the close of a story in Woman's Fiction. Given slavery's reality, it is impossible for the three Antebellum heroines to end their narratives reunited with their respective families.

The heroines of both Eras discussed in this thesis have lost either both parents or one parent: Mary Prince is made an orphan by the slave system, Frado's black father dies and she is then abandoned by her white mother, Linda Brent loses both parents as well as her good-hearted mistress, Iola Leroy loses her father because of yellow fever, Sappho's parents die at the hands of a mob, and Megda grows up without a father. The authors' representation of their heroines as orphans mirrors two things, the high death rate in the 19th century and the heroines' common literary parentage in the famous orphans of literature, such as Moll Flanders, Oliver Twist, Jane Eyre, Heathcliff, and many others.

The heroines of the Antebellum Era narratives all have to pass through several stages on their individual ways to freedom. First, they have to become aware of their situation as slave, then to go through a period of immense suffering at the hands of their masters or mistresses. These trials can be endured only through their growing knowledge of God's eternal justice and their gaining of literacy. The word of God and the newly acquired knowledge of reading give power and strength to the slaves, who finally decide to defy their masters and/or mistresses by daring to defend themselves and to escape.

The three Woman's Era heroines, Iola Leroy, Sappho, and Megda, all have to overcome some personal obstacles in order to find happiness. Iola Leroy has to realize, painfully, that she does not belong to the master class. By becoming aware of her connection with the 'despised' race and by seeing the slave's reality with different eyes - those of a slave and not of a slaveholder's daugher - Iola Leroy finds the strength to reject a white man's offer of marriage. This heroine's rejection of a life of ease and luxury within America's white society emphasizes Harper's belief that the black race can advance in corpore only by the individual sacrifice of each member. However, Iola Leroy's love for and final marriage to Dr. Latimer, who like herself had rejected an offer which would have allowed him to pass from black into white society, recompenses her for her sacrifice. By representing her major characters as mulattoes who do not accept 'passing' as a solution to their problems, Harper clearly implies that the mulatto's position should place him/her within the ranks of the black population.

Sappho, similarly to Iola Leroy, is a mulatto of extraordinary beauty. And like Iola Leroy, who first had to become aware of her black roots and the common experience she shares with the black race, Sappho also has to return from the North to the South in order to face the horrors of her past (i.e. her rape by her white uncle), by acknowledging her child. Iola Leroy's sudden awareness of her black origin and Sappho's awareness of her double victimization - at the hands of a white man in the South and of a black man in the North - make them realize their difference as blacks and as women. Their return back South to the place of their origin is highly metaphorical, and expresses the authors' belief that only the characters' understanding and acceptance of their individual 'histories' - as rooted in the black experience - will finally enable them to comprehend themselves more fully. This North-South move is in contrast to the South-North move in Richard Wright's *Black Boy* and Ralph Elllison's *Invisible Man*, whose black protagonists go North in order to find out who they are. These two novels are deeply rooted within the blacks' collective history while transcending the topos of the fugitive slave's escape from slavery, to a black adolescent's 'flight' from a South which hinders the full development of his personality:

> Not only had the southern whites not known me, but, more important still, as I had lived in the South I had not had the chance to learn who I was. The pressure of southern living kept me from being the kind of person that I might have been. I had been what my surroundings had demanded, what my family - conforming to the dictates of the whites above them - had exacted of me, and what the whites had said that I must be. Never being fully able to be myself, I had slowly learned that the South could recognize but a part of a man, could accept but a fragment of his personality, and all the rest - the best and deepest things of heart and mind - were tossed away in blind ignorance and hate.
>
> I was leaving the South to fling myself into the unknown, to meet other situations that would perhaps elicit from me other responses. And if I could meet enough of a different life, then, perhaps, gradually and slowly I might understand it, might come to know what its rigours had done to me, to its children. (Richard Wright, *Black Boy* 294)

With their heroines' cathartic return to the South, their place of origin, *Iola Leroy* and *Contending Forces* anticipate the novels published by the new generation of black women in the late 1960s, and particularly in the 1980s.[1] These novels are set in the South or in the Caribbean, focusing on the black community and the black characters' increasing, and thus healing, awareness of their connection with a collective past (Africa, the Middle Passage, slavery, the Underground Railroad, segregation, the Civil Rights Movement).

Kelley's heroine, Megda, develops in quite a different way to Iola Leroy and Sappho. Here, the author's ultimate goal is to portray an adolescent's difficulty in acquiring faith. Thus she describes Megda's path, from her outright rejection of religion, to her conversion to the Baptist faith and her increasing awareness of her own limits, to her total reliance on God as the only source of her strength. Megda and her community seem to exist outside of the historical and social reality of the 19th-century blacks, because nothing refers the reader to a common black experience as in *Iola Leroy* and *Contending Forces*. But whereas the two latter novels describe their heroines' physical and mental journey to their black roots, which thus strengthens their awareness, the former depicts a soul's journey from adolescence to full womanhood and from darkness to heavenly salvation. Finally, the three Woman's Era heroines all find happiness within their respective families, which are closely connected to the (black) community.

The writers of the two Eras have in common that they create heroines who - with the exception of Megda - are deeply rooted within the blacks' collective history. By depicting the heroines' quest for liberty in the Antebellum Narratives, and their quest for happiness in the Woman's Era novels, the authors combine the black woman's reality with the classic models derived from English and American fiction. This unique blend of Afro-American elements combined with elements taken from 'Early Fiction', 19th-century English Fiction, and Woman's Fiction, enlarges the possibilities of the black heroine's characterization in 19th-century literature. The study of contemporary black women writers such as Angelou, Marshall, Morrison, Walker, and Naylor, could indicate if and how these early African-American

1 Maya Angelou's *I Know Why the Caged Bird Sings*, Paule Marshall's *The Chosen Place, The Timeless People*, and *Praisesong for the Widow*, Alice Walker's *Meridian*, and *The Color Purple*, Toni Morrison's *Beloved*, and Gloria Naylor's *Mama Day*.

women writers have exerted an influence on the writers of the 20th century.

The Heroine's Source of Strength: From Individual to Community

The slaves' source of strength for action consisted in their increasing awareness of the injustices inflicted upon them by the slave system, and in the knowledge of the alphabet which allowed them to read the Bible. Their reading of the scriptures opened up for them a new 'reality', a new world which informed them about the equality of the races and denied that serfdom was the lot of the black race, as claimed by the master class. The slaves thus felt strengthened and confirmed by an authority which was above that of their masters. This questioning of the slaves' peculiar situation triggers their decision to flee to the free North. Mary Prince, Frado, and Linda Brent also gain their strength from the same sources. Reading, for Frado, reveals a source of information which gives her "a new impulse" and makes herself feel "capable of elevation" (Harriet Wilson 124). In her search for identity (escape), the importance of a character's knowledge of reading and writing is further developed in *The Color Purple*: "Us both be hitting Nettie's schoolbooks pretty hard, cause us know we got to be smart to git away" (19). In her letters to God, and later to her sister Nettie, Celie opens a dialogue which broadens her horizon, giving her insight into other cultures (Africa), into her own Afro-American culture, and into herself. By writing about her problems and by believing in God's power to intervene and change her life, Celie finds a sense in her life and thus is able to survive.

The Slave Narrative's metaphor of literacy - which implies the journey from darkness and bondage to the light of knowledge, growing self-awareness, freedom, and humanity - is taken up by the Woman's Era novels. The spokespersons of *Iola Leroy*, *Contending Forces*, and *Megda* are in accord with the view prevailing at the end of the last century, that the moral and formal education of the black citizens would eliminate America's racial problems. Thus Iola Leroy, Sappho, and Megda, having had the privilege of belonging to an intellectual elite, feel the urge to transmit their knowledge to others of their race in order to improve the ex-slaves' miserable condition. Iola Leroy was a teacher in the South shortly after the war, but was forced to resign due to failing health. Her greatest wish is to "do something of lasting service for the race". Her future husband suggests that she should "write a good, strong book ... [and that] out of the race must come its own thinkers and writers" (Harper 262/263). Iola Leroy does not write a book, but she returns with her husband to the South as a teacher of domestic science and as a guide for her people. Sappho has first to acknowledge her child and fulfil a mother's duties, before she becomes a governess in the South. She will finally join her husband in the endeavour to establish "a school which should embrace every known department of science, where the Negro youth of ability and genius could enter without price" (Hopkins 386). Before her marriage, Megda becomes a teacher at her former high school, and after her marriage joins her husband in his work as a minister of their community, by guiding the members of her community on their way to heavenly salvation.

This thesis has demonstrated that the Slave Narratives authored by women focus significantly on the nurturing relationships which the slave woman experiences with mothers, other women slaves, grandmothers, good mistresses, and white women, during her quest for independence and freedom; the narratives authored by men, on the other hand, concentrate on the slave's solitary and heroic escape. The woman slave's nurturing relationship to other women, black or white, slave or ex-slave, is an important source of strength on her way to freedom. Mary Prince, Frado, and Linda Brent, however, lack the support of strong (black) communities like those pictured in the three Woman's Era novels. Linda Brent's southern town, with her grandmother's influence and protection, comes perhaps closest to the representation of the communities of the later novels. Thus it can be maintained that the heroines of the Antebellum Era are represented as individuals who derive their power to survive from the nurturing support of single women, whereas the Woman's Era heroines gain their energy from the particular black community in which they live and work.

Iola Leroy's source of strength comes at first from her black mother, who tells her to turn for support and guidance to the black race. When sold away from her family, she derives hope from her conviction that one day she will find her mother and brother again. She finds not only them, but also an uncle and a grandmother. This newly found family gives her support and the strength to face the difficulties of racism, segregation, and the unemployment of blacks in the North. A further source of strength is Iola Leroy's political engagement for the blacks' cause.

Sappho's source of strength is the community of nuns in a convent in New Orleans, who give her a new identity and help her to heal the wounds of her rape. The Smiths' boarding-house is a further community in which Sappho feels at home and where she tries to forget her terrible past.

Megda can find salvation and happiness only because of her community's support. Her conversional experience gives her strength to help others in her community.

The heroines of the Antebellum Era are deprived of their families, and thus of a black community because of the slave system - and in Frado's case because of her mother's ostracism. Therefore at the end of their accounts, these heroines are separated from families, friends, and their southern home. Iola Leroy and Sappho are also robbed of their families as a result of slavery, but in the end they either create their own community, as in Iola Leroy's case, or a family, as in *Contending Forces*.

The heroines' source of strength changes between the Antebellum Era and the Woman's Era. Whereas during the former, the heroines derived their power to survive from individual people, mostly women, the heroines of the latter Era derive their power from the communities they help to create (*Iola Leroy*) or in which they already live (*Contending Forces* and *Megda*).

The Representation of Reality: From Race to Colour

Mary Prince, Wilson, Jacobs, and other black women writers of the Antebellum Era tried to create and invent heroines who would refute the black woman's negative and stereotyped image as a seducer, a 'mammy' figure, or a victim. Within the formal boundary of the Slave Narrative and Woman's Fiction, these authors nevertheless managed to depict heroines who can be seen as the representatives of a shared experience, an experience unparalleled in any other literary tradition.

The black heroines' constant consciousness of their situation, and their direct comparison with the 'master class', above all with their white mistresses, foregrounds the close relationship between the two races. Inevitably the question of race and the consequences of belonging to one race is a prominent issue in the Antebellum Narratives. The heroines' white mistresses, Mrs. Wood, Mrs. Bellmont, and Mrs. Flint, are the representatives of 'True Womanhood'. However, by relating the cruelties inflicted on the three Antebellum heroines by their white mistresses, the authors question and erode the cult of 'True Womanhood'. Linda Brent thus analyses the ambiguity and hypocrisy of her mistress: "Mrs. Flint was totally deficient in energy. She had not strength to superintend her household affairs; but her nerves were so strong, that she could sit in her easy chair and see a woman whipped, till the blood trickled from every stroke of the lash" (22). Frado innocently questions God's authority and infallibility by her surprising statement that she does not want to go to heaven because she would meet the cruel Mrs. Bellmont there. By actively comparing the black woman's life with the white woman's, and by questioning their slaveholders' Christianity, the three Antebellum protagonists manage to survive in an environment which regards black people as inferior, and black women even as immoral. The slaves' unique experience produced a literature which in the first place helped to assert the blacks' existence and humanity. Thus the Slave Narrative is the black's voice which says: 'I am black and I exist'. Slavery's reality, as well as the use of the Slave Narrative as a form of abolitionist propaganda, forced the narrators to define themselves or their heroines in relation to the master class.

The three authors of the Woman's Era, who published their novels thirty and more years after Harriet Jacob's *Incidents*, depict their (black) heroines as almost white, or even 'dazzling white' as in *Megda*. Although in appearance Iola Leroy and Sappho closely resemble the white heroines of Woman's Fiction, their strong political statements against lynching, segregation, the employment barrier for blacks in the North, and the disenfranchisement of blacks connect them unmistakably and uncompromisingly with America's Afro-American population. Harper, Hopkins, and Kelley had to portray their heroines according to the models of Woman's Fiction, because they wrote for an audience who should be able to identify with the (black) heroines' trials. Therefore the four virtues of purity, piety, domesticity, and submissiveness, according to which a 'True Woman' had to live, were, of course, also adopted in part by Iola Leroy, Sappho, and Megda. However, they seem to be able to do without the fourth virtue, as they all live on an equal basis with their respective husbands. Harper's, Hopkins', and Kelley's preoccupation with skin colour and 'Caucasian' features clearly mirrors the authors' reality. Confronted, on the one hand, with colour prejudice in every field of society in the North and, on the other hand, with defamation and death in the South, these authors tried to find ways to express and thus to project their personal anxieties onto a literary platform.

The different realities to which the writers of the two Eras were subjected also find expression in their respective works. The Antebellum texts concentrate more on the difference between the black and the white races as a direct result of slavery, whereas the Woman's Era novels transcend the blacks' specific everyday problems to focus on more general predicaments by their use (and sometimes even excessive use) of colour, Caucasian features, and human virtues.

Final Remarks: The Re-Discovery of a Tradition

As a result of this analysis of a representative group of black women writers from Mary Prince (1831) to Hopkins (1900), it can be concluded that, from the Antebellum Era to the Woman's Era, each individual author and each individual text contributes to a movement towards increasing literary independence. The re-discovery of these 'early' women and their work made it possible to first detect and then study the intrinsic features of early African-American woman's fiction in this thesis. These black women authors, we can see, were influenced in part by English and American literature and the African oral tradition. However, their specific experiences as black women in 19th-century America triggered a literature which - in form, plot, message, and characterization - differed from that of their black male contemporaries. This difference, which many scholars had not noticed or considered worth mentioning, gave insight into a distinct experience within the African-American literary tradition. This experience common to the black women, from Mary Prince to Pauline

Hopkins, finds expression in the representation of their heroines. They are portrayed as women who actively shape their own lives, while fighting injustice and prejudice. The Woman's Era heroines work - on an equal base with their husbands - for a common cause; the abolition of segregation, mob rule, voting restrictions, and social ostracism. The black heroine's development from 1831 to 1900 emphasizes the literary sisterhood of African-American women writers. The great impact of this sisterhood across generations and even centuries can be felt, cherished and enjoyed when reading the works of Zora Neale Hurston, Paule Marshall, Toni Morrison, Alice Walker and Gloria Naylor.

Bibliography of Primary Sources

A Selective List of Works by African-American Women Writers from the 18th to the 20th Centuries

Albert, Octavia V. Rogers. *The House of Bondage: Or, Charlotte Brooks and Other Slaves*. New York: Hunt & Eaton, 1890. Introd. Frances Smith Foster. The Schomburg Library. New York: Oxford UP, 1988.

Ammons, Elizabeth, collector. *Short Fiction by Black Women, 1900-1920*. The Schomburg Library. New York: Oxford UP, 1991.

Andrews, William L., ed. *Sisters of the Spirit: Three Black Women's Autobiographies of the Nineteenth Century*: [Jarena Lee; Mrs. Zilpha Elaw; Mrs. Julia A. J. Foote]. Bloomington: Indiana University Press, 1986.

Angelou, Maya. *I Know Why the Caged Bird Sings*. 1969. New York: Bantam Books, 1971.

Brown, Hallie Q., comp. and ed. *Homespun Heroines and Other Women of Distinction*. Xenia, Ohio: Aldine Publishing Company, 1926. Introd. Randall K. Burkett. The Schomburg Library. New York: Oxford UP, 1988.

Brown, Josephine. *Biography of an American Bondman, by His Daughter*. Boston: R. F. Wallcut, 1856. In: *Two Biographies by African-American Women*.

Burton, Annie L. *Memories of Childhood's Slavery Days*. Boston: Ross Publishing Company, 1909. In: *Six Women's Slave Narratives*.

Busby, Margaret, ed. *Daughters of Africa: An International Anthology of Words and Writings by Women of African Descent from the Ancient Egyptian to the Present*. London: Jonathan Cape, 1992.

Bush-Banks, Olivia Ward. *The Collected Works of Olivia Ward Bush-Banks*. Comp. and ed. Bernice F. Guillaume. The Schomburg Library. New York: Oxford UP, 1991.

Collected Black Women's Narratives: [N. Prince (1853); L. Picquet (1861); B. Veney (1889); S. K. Taylor (1902)]. Introd. Anthony G. Barthelemy. The Schomburg Library. New York: Oxford UP, 1988.

Cooper, Anna Julia. *A Voice from the South. By a Black Woman of the South.* Xenia, Ohio: Aldine Printing House, 1892. Introd. Mary Helen Washington. The Schomburg Library. New York: Oxford UP, 1988.

Delaney, Lucy A. *From the Darkness Cometh the Light: Or, Struggles for Freedom.* St. Louis, MO: J. T. Smith, 1891. In: *Six Women's Slave Narratives.*

Drumgoold, Kate. *A Slave Girl's Story.* Brooklyn-New York, n.p., 1898. In: *Six Women's Slave Narratives.*

Dubois, Silvia [C. W. Larison]. *Silvia Dubois, a Biografy of the Slav Who Whipt Her Mistres and Gand Her Fredom.* Ringos, NJ: by the author, 1883. Ed. Jared C. Lobdell. The Schomburg Library. New York: Oxford UP, 1988.

Dunbar-Nelson, Alice. *The Works of Alice Dunbar-Nelson*, 3 vols. Ed. Gloria T. Hull. The Schomburg Library. New York: Oxford UP, 1988.

---. *Give Us Each Day. The Diary of Alice Dunbar-Nelson.* Ed. Gloria T. Hull. New York: W. W. Norton, 1984.

Fauset, Jessie Redmon. *Plum Bun: A Novel Without a Moral.* 1928. Introd. Deborah E. McDowell. London & Boston: Pandora Press, 1985.

---. *The Chinaberry Tree: A Novel of American Life.* 1931. New York: AMS Press, 1969.

Gates, Henry Louis, Jr., gen. ed. *The Schomburg Library of Nineteenth-Century Black Women Writers.* 30 vols (with a Supplement: 10 vols.). New York: Oxford UP, 1988 & 1991.

Grimké, Angelina Weld. *Selected Works of Angelina Weld Grimké.* Ed. Carolivia Herron. The Schomburg Library. New York: Oxford UP, 1991.

Grimké, Charlotte Forten. *The Journals of Charlotte Forten Grimké.* New York: Norton, 1981. Ed. Brenda Stevenson. The Schomburg Library. New York: Oxford UP, 1988.

Harper, Frances Ellen Watkins. *A Brighter Coming Day. A Frances Ellen Watkins Harper Reader.* Ed. Frances Smith Foster. New York: The Feminist Press, 1990.

---. *Complete Poems of Frances E. W. Harper.* Ed. Maryemma Graham. The Schomburg Library. New York: Oxford UP, 1988.

---. *Iola Leroy, Or, Shadows Uplifted*. Philadelphia: Garrigues Brothers, 1892 (1893 2nd ed.). Introd. Frances Smith Foster. The Schomburg Library. New York: Oxford UP, 1988.

--- [Watkins]. "The Slave Mother". 1857. *A Brighter Coming Day. A Frances Ellen Watkins Harper Reader*. 58-59.

--- [Watkins]. "The Two Offers." *Anglo-African Magazine* Sept. 1859: 288-91; Oct. 1859: 311-13.

---. "Woman's Political Future." *Black Women in Nineteenth-Century American Life. Their Words. Their Thoughts. Their Feelings*. Bert James Loewenberg and Ruth Bogin. 244-247.

Hopkins, Pauline E. *Contending Forces: A Romance Illustrative of Negro Life North and South*. Boston: The Colored Co-operative Publishing Co., 1900. Introd. Richard Yarborough. The Schomburg Library. New York: Oxford UP, 1988.

--- [Sarah A. Allen]. "Hagar's Daughter. A Story of Southern Caste Prejudice." *Colored American Magazine* Mar. 1901 - Mar. 1902. In: *The Magazine Novels of Pauline Hopkins*. 1-284.

---. "Of One Blood. Or, the Hidden Self." *Colored American Magazine* Nov. 1902 - Nov. 1903. In: *The Magazine Novels of Pauline Hopkins*. 439-621.

---. *Slaves' Escape: or the Underground Railroad*. Boston: Oakland Garden, 5 July 1880; edited and revised as *Peculiar Sam, or the Underground Railroad*, n.d.

---. *The Magazine Novels of Pauline Hopkins*. Introd. Hazel V. Carby. The Schomburg Library. New York: Oxford UP, 1988.

---. "Winona. A Tale of Negro Life in the South and Southwest." *Colored American Magazine* May 1902 - Oct. 1902. In: *The Magazine Novels of Pauline Hopkins*. 285-437.

Hurston, Zora Neale. *Mules and Men*. Bloomington: Indiana University Press, 1935.

---. *Their Eyes Were Watching God*. 1937. Urbana & Chicago: University of Illinois Press, 1978.

Jackson, Mattie J. *The Story of Mattie Jackson*. Lawrence: Sentinel Office, 1866. In: *Six Women's Slave Narratives*.

Jacobs, Harriet [Linda Brent]. *Incidents in the Life of a Slave Girl. Written by Herself.* Ed. L. Maria Child. Boston: by the author, 1861. Introd. Valerie Smith. The Schomburg Library. New York: Oxford UP, 1988.

---. *Incidents in the Life of a Slave Girl. Written by Herself.* Ed. and introd. Jean Fagan Yellin. Cambridge, MA & London: Harvard UP, 1987.

---. *Incidents in the Life of a Slave Girl. Written by Herself.* In: *The Classic Slave Narratives.* Gates 333-515.

Johnson, A. E. *Clarence and Corinne; Or, God's Way.* Philadelphia: American Baptist Publication Society, 1890. Introd. Hortense J. Spillers. The Schomburg Library. New York: Oxford UP, 1988.

---. *The Hazeley Family.* Philadelphia: American Baptist Publication Society, 1894. Introd. Barbara Christian. The Schomburg Library. New York: Oxford UP, 1988.

Kanwar, Asha, ed. *The Unforgetting Heart: An Anthology of Short Stories By African American Women (1859-1993).* San Francisco: aunt lute books, 1993.

Keckley, Elizabeth. *Behind the Scenes. Or, Thirty Years a Slave, and Four Years in the White House.* New York: n.p., 1868. Salem, NH: Ayer Company, Publishers, Inc., 1985.

Kelley, Emma Dunham. *Megda.* Boston: James H. Earle, 1891. Introd. Molly Hite. The Schomburg Library. New York: Oxford UP, 1988.

Kelley-Hawkins, Emma D. *Four Girls at Cottage City.* Boston: James H. Earle, 1898. Introd. Deborah E. McDowell. The Schomburg Library. New York: Oxford UP, 1988.

Larsen, Nella. *Quicksand and Passing.* Ed. and introd. Deborah E. McDowell. American Women Writers Series. New Brunswick & New Jersey: Rutgers University Press, 1986.

Loewenberg, Bert James, and Ruth Bogin, eds. *Black Women in Nineteenth-Century American Life. Their Words. Their Thoughts. Their Feelings.* 1976. University Park and London: The Pennsylvania State University Press, 1978.

Marshall, Paule. *Praisesong for the Widow.* London: Virago Press, 1983.

---. *The Chosen Place, The Timeless People.* 1969. New York: Vintage Books, 1984.

McMillan, Terry, ed. *Breaking Ice: An Anthology of Contemporary African-American Fiction*. London: Vintage, 1990.

Morrison, Toni. *Beloved*. 1987. London: Picador, 1988.

---. *The Bluest Eye*. 1970. Reading: Triad/Granada, 1981.

Mossell, N. F. *The Work of the Afro-American Woman*. Philadelphia: George S. Ferguson Co., 1894. Introd. Joanne Braxton. The Schomburg Library. New York: Oxford UP, 1988.

Naylor, Gloria. *Mama Day*. New York: Ticknor and Fields, 1988.

"Old Elizabeth." *Memoir of Old Elizabeth, a Coloured Woman*. Philadelphia: Collins, Printer, 1863. In: *Six Women's Slave Narratives*.

Petry, Ann. *The Street*. 1946. Boston: Beacon Press, 1985.

Picquet, Louisa. [H. Mattison]. *Louisa Picquet, The Octoroon: A Tale of Southern Slave Life*. New York: by the author, 1861. In: *Collected Black Women's Narratives*.

Plato, Ann. *Essays; Including Biographies and Miscellaneous Pieces, in Prose and Poetry*. Hartford: by the author, 1841. Introd. Kenny J. Williams. The Schomburg Library. New York: Oxford UP, 1988.

Potter, Eliza. *A Hairdresser's Experience in High Life*. Cincinnati: by the author, 1859. Introd. Sharon G. Dean. The Schomburg Library. New York: Oxford UP, 1991.

Prince, Mary. *The History of Mary Prince, a West Indian Slave. Related by Herself*. London: F. Westley & A. H. Davis, 1831. In: *Six Women's Slave Narratives*.

---. *The History of Mary Prince, a West Indian Slave. Related by Herself*. In: *The Classic Slave Narratives*. Gates 183-242.

Prince, Nancy. *A Narrative of the Life and Travels of Mrs. Nancy Prince. Written by Herself*. Boston: by the author, 1850 (1853 2nd ed.). In: *Collected Black Women's Narratives*.

Rollin, Frank [Frances] A. *Life And Public Services of Martin R. Delany*. Boston: Lee & Shephard, 1883 (orig. pub. 1868). In: *Two Biographies by African-American Women*.

Seacole, Mary. *Wonderful Adventures of Mrs. Seacole in Many Lands*. London: James Blackwood, Paternoster Row, 1857. Introd. William L. Andrews. The Schomburg Library. New York: Oxford UP, 1988.

Sewell, May Wright, ed. *World's Congress of Representative Women: A Historical Resume*. Chicago: Rand McNally, 1894.

Six Women's Slave Narratives: [M. Prince (1831); Old Elizabeth (1863); M. J. Jackson (1866); L. A. Delaney (1891); K. Drumgoold (1898); A. L. Burton (1809)]. Introd. William L. Andrews. The Schomburg Library. New York: Oxford UP, 1988.

Smith, Amanda Berry. *An Autobiography of Mrs. Amanda Smith: The Colored Evangelist*. Chicago: Meyer & Brother, 1893. Rpt. as *An Autobiography: The Story of the Lord's Dealings with Mrs. Amanda Smith the Colored Evangelist*. Introd. Jualynne E. Dodson. The Schomburg Library. New York: Oxford UP, 1988.

Spiritual Narratives: [M. W. Stewart (1835); J. Lee (1848); J. A. J. Foote (1886); V. W. Broughton (1907)]. Introd. Sue E. Houchins. The Schomburg Library. New York: Oxford UP, 1988.

Stewart, Maria W. *Productions of Mrs. Maria W. Stewart*. Boston: n.p., 1835.

Taylor, Susie King. *Reminiscences of My Life in Camp with the 33d United States Colored Troops Late 1st S. C. Volunteers*. Boston: by the Author, 1902. In: *Collected Black Women's Narratives*. The Schomburg Library. New York: Oxford UP, 1988.

Tillman, Katherine Davis Chapman. *Works of Katherine Davis Chapman Tillman*. Ed. Claudia Tate. The Schomburg Library. New York: Oxford UP, 1991.

Truth, Sojourner. *The Narrative of Sojourner Truth, a Northern Slave, Emanci-pated from Bodily Servitude by the State of New York in 1828. Narrated to Olive Gilbert, Including Sojourner Truth's Book of Life, and a Dialogue*. Boston: by the author, 1850. Rpt. as *Narrative of Sojourner Truth; a Bondswoman of Olden Time, with a History of Her Labors and Correspondence Drawn from her "Book of Life"*. Introd. Jeffrey C. Stewart. The Schomburg Library. New York: Oxford University Press, 1991.

Two Biographies by African-American Women. Introd. William L. Andrews. The Schomburg Library. New York: Oxford UP, 1991.

Veney, Bethany. *The Narrative of Bethany Veney: A Slave Woman*. Worcester, MA: by the author, 1889. In: *Collected Black Women's Narratives*.

Walker, Alice. *I Love Myself When I Am Laughing ... : A Zora Neale Hurston Reader*. Old Westbury, N.Y.: The Feminist Press, 1979.

---. "Looking for Zora." *In Search of Our Mothers' Gardens.* 1983. London: The Women's Press, 1984. 93-116.

---. *Meridian.* 1976. London: The Women's Press, 1982.

---. *The Color Purple.* 1982. New York: Washington Square Press, 1983.

---. "Zora Neale Hurston: A Cautionary Tale and a Partisan View." *In Search of Our Mothers' Gardens.* 1983. London: The Women's Press, 1984. 83-92.

Washington, Mary Helen. *Invented Lives: Narratives of Black Women: 1860-1960.* 1987. London: Virago Press, 1989.

---, ed. *Midnight Birds: Stories of Contemporary Black Women Writers.* New York: Anchor Press, 1980.

Wells-Barnett, Ida B. [Iola]. *Selected Works of Ida B. Wells-Barnett.* Comp. Trudier Harris. The Schomburg Library. New York: Oxford UP, 1991.

---. *Southern Horrors: Lynch Law in All Its Forms.* 1892. Rpt. as *On Lynchings. Southern Horrors. A Red Record. Mob Rule in New Orleans.* The American Negro. His History and Literature. New York: Arno Press & The New York Times, 1969.

Wheatley, Phillis. *Poems on Various Subjects, Religious and Moral.* London: A. Bell, Bookseller, Aldgate, 1773 (1786 1st pub. in America). Rpt. as *The Collected Works of Phillis Wheatley.* Ed. John C. Shields. The Schomburg Library. New York: Oxford UP, 1988.

Wilson, Harriet E. ["Our Nig"]. *Our Nig; Or, Sketches from the Life of a Free Black, in a Two-Story White House, North. Showing That Slavery's Shadows Fall Even There.* Boston: Geo. C. Rand & Avery, 1859. Ed. and introd. Henry Louis Gates. New York: Random House, 1983.

Works by Other Authors from the English Speaking World

Abrahams, Roger D., ed. *Afro-American Folktales: Stories from Black Traditions in the New World*. New York: Pantheon Books, 1985

Alcott, Louisa May. *Alternative Alcott*. American Women Writers Series. New Brunswick & London: Rutgers University Press, 1988.

---. *Little Women*. 1868. New York: Simon & Schuster, 1982.

---. *Work: A Story of Experience*. 1872. In: *Alternative Alcott*. 237-349.

Andrews, William L., ed. *Journeys in New Worlds: Early American Women's Narratives*. Madison: The University of Wisconsin Press, 1990.

Baldwin, James. *Go Tell It on the Mountain*. 1952. New York: Dell Publishing Co., 1977.

Bibb, Henry. *Narrative of the Life and Adventure of Henry Bibb, an American Slave*. New York: by the author, 1849. In: *Puttin' On Ole Massa*. Osofski 51-171.

Brontë, Charlotte. *Jane Eyre*. 1847. Harmondsworth: Penguin, 1985.

Brontë, Emily. *Wuthering Heights*. 1847. Harmondsworth: Penguin, 1987.

Brown, William Wells. *Clotel; Or, The President's Daughter: A Narrative of Slave Life in the United States*. London: Partridge & Oakey, 1853.

---. *Clotelle; Or, The Colored Heroine. A Tale of the Southern States*. 1867. Miami: Mnemosyne Publishing Inc., 1969.

---. *Narrative of William Wells Brown, a Fugitive Slave, Written by Himself*. Boston: Boston Anti-Slavery Office, 1847. In: *Puttin' On Ole Massa*. Osofski 172-223.

Chapman, Abraham. *Steal Away: Slaves Tell Their Own Stories*. 1971. London: Benn, 1973.

Child, Lydia Maria. *An Appeal in Favor of Americans Called Africans*. 1836. The American Negro His History and Literature. New York: Arno Press & The New York Times, 1968.

---. *Letters of Lydia Maria Child: With a Biographical Introduction By John G. Whittier and An Appendix by Wendell Phillips.* 1883. New York: AMS Press, 1971.

Chopin, Kate. *The Awakening*. 1899. London: Everyman's Library, 1992.

Cummins, Maria Susanna. *The Lamplighter*. 1854. American Women Writers Series. New Brunswick & London: Rutgers University Press, 1988.

Defoe, Daniel. *Moll Flanders*. 1722. Harmondsworth: Penguin, 1983.

---. *Robinson Crusoe*. 1719. Harmondsworth: Penguin, 1986.

Delany, Martin R. *Blake: Or, The Huts of America*. 1859. Boston: Beacon Press, 1970.

Douglass, Frederick. "The Heroic Slave." *Autographs for Freedom*. Boston, Cleveland & London: The Rochester Ladies' Anti-Slavery Society, 1853. In: *Steal Away*. Chapman 131-181.

---. *The Narrative of the Life of Frederick Douglass, an American Slave. Written by Himself.* Boston: Anti-Slavery office, 1845. New York: Anchor Press/Doubleday, 1963.

Du Bois, W.E.B. *The Souls of Black Folk*. 1903. Introd. Herbert Aptheker. Millwood, N.Y.: Kraus-Thomson Organization Ltd., 1973.

---. "The Talented Tenth." Booker T. Washington, *The Negro Problem* 31-75.

Eliot, George. *Adam Bede*. 1859. Harmondsworth: Penguin, 1885.

Ellison, Ralph. *Invisible Man*. 1952. Harmondsworth: Penguin, 1978.

Equiano, Olaudah [Gustavus Vassa]. *The Interesting Narrative of the Life of Olaudah Equiano, or Gustavus Vassa, the African. Written by Himself.* London: by the author, 1789. In: *The Classic Slave Narratives*. Gates 1-182.

Grayson, William John. *The Hireling and Slave*. 1851. Charleston: John Russell, 1854.

Gyles, John. *Memoirs of Odd Adventures, Strange Deliverances, etc. in the Captivity of John Gyles, Esq., Commander of the Garrison on St. George's River*. Boston: n.p.,1736. In: *Puritans among the Indians*. Vaughan & Clark 93-131.

Hammon, Briton. *A Narrative of the Uncommon Sufferings, and Surprizing [sic] Deliverance of Briton Hammon, A Negro Man, ...* Boston: Green and Russel, 1760.

Hawthorne, Nathaniel. *The Scarlet Letter.* 1850. Harmondsworth: Penguin, 1986.

Henson, Josiah. *The Life of Josiah Henson, Formerly a Slave Now an Inhabitant of Canada.* 1849. Rpt. as *Truth Stranger Than Fiction: Father Henson's Story of His Own Life; with an Introduction By Mrs. H. B. Stowe.* Boston: J. P. Jewett and Company, 1858. In: *Steal Away.* Chapman 86-102.

Johnson, James Weldon. *The Autobiography of an Ex-Coloured Man.* 1927. Introd. Carl Van Vechten. New York: Alfred A. Knopf, 1976.

Kennedy, John Pendleton. *Swallow Barn; Or, A Sojourn in the Old Dominion.* 1832. Introd. Lucinda H. MacKethan. Baton Rouge & London: Louisiana State University Press, 1986.

Northup, Solomon. *Twelve Years a Slave: Narrative of Solomon Northup.* Auburn, New York, Buffalo, and London: Derby and Miller, 1853. In: *Puttin' On Ole Massa.* Osofski 225-406.

Osofski, Gilbert, ed. *Puttin' On Ole Massa: The Slave Narratives of Henry Bibb, William Wells Brown, and Solomon Northup.* New York: Harper & Row, Publishers, 1969.

Page, Thomas Nelson. *In Ole Virginia. Or, Marse Chan and Other Stories.* 1887. Southern Literary Classics Series. Chapel Hill: The University of North Carolina Press, 1969.

Randolph, J. Thornton. *The Cabin and Parlor; or, Slaves and Masters.* 1852. The Black Heritage Library Collection. Freeport: Books for Libraries Press, 1971.

Richardson, Samuel. *Pamela; Or, Virtue Rewarded.* 1740. Harmondsworth: Penguin, 1980.

Rowlandson, Mary. *A Narrative of the Captivity, Sufferings and Removes of Mrs. Mary Rowlandson.* 1682. Boston: John Boyle's Printing-Office, 1773. In: *Puritans among the Indians.* Vaughan & Clark 29-75.

Rush, Caroline E. *The North and South: Or, Slavery and Its Contrasts.* 1852. Freeport, New York: Books for Libraries Press, 1971.

Simms, William Gilmore. *The Yemassee: A Romance of Carolina.* 1835. New Haven, Conn.: College & University Press, 1964.

---. *Woodcraft: Or, Hawks About the Dovecote: A Story of the South at the Close of the Revolution [The Sword and the Distaff]*. 1852. The Masterworks of Literature Series. Ed. Charles S. Watson. Albany, New York: New College and University Press, 1983.

Smollett, Tobias. *The Adventures of Roderick Random*. 1748. New York: Oxford UP, 1981.

Southworth, E.D.E.N. *The Hidden Hand: Or, Capitola the Madcap*. 1888. American Women Writers Series. New Brunswick & London: Rutgers University Press, 1988.

Still, William. *The Underground Railroad*. 1872. The American Negro. His History and Literature. New York: Arno Press & The New York Times, 1968.

Stowe, Harriet Beecher. *Uncle Tom's Cabin*. 1852. New York: Signet, 1966.

Swift, Jonathan. *Gulliver's Travels*. 1726. Harmondsworth: Penguin, 1987.

Vaughan, Alden T., and Edward W. Clark, eds. *Puritans among the Indians: Accounts of Captivity and Redemption 1676-1724*. Cambridge, MA & London: Belknap Press, 1981.

Warner, Susan [Elizabeth Wetherell]. *The Wide, Wide World*. 1850. New York: The Feminist Press, 1987.

Washington, Booker T, et al., eds. *The Negro Problem: A Series of Articles by Representative Negroes of Today* 1903. Rpt. as *The Negro Problem*. Pref. August Meier. New York: Arno Press & The New York Times, 1969.

---. *Up from Slavery*. 1901. New York: Bantam, 1963.

Webb, Frank J. *The Garies and Their Friends*. 1857. The American Negro His History and Literature. New York: Arno Press & The New York Times, 1969.

Whittier, John Greenleaf. *Anti-Slavery Poems: Songs of Labor and Reform*. 1888. New York: Arno Press & The New York Times, 1969.

Wright, Richard. *American Hunger*. 1977. New York: Harper & Row, 1983.

---. *Black Boy*. 1945. London: Picador Classics, 1988.

---. *Native Son*. 1940. Harmondsworth: Penguin, 1981.

Bibliography of Secondary Sources

Abel, Elizabeth. "Black Writing, White Reading: Race and the Politics of Feminist Interpretation." *Critical Inquiry* 19 (1993): 470-498.

Ammons, Elizabeth. *Conflicting Stories: American Women Writers at the Turn into the Twentieth Century*. New York & Oxford: Oxford UP, 1992.

Andrews, William L., ed. *African American Autobiography: A Collection of Critical Essays*. Englewood Cliffs, New Jersey: Prentice Hall, 1993.

---. "Dialogue in Antebellum Afro-American Autobiography." Olney 89-98.

---. Introduction. *Six Women's Slave Narratives*. The Schomburg Library. New York: Oxford UP, 1988. xxix-xli.

Bain, Robert, and Joseph M. Flora, eds. *Fifthy Southern Writers Before 1900: A Bio-Bibliographical Sourcebook*. New York: Greenwood Press, 1987.

Baldwin, James. "Everybody's Protest Novel." *Partisan Review* 16 (1949): 578-85.

Baym, Nina. Introduction. *The Lamplighter*. By Maria Susanna Cummins. ix-xxxi.

---. "The Madwoman and Her Languages: why i don't do feminist theory." Warhol & Herndl 154-167.

---. *Woman's Fiction: A Guide to Novels by and about Women in America, 1820-1870*. 1978. Ithaca & London: Cornell UP, 1993.

Bell, Bernard W. *The Afro-American Novel and Its Tradition*. Amherst: The University of Massachusetts Press, 1987.

Bercovitch, Sacvan, ed. *Reconstructiong American Literary History*. Cambridge, MA & London: Harvard UP, 1986.

Berlant, Lauren. "The Queen of America Goes to Washington City: Harriet Jacobs, Frances Harper, and Anita Hill." *American Literature* 65.3 (1993): 549-574.

Berry, Mary Frances, and John W. Blassingame. *Long Memory: The Black Experience in America*. New York & Oxford: Oxford UP, 1982.

Berzon, Judith R. *Neither White Nor Black: The Mulatto Character in American Fiction*. New York: New York University Press, 1978.

Birch, Eva Lennox. *Black American Women's Writing: A Quilt of Many Colours*. New York & London: Harvester Wheatsheaf, 1994.

Blassingame, John W., ed. *New Perspectives on Black Studies*. Urbana: University of Illinois Press, 1971.

---. *The Slave Community: Plantation Life in the Antebellum South*. 1972. New York: Oxford UP, 1974.

Bone, Robert. *The Negro Novel in America*. 1958. New Haven & London: Yale UP, 1973.

Brawley, Benjamin. *The Negro Genius: A New Appraisal of the Achievement of the American Negro in Literature and the Fine Arts*. 1937. New York: Biblo & Tannen, 1966.

Braxton, Joanne M., Andrée Nicola Mc Laughlin, eds. *Wild Women in the Whilrlwind: Afra-American Culture and the Contemporary Literary Renaissance*. New Brunswick & New Jersey: Rutgers University Press, 1990.

Brodzki, Bella, and Celeste Schenk, eds. *Life/Lines: Theorizing Women's Autobiography*. Ithaca & London: Cornell UP, 1988.

Brown, Sterling A., Arthur P. Davis, and Ulysses Lee, eds. *The Negro Caravan: Writings by American Negroes*. 1941. Rpt. New York: Arno & The New York Times, 1970.

---, eds. *The Negro in American Fiction*. 1937. New York: Argosy-Antiquarian Ltd., 1969.

Bullock, Penelope L. *The Afro-American Press: 1838-1909*. Baton Rouge: Louisiana State University Press, 1981

Campbell, Jane. "Pauline Elizabeth Hopkins." Harris, *DLB* 164-173.

Carby, Hazel. *Reconstructing Womanhood: The Emergence of the Afro-American Woman Novelist*. New York: Oxford UP, 1987.

Cawelti, John G. *Adventure, Mystery, and Romance: Formula Stories as Art and Popular Culture*. Chicago & London; U of Chicago P, 1976.

Christian, Barbara. "The Use of History: Frances Harper's *Iola Leroy, Shadows Uplifted*." *Black Feminist Criticism. Perspectives on Black Women Writers*. New York: Pergamon Press, 1985. 165-170.

---. *Black Women Novelists: The Development of a Tradition, 1892-1976*. Westport & London: Greenwood Press, 1980.

Curtis, David A. "Chronology of Harriet E. Adams Wilson." Wilson xiii-xxvii.

Curtis, David A., Henry Louis Gates, Jr. "Establishing the Identity of the Author of Our Nig." Braxton & Mc Laughlin 48-69.

Davis, Charles T., and Henry Louis Gates, Jr., eds. *The Slave's Narrative*. New York: Oxford UP, 1985.

Dearborn, Mary V. *Pocahontas's Daughters: Gender and Ethnicity in American Culture*. New York & Oxford: Oxford UP, 1986.

Dobson, Joanne. Introduction. *The Hidden Hand*. By E.D.E.N. Southworth. xi-xli.

Dodson, Howard. A Note from the Schomburg Center. *The Schomburg Library of Nineteenth-Century Black Women Writers*. New York: Oxford UP, 1988. xxiii-xxvi.

Draper, James P., ed. *Black Literature: Criticism*. 3 vols. Detroit: Gale Research Inc., 1992.

Eisenstein, Hester. *Contemporary Feminist Thought*. 1984. London & Sydney: Unwin Paperbacks, 1988.

Elder, Arlene A. *The "Hindered Hand": Cultural Implication of Early African-American Fiction*. Westport & London: Greenwood Press, 1978.

Ernest, John. "From Mysteries to Histories: Cultural Pedagogy in Frances E. W. Harper's *Iola Leroy*." *American Literature* 64.3 (1992): 497-518.

Faust, Drew Gilpin, ed. *The Ideology of Slavery: Proslavery Thought in the Antebellum South, 1830-1860*. Baton Rouge & London: Louisiana State University Press, 1981.

Fetterley, Judith. *Provisions: A Reader from 19th-Century American Women*. Bloomington: Indiana UP, 1985.

Foster, Frances Smith. "Adding Color and Contour to Early American Self-Portraitures: Autobiographical Writings of Afro-American Women." Pryse 25-38.

---. "Harriet Jacobs's *Incidents* and the 'Careless Daughters' (and Sons) Who Read It." Warren 92-107.

---. *Witnessing Slavery: The Development of Ante-bellum Slave Narratives*. Westport & London: Greenwood Press, 1979.

---. *Written by Herself: Literary Production by African American Women, 1746-1892*. Bloomingston & Indianapolis: Indiana UP, 1993.

Fox-Genovese, Elizabeth. *Within the Plantation Household: Black and White Women of the Old South.* Chapel Hill & London: The University of North Carolina Press, 1988.

Freimarck, Vincent, and Bernard Rosenthal, eds. *Race and the American Romantics*. New York: Schocken Books, 1971.

Friedan, Betty. *The Feminine Mystique*. 1963. Harmondsworth: Penguin, 1965.

Gates, Henry Louis, Jr. *Black Literature and Literary Theory*. New York & London: Methuen, 1984.

---. gen. ed. Foreword in Her Own Write. *The Schomburg Library of Nineteenth-Century Black Women Writers*. 30 vols. New York: Oxford UP, 1988. vii-xxii.

---, Foreword to the Schomburg Supplement. *The Schomburg Library of Nineteenth-Century Black Women Writers*. 10 vols. New York: Oxford UP, 1991. ix-xii.

---, ed. Introduction. *The Classic Slave Narratives*. New York: New American Library, 1987. ix-xviii.

---, ed. "Introduction and Notes to the Text." *Our Nig*. By Harriet E. Wilson. New York: Random House, 1983. xi-lv and *iii-xi*.

---, ed. *"Race," Writing, And Difference*. Chicago & London: The University Press, 1985.

---, ed. *Reading Black, Reading Feminist: A Critical Anthology*. Harmondsworth: Meridian, 1990.

---. *The Signifying Monkey: A Theory of Afro-American Criticsm*. New York & Oxford: Oxford UP, 1988.

---. "The Trope of a New Negro and the Reconstruction of the Image of the Black." *Representations* 24 (Fall 1988): 129-155.

Gayle, Addison, Jr. *The Way of the New World: The Black Novel in America*. Garden City: Anchor Press, 1975.

Gloster, Hugh M. *Negro Voices in American Fiction*. 1948. New York: Russell & Russell, 1965.

Graham, Maryemma. "The Origins of Afro-American Fiction." *American Antiquarian Society*. 100 (1990): 231-249.

Greenblatt, Stephen, and Giles Gunn, eds. *Redrawing the Boundaries: The Transformation of English and American Literary Studies*. New York: The Modern Language Association of America, 1992.

Grossberg, Lawrence, Cary Nelson, and Paula A. Treichler, eds. *Cultural Studies*. New York & London: Routledge, 1992.

Gwin, Minrose C. "Green-eyed Monsters of the Slavocracy: Jealous Mistresses in Two Slave Narratives." Pryse & Spillers 39-52.

Harris, Susan K. *19th-Century American Women Novels: Interpretative Strategies*. Cambridge & New York: Cambridge UP, 1990.

Harris, Trudier, ed. *Dictionary of Literary Biography: Afro-American Writers Before the Harlem Renaissance*. Vol. 50. Detroit: Gale Research Company, 1986.

Hemenway, Robert E. *Zora Neale Hurston: A Literary Biography*. Urbana: University of Illinois Press, 1977.

Holloway, Karla F. C. "Economics of Space: Markets and Marketability in *Our Nig* and *Iola Leroy*." Warren 126-140.

Holt, Thomas C. "The Political Uses of Alienation: W. E. B. Du Bois on Politics, Race, and Culture, 1903-1940." *American Quarterly* 42 (1990): 301-323.

Hull, Gloria T., Patricia Bell Scott, and Barbara Smith, eds. *All the Women Are White, All the Blacks Are Men, But Some of Us Are Brave: Black Women's Studies*. New York: The Feminist Press, 1982.

Humphreys, Debra. "Power and Resistance in Harriet Jacobs' *Incidents in the Life of a Slave Girl*." Singley & Sweeney 143-155.

Jackson, Blyden. *A History of Afro-American Literature. Volume I: The Long Beginning, 1746-1895.* Baton Rouge & London: Louisiana State University Press, 1989.

Jefferson, Margo. "Down & Out & Black in Boston." *The Nation* 236 (1983): 675-677.

Jones, Gayl. *Liberating Voices: Oral Traditon in African American Literature*. Cambridge, MA & London: Harvard UP, 1991.

Kelley, Mary. *Private Woman, Public Stage: Literary Domesticity in Nineteenth-Century America*. New York & Oxford: Oxford UP, 1984.

Lauter, Paul, gen. ed. *The Heath Anthology of American Literature*. 2 vols. Lexington, MA & Toronto: Heath, 1990.

Lentricchia, Frank, and Thomas McLaughlin, eds. *Critical Terms for Literary Study*. Chicago & London: U of Chicago P, 1990.

Levine, Lawrence W. *Black Culture and Black Consciousness: Afro-American Folk Thought from Slavery to Freedom*. 1977. New York: Oxford Up, 1978.

Lewis, Vashti. "The Near-White Female in Frances Ellen Harper's *Iola Leroy*: Public Image Versus Private Reality." *Phylon*. 45.4 (1994): 314-322.

Lindberg-Seyersted, Brita. "The Color Black: Skin Color as Social, Ethical, and Esthetic Sign in Writings by Black American Women." *English Studies* 73.1 (1992): 51-67.

Mainiero, Lina, and Langdon Lynne Faust, eds. *American Women Writers: A Critical Reference Guide from Colonial Times to the Present*. 4 vols. New York: Frederick Ungar Publishing Co., 1979-1982.

McDowell, Deborah E. "New Directions for Black Feminist Criticism." Showalter 186-199.

McDowell, Deborah E., and Arnold Rampersad. *Slavery and the Literary Imagination*. Baltimore & London: The Johns Hopkins UP, 1989.

MacKethan, Lucinda H. "Plantation Fiction, 1865-1900." *The History of Southern Literature*. Gen. ed. Louis D. Rubin, Jr. Baton Rouge & London: Louisiana State University Press, 1985. 209-218.

Margolies, Edward, and David Bakish. *Afro-American Fiction, 1853-1976*. Detroit: Gale Research Company, 1979. Vol. 25 of *American Literature, English Literature, and World Literatures in English: An Information Guide Series*.

McFeely, William S. *Frederick Douglass*. New York & London: Norton, 1991.

Meier, August. *Negro Thought in America, 1880-1915*. Ann Arbor: University of Michigan Press, 1963.

Mitchell, Sally. *The Fallen Angel: Chastity, Class and Women's Reading, 1835-1880*. Bowling Green: Bowling Green University Popular Press, 1981.

Mullen, Harryette. "Runaway Tongue: Resistant Orality in *Uncle Tom's Cabin, Our Nig, Incidents in the Life of a Slave Girl*, and *Beloved*." Samuels 244-264.

Neff-Mayson, Heather. *Redemption Songs: The Voice of Protest in the Poetry of Afro-Americans: 1760-1880*. Diss. Swiss Studies in English 116. Bern: Francke Verlag, 1989.

Nelson, Dana D. *The Word in Black and White: Reading "Race" in American Literature, 1638-1867*. New York & Oxford: Oxford UP, 1992.

Olney, James. "'I Was Born': Slave Narratives, Their Status as Autobiography and as Literature." Davis & Gates 148-175.

---, ed. *Studies in Autobiography*. New York & Oxford: Oxford UP, 1988.

Ong, Walter J. *Orality and Literacy*. London & New York: Methuen, 1982.

Peterson, Carla L. "'Doers of the World': Theorizing African-American Women Writers in the Antebellum North." Warren 183-202.

Petter, Henri. *The Early American Novel*. Ohio State University Press, 1971.

Pryse, Marjorie, and Hortense J. Spillers, eds. *Conjuring: Black Women, Fiction, and Literary Tradition*. Bloomington: Indiana UP, 1985.

Reising, Russell. *The Unusable Past: Theory and the Study of American Literature*. New York & London: Methuen, 1986.

Ridgely, J.V. *Nineteenth-Century Southern Literature*. Lexington: The University Press of Kentucky, 1980.

Rogers, Katharine M., ed. *The Meridian Anthology of Early American Women Writers: From Anne Bradstreet to Louisa May Alcott, 1650-1865*. Harmondsworth: Meridian, 1991.

Rubin, Louis D., Jr. *The Edge of the Swamp: A Study in the Literature and Society of the Old South*. Baton Rouge & London: Louisiana State University Press, 1989.

Ruoff, A. LaVonne Brown, and Jerry W. Ward, eds. *Redefining American Literary History*. New York: The Modern Language Association of America, 1990.

Samuels, Shirley, ed. *The Culture of Sentiment: Race, Gender, and Sentimentality in Nineteenth-Century America*. New York & Oxford: Oxford UP, 1992.

Sanchez-Eppler, Karen. "Bodily Bonds: The Intersecting Rhetorics of Feminism and Abolition." *Representations* 24 (Fall 1988): 28-59.

Showalter, Elaine. Introduction. *Alternative Alcott*. By Alcott. ix-xliii.

---, ed. *The Feminist Criticism: Essays on Women, Literature, and Theory*. London: Virago Press, 1986.

Singley, Carol J., and Susan Elizabeth Sweeney, eds. *Anxious Power: Reading, Writing, and Ambivalence in Narrative by Women*. Albany: State U of New York P, 1993.

Smith, Barbara. "Toward a Black Feminist Criticism." Showalter 168-185.

Smith, Valerie. Introduction. *Incidents in the Life of a Slave Girl*. By Harriet Jacobs. New York: Oxford UP, 1988. xxvii-xl.

---. "'Loopholes of Retreat': Architecture and Ideology in Harriet Jacobs's *Incidents in the Life of a Slave Girl* ." Gates, *Reading Black, Reading Feminist* 212-226.

---. *Self-Discovery and Authority in Afro-American Narrative*. Cambridge, MA & London: Harvard UP, 1987.

Starling, Marion Wilson. *The Slave Narrative: Its Place in American History*. 1981. Washington, D.C.: Howard University Press, 1988.

Still, William. Introduction. *Iola Leroy, Or Shadows Uplifted*. By Frances Ellen Watkins Harper. Philadelphia: Garrigues Brothers, 1892 (1893 2nd ed.). 1-3.

Stringfellow, Thornton. "A Brief Examination of Scripture Testimony on the Institution of Slavery." Faust 136-167.

Tate, Claudia. *Domestic Allegories of Political Desire: The Black Heroines's Text at the Turn of the Century*. New York & Oxford: Oxford UP, 1992.

---. "Pauline Hopkins: Our Literary Foremother." Pryse & Spillers 54-66.

Tise, Larry E. *Proslavery: A History of the Defense of Slavery in America, 1701-1840*. Athens & London: The University of Georgia Press, 1987.

Tompkins, Jane. *Sensational Designs: The Cultural Work of American Fiction: 1790-1860*. New York & Oxford: Oxford UP, 1985.

---. Afterword. *The Wide, Wide World*. By Susan Warner.

Wald, Carol. *Myth America: Picturing Women 1865-1945*. New York: Pantheon Books, 1975.

Ward, John William. Afterword. *Uncle Tom's Cabin*. By Harriet Beecher Stowe.

Warhol, Robyn R., and Diane Price Herndl, eds. *Feminism: An Anthology of Literary Theory and Criticism*. New Brunswick & New Jersey: Rutgers University Press, 1991.

Warren, Joyce W., ed. *The (Other) American Traditions: Nineteenth-Century Women Writers*. New Brunswick & New Jersey: Rutgers University Press, 1993.

Warren, Kenneth W. *Black and White Strangers: Race and American Literary Realism*. Chicago & London: U of Chicago P, 1993.

Washington, Mary Helen. Introduction. *A Voice from the South*. By Anna Julia Cooper. New York: Oxford UP, 1988. xxvii-liv.

Watson, Carole McAlpine. *Prologue: The Novels of Black American Women, 1891-1965*. Westport & London: Greenwood Press, 1985.

Welter, Barbara. "Coming of Age in America: The American Girl in the Nineteenth Century." *Dimity Convictions: The American Woman in the Nineteenth Century*. Athens: Ohio University Press, 1976. 3-20.

---. "The Cult of True Womanhood: 1800-1860." *Dimity Convictions: The American Woman in the Nineteenth Century*. Athens: Ohio University Press, 1976. 21-41.

White, Barbara A. "'Our Nig' and the She-Devil: New Information about Harriet Wilson and the 'Bellmont' Family." *American Literature* 65.1 (1993): 19-52.

Wilkerson, Margaret B. "Excavating Our History: The Importance of Biographies of Women of Color." *Black American Literature Forum* 24.1 (1990): 73-84.

Winter, Kari J. *Subjects of Slavery, Agents of Change: Women and Power in Gothic Novels and Slave Narratives, 1790-1865.* Athens & London: The University of Georgia Press, 1992.

Yellin, Jean Fagan. "Texts and Contexts of Harriet Jacobs' Incidents in the Life of a Slave Girl: Written by Herself." Davis & Gates 262-282.

---. *The Intricate Knot: Black Figures in American Literature, 1776-1863.* New York: New York University Press, 1972.

---. *Women and Sisters: The Antislavery Feminists in American Culture.* New Haven & London: Yale UP, 1989.

Yellin, Jean Fagan, and Cynthia D. Bond, comp. *The Pen Is Ours. A Listing of Writings by and about African-American Women before 1910. With Secondary Bibliography to the Present.* Schomburg Library. New York: Oxford UP, 1991.